WHOSE MAN

IN HAVANA?

Latin American and Caribbean Series

Hendrik Kraay, General Editor

ISSN 1498-2366 (PRINT), ISSN 1925-9638 (ONLINE)

This series sheds light on historical and cultural topics in Latin America and the Caribbean by publishing works that challenge the canon in history, literature, and postcolonial studies. It seeks to print cutting-edge studies and research that redefine our understanding of historical and current issues in Latin America and the Caribbean.

UNIVERSITY OF CALGARY
Press

WHOSE MAN IN HAVANA?

Adventures from the Far Side of Diplomacy

JOHN W. GRAHAM

UNIVERSITY OF CALGARY
FACULTY OF ARTS
Latin American Research Centre

Latin American and Caribbean Series
ISSN 1498-2366 (Print) ISSN 1925-9638 (Online)

© 2015 John W. Graham
University of Calgary Press
2500 University Drive NW
Calgary, Alberta
Canada T2N 1N4
www.uofcpress.com

LIBRARY AND ARCHIVES CANADA CATALOGUING IN PUBLICATION

Graham, John W. (John Ware), 1934-, author
    Whose man in Havana? : adventures from the far side of diplomacy / John W. Graham.

(Latin American and Caribbean series, 1498-2366 ; no. 12)
Includes bibliographical references and index.
Issued in print and electronic formats.
ISBN 978-1-55238-824-2 (paperback).—ISBN 978-1-55238-826-6 (pdf).—
ISBN 978-1-55238-827-3 (epub).—ISBN 978-1-55238-828-0 (mobi).—
ISBN 978-1-55238-825-9 (open access pdf)

    1. Graham, John W. (John Ware), 1934-. 2. Diplomats—Canada—Biography. 3. Ambassadors—Canada—Biography. 4. Canada—Foreign relations—1945-. I. Title. II. Series: Latin American and Caribbean series ; no. 12

FC601.G748A3 2015   327.2092   C2015-906730-8
                                             C2015-906731-6

The University of Calgary Press acknowledges the support of the Government of Alberta through the Alberta Media Fund for our publications. We acknowledge the financial support of the Government of Canada through the Canada Book Fund for our publishing activities. We acknowledge the financial support of the Canada Council for the Arts for our publishing program.

Canada Council   Conseil des Arts
for the Arts   du Canada

Printed and bound in Canada by Houghton Boston
♻ This book is printed on 55lb Rolland Enviro 100 paper

Cover design, page design, and typesetting by Melina Cusano.
Cover linocut and all other linocuts, maps, and sketches by John W. Graham.

For Judy

"[The Colossus] saw the humorous aspect of everything, which is the real test of the tragic sense."

Henry Miller, *The Colossus of Maroussi*

(ONTENTS

BOOK TWO

FOREWORD

John Graham's memoir is a joyous guide to a life in the Canadian foreign service, and reassuringly he also shows that there is a life after bureaucracy. Graham joined the foreign service when becoming a Canadian diplomat was thought to be a Good Thing. Canada's Department of External Affairs managed to look glamorous from the outside, and proved to be interesting and often strenuous from the inside. Though the foreign service had its share of clunks and incompetents, and ran a few posts that competed with Devil's Island for isolation and discomfort, it was usually much better than that, and there were real rewards – not the least of which was to join an international profession that required its members always to understand the other point of view and not simply to parrot instructions from head office in Ottawa.

Diplomatic life could be pleasant. There were indeed parties and receptions and dinners. Other diplomats from other countries could be, and often were intelligent, good company, and sometimes lifelong friends. It could also be stressful, as Graham shows, hair-raising, and occasionally tragic – as he also shows. Life abroad with allowances was mitigated by home duty: ice and snow in Ottawa, and quite often a modest lifestyle. It was (and is) the equivalent of the slave riding in a chariot with a Roman conqueror, whispering in his ear, "Remember, you are but mortal."

Canadian foreign policy when Graham was a diplomat was run from a smallish ministry that had been originally attached to the prime minister's office (with a lower case "o" at a time when it had not achieved the grandeur and size it has today). That meant it was located in a neo-Gothic pile, the East Block of Canada's Parliament buildings, where prime ministers could keep an eye on it. Indeed for almost forty years the prime minister was also styled "Secretary of State for External Affairs" to distinguish him from the "Secretary of State," who handled patents and other forms.

In the 1940s, "the Department" (all such entities were called departments before ascending in nomenclature to be "ministries") acquired its own minister, and two of them, Louis St. Laurent and Lester B. Pearson, went on to be prime minister: it seemed a natural step. Pearson even collected a Nobel Peace Prize as he passed Go.

Under the minister came the under-secretary, the deputy minister. The under-secretary was a homebody, minding the store, running errands ("interfacing" today) between the political and the bureaucratic, rewarding, punishing, stretching budgets and generally keeping his fractious brood in line. He (for they were all male in Graham's period) occasionally had to suppress bad ideas from ambitious ambassadors. "For the son-of-a-bitch," one under-secretary growled when an ambassador in Cuba produced a plan for harmony between the United States and communist Cuba. In that case his staff calmed the enraged deputy minister, but sometimes diplomats found themselves abruptly yanked and returned to Ottawa to contemplate life from within the department's Historical Division.

It was understood that ministers, and more broadly the cabinet, made policy, and the diplomats executed it. It was also their function to give advice, as practically as possible, for ministers to adopt or disregard. As a general rule, however, the advice bore some resemblance to the policy adopted, and the policy, in turn, helped shape the advice. For that to be so, there had to be some common ground or at least mutual confidence.

Most day-to-day work sailed comfortably under the ministerial radar. Readers will find very few ministerial irruptions in Graham's volume, and rightly so. Diplomats on post had considerable freedom to conduct their work as they saw best, disturbed only by very infrequent visits from superiors from headquarters or sorties by ministers in search of trade and publicity. An ambassador or high commissioner could address the local Drones Club or Meathead Society and nobody in Ottawa would be any the worse – in fact, better for not following up on such mundane details.

Common ground and mutual confidence also applied to relations among foreign missions in a given capital. Sometimes this was necessary for survival or more usually comfort, pooling supplies, or shopping at the same commissary. This shared cordiality even applied to contacts with officials from one or another of Canada's official enemies, such as the Soviet Union. But even Soviet ambassadors might have opinions, and sometimes social charms, which were worth harvesting.

Graham represented "Canada" – the combination of geography and demographics and economy and strategy that made up the country. "Canada" was not just a projection of domestic politics, though ambassadors were assumed not to contradict the explicit policy of the government of the day. Diplomats from other countries often admired the ability of their Canadian counterparts to sail past political tests and witch-hunts. One very senior American diplomat wished he could have moved: "I would have felt comfortable serving in the Canadian Foreign Service, and I felt I knew enough people that it was a conceivable thing."*

Canadians in the eyes of other diplomats had a characteristic negotiating style. According to the same witness, "There is something special about the Canadians which you cannot transpose to many other situations, and that is at a point where we would appear to face irreconcilable difference over something, the Canadians were people you could sit down with over a cup of coffee or a beer and talk and say, 'Now come on. We've got to find our way through all this.' They have a nice genius for knowing when to move on from total hard-line position to search for a compromise that's palatable to both sides, and they showed it many times."

Reading Graham is to contemplate many good beers – fine ales, to be sure. It is reminiscence not only of a career well spent, but of a foreign service and a Canada that deserve commemoration and if possible replication.

Robert Bothwell
September 2015

---

*George Vest, stationed in the US embassy in Ottawa, 1951–54, desk officer for Canada in the State Department, 1954–57. Vest later became Inspector-General of the Foreign Service.

PREFACE

Every morning when I am at home I greet Cuthbert in twelve languages. Cuthbert is our thirty-five-year-old Amazon parrot, and the languages are Arabic, Arawak (from his home in Guyana), Aymara, Bosnian, Cantonese, Czech, Greek, Guarani, Japanese, Kyrgyz, Mam, and Quechua. As I am not a gifted linguist, the greeting in these languages is only "Good morning," but Cuthbert, a unilingual anglophone who is known as Maggie to the rest of the family, seems to enjoy the performance. He spreads his spectacular tail feathers, dilates both irises, and waves a claw to acknowledge the greeting. It is a curious routine, and I suppose that I do it not just out of habit but in remembrance of fascinating times in fascinating places. I think the family would be relieved if I were to stop, but I like to believe that Cuthbert would be disappointed.

This book is about unusual and often extraordinary experiences in many of the places these languages are spoken – half of them as a Canadian diplomat, the other half as a member of international and non-governmental organizations, with one as a private traveller. Because it was originally conceived as an 'entertainment' and not a treatise on diplomacy, I have focused mostly on the lighter side of people and places. But almost everywhere the dark side intrudes, especially the man-made dark side. The intersection of both sides is black comedy, and there is a great deal of that. Substance slips in from time to time.

In the fifties and sixties, young officers in the Department of External Affairs were invited to tell the Personnel Division where they would like to be posted. Like many of my colleagues, I wrote London, Paris, and Washington on the form, naively thinking that the mark I could make in those places would be visible to my superiors in Ottawa. Of course the Department never read these requests, and eventually I learned not to be disappointed by assignments to non-A-list countries. Off the beaten track is often more fun, as I hope these pages will reveal, and I quickly developed a taste for exotic cultures. I was lucky to take my apprenticeship in the Dominican Republic and Cuba, and professionally fortunate also in my timing. These were two very different dictatorships: the one on the right ended in assassination, and the other, on the left, almost ignited an East–West holocaust. Even in fantasy I could not have imagined that I would be sent to Cuba after the missile crisis to spy on Soviet military operations, and that the mission (not me) would have the blessing of the president of the United States and the prime minister of Canada.

It was only after I gave up completing these forms that we were sent to London and, much later, Washington. Over two postings we had seven golden years in London full of cherished memories, including the birth of two of our children, and, much later, three years in Washington. But only one of the London and none of the Washington stories make the cut for this book.

Readers may be surprised that the volume contains almost as many stories from my post-diplomatic career as from the years when I was in government harness. After my departure from the foreign service I sometimes pushed for particular assignments, but on the whole the appointments and their destinations were serendipitous – more good luck than good management. For this project it has also proved invaluable that about twenty years ago I acquired the habit of buying a fresh notebook in advance of each expedition. Some stories are from memory, but they are supported by fact-checking with Library and Archives Canada, Google, and friends. Several have been previously published. Most are mined from my stack of notebooks – saved and boxed by my wife, Judy, and from scrapbooks assembled by her. The dialogue resembles the original conversations, but it is not an accurate reproduction of them. Some names are changed or not given, for reasons that will be obvious, but most names are real. The incidents speak for themselves. There has been no invention, and if there has been embroidery it is a flaw of memory, not of intent.

The list of people to whom I am indebted for their support of this enterprise is long and deep. For at least twenty years, friends and mentors have said – some, probably, because they had heard the same story too many times – "For God's sake, write it down." These include Simon Wade, Sharon Edwards, Louise Muise, and Reed Whittemore, a former US poet laureate, who provided critical guidance and encouragement at the Writer's Center in Bethesda, Maryland; Paul Mackan, who performed a similar role in classes offered by the Ottawa Board of Education; John Meisel, Denis Smith, and George Post, who went through every page and produced a wealth of invaluable criticism; Don Munton, who found several of my Havana telegrams in the Kennedy Library in Boston; the Rt. Hon. Joe Clark, who authorized the use of his responses in an exchange of correspondence and provided counsel, Greg Donaghy, Julie Fournier from Foreign Affairs, Patrick Belanger from the Foreign Affairs library and Lana Merifield from the Library and Archives Canada, whose toil on my behalf bore fruit with declassified material; Sharleen Tattersfield, who helped make up for my technological failings by scanning and transmitting many illustrations; Paul Durand, James Bartleman, John Kneale, and Jean-Paul Hubert, who encouraged, helped with revision and spotted errors; Stephen Randall, who made the key introduction to the University of Calgary Press, Hendrik Kraay of that university, who had confidence in the project, Peter Enman, editor at the university's press, Melina Cusano, who provided design and the frame for the cover page illustration, Paul Dole, who instigated advance publicity, Douglas Campbell who sanded rough surfaces, and Joe Choi for timely tech support. The chapter on mediation in the Dominican Republic would not have emerged without generous help from Monsignor Agripino Nunez Collado, Juan Bolivar Diaz, and Michael Skol. Other support was provided by Lisa Chartrand, who insisted that I include maps, and Eric Bergbusch, who provided ideas and suggested that I remove some cluttered thinking. My greatest debt is to Judy, to whom this book is dedicated, and without whose wisdom, skill, and sorely tested forbearance it would never have happened.

Literary debts invariably run in other directions. Over many years I have been drawn to the enchantment of first-class travel writers. I have in mind such people as Isabella Bird, William Dalrymple, Edith Durham, Rebecca West, and particularly those such as Lawrence Durrell, his brother Gerald, and Patrick Leigh Fermor, who manage their stories with self-deprecating humour. Spike Milligan is on this list, but in a separate category: the gloriously inane. Four of these writers (Lawrence Durrell, Durham, Leigh Fermor, and West) devoted space to the Balkans, the focus of five of my chapters. This is rich memoir ground, vividly cross-hatched with light and dark. To these authors my debt is a sort of unrequited admiration.

I wish to acknowledge the following for their generosity in permitting the reproduction of previously published material: Fitzhenry and Whiteside; Bernardo Vega of *La Fundación Cultural Dominicana*; *bout de papier, Canada's Magazine of Diplomacy and Foreign Service*; the *Scarboro Missions Magazine*; and the *Manor Park Chronicle*.

BOOK ONE

DOMINICAN REPUBLIC

Voyage to a Different Planet

I was twenty-one and in my last year at Queen's University when I took my exams, and was subsequently interviewed, for the Canadian foreign service. To my surprise, I was accepted. The outcome of these exams has always seemed to me like the fortuitous click of a roulette wheel. A year later, in 1957, I joined the Department of External Affairs, then lodged in the splendid and as yet ungentrified East Bloc on Parliament Hill. After a year's leave of absence to complete a degree at Cambridge and a year in the Legal Division, I was assigned to my first posting, which is where this narrative begins.

In late August 1960, I was summoned to the office of Eustace McGaughey, the head of personnel in the Department of External Affairs. McGuff, as he was known, greeted me and asked me to sit down.

"Graham," he said, "it's time for you to go abroad. The department is going to assign you to a very responsible job. We are going to send you …" – he glanced at the paper on his desk – "… to Soodad Truejello." After a pause, he muttered, "Where the hell is that?"

I knew where it was, and my heart sank. Ciudad Trujillo was the capital of the Dominican Republic. For five hundred years it had been "Santo Domingo," until the hemisphere's most ruthless and megalomaniacal dictator, Generalissimo Rafael Trujillo Molina, renamed it after himself. I was naively expecting a more conventional orbit – London, Rome, maybe Delhi. If the head of personnel didn't know about the country I was going to, it was hardly at the leading edge of Canadian overseas engagement.

My next visit was to Yvon Beaulne, the head of the newly established Latin American Division. He greeted me warmly. A jovial and distinguished veteran of the foreign service, he spoke glowingly of the professional and personal joys of a Latin American posting. My gloom was lifting when Beaulne asked, "Are you armed?"

"Armed?" I said in surprise.

Beaulne explained, "When I arrive in a new house in a new country, I go into the garden and empty the chamber of my revolver into the flower beds. This ensures that any villains in the neighbourhood will know what to expect."

Three weeks later, while on a visit to my mother in Toronto, I walked into a gun store on Yonge Street and asked the salesman if he could show me an "inexpensive" pistol. Twenty dollars seemed a good price for a used .25-calibre revolver – known in those days as a "Saturday night special." The next day I took the pistol to an RCMP office for registration. The corporal who examined it asked what my intention was.

"Intention?" I replied peevishly. "Self-defence."

"Hmm," said the corporal, glancing at the pistol in his hand. "If your intention is to commit suicide, this would be a good choice." He showed me the inside of the barrel, which was so worn that it no longer fit precisely with the cartridge chamber. Back at the gun store, the clerk was pleased to see me. I left with a brand-new 7mm Browning automatic, two small cartons of cartridges, and no instructional pamphlet.

Another important part of my preparation was learning the language. Twice a week I took Spanish from a young (and very attractive) Venezuelan woman. It was probably in the course of my third lesson that she gave me an exercise based on a key word. The word was "*queso*," which in the rudimentary state of my vocabulary I mistook for the word "*beso*" (kiss). *Queso* is, of course, the word for cheese, and the basis of a misunderstanding that could have terminated my tuition. "Do you like *queso*?"

Startled, I said something like, "Err, yes."

"What sort of *queso* do you like?"

I was still taken aback, and because I did not respond to this question, she asked if I liked Dutch *queso*. Using my few bits of Spanish, I tried to reply that I had no experience with Dutch *queso*. Reddening, and pulled increasingly between anticipation and anxiety, I admitted that I liked English *queso*. By the time the exercise moved on to French *queso*, at the point where I thought she would tear my clothes off, she recognized my confusion, and the lesson ended in laughter.

A month later I flew from New York with Pan American Airways – itself a small adventure, because it was my first time on a jet passenger liner. I was met at the new Generalissimo Rafael Trujillo airport by my predecessor, Leopold Lapin, and his friend Philip Bernstein. Philip, who would become my friend, was an elderly British businessman and the only person I have known, before or since, who regularly took snuff. About once every twenty minutes Philip would take some from a small ivory snuff box, insert a pinch into a nostril, and sneeze into a yellowing handkerchief.

Leopold, with whom I was having a short overlap, was unusual. By no stretch of the imagination could he be described as a stereotypical diplomat. He was voluble, tactile, and exuberant about his passions, his likes, and his dislikes. And he was delightful, but as a vaguely Presbyterian product I was taken aback by him – and soon by just about everything else. The airport was an initiation. Leopold was wearing a *guayabera* (a tropical shirt worn untucked), which hid the pistol that was tucked into his belt. As he explained it, the pistol was definitely for self-defence. He had been attending the funerals of persons liquidated by the secret police, and, as he admitted, he had become paranoid about the possibility that his increasingly visible detestation of the regime would lead to an attempt on his own life. It is unlikely that he would have been targeted, but the news released on November 23, the day of my arrival, that the three well-known and respected Mirabel sisters had died in a motor accident, drove his point home. The sisters were clandestine members of a very small, brave, and largely suicidal group dedicated to the overthrow of the regime. Everyone took it for granted that the news item about the motor accident was just a cover story, and that the sisters had been tortured and killed by the secret police.

I was beginning to grasp that I was on a different planet when we left Generalissimo Trujillo Airport (the father), turned onto Lieutenant General Ramfis Trujillo Highway (the elder son), drove across Rhadames Trujillo Bridge (the younger son), left Ensanche Molina (the mother) on our right, and entered the capital, Ciudad Trujillo.

Leopold's List

Leopold left me several legacies. The first was the one-bedroom, well-located house that he had been renting from Franz Naescher, his Liechtensteiner landlord, and that he had persuaded him to let me have. Built of wood, brick, tile, and local marble on the model of a Pyrenees chalet as imagined by a Spanish painter and constructed by an Italian marble worker, the house was a small jewel – unless you were concerned about air conditioning and hot water. For purity of form, there was no glass in the windows, only wooden spokes and louvres. The showers were unheated. Naescher, an astute collector of Latin American painting, hung the overflow of his collection, including a gorgeous Wilfredo Lam, now Cuba's most famous and most expensive painter, on the chalet's walls.

The second legacy was Mamouna Altagracia Corazón de Jesús. Mamouna was Leopold's dog, a six-months-old Creole bitch. The name was a puzzle. Mamouna is the name of a hotel in Casablanca, and the longer bit was the result of Leopold's experience with young Dominican ladies with exalted religious nomenclature. Leopold explained: the dog was a virgin; the girls weren't.

Mamouna was a delight, and remained with me and then with my family for several postings, before finally expiring in London. However, she did not remain virginal for long. In fact, much like her namesakes, she greatly enjoyed reproductive activity and produced many litters of puppies. It seemed appropriate to me, and my wife later agreed, to maintain the sacrilegious tradition. Mamouna's first union was with a dog left with me by my girlfriend's parents. The girl's mother was a Dutch woman whose husband had been killed in Sumatra by the Japanese, and her stepfather, Otto, was a former Luftwaffe squadron leader, and allegedly for a short time a member of Hitler's personal squadron, *Die Fliegerstaffel des Führers*. (He had been hired to train pilots for Trujillo's air force.) The dog's name was Terry. He soon became Terry de la Inmaculada Concepción. Their progeny included Maximo Milagro de la Alta Caridad, and Dulce Aroma de los Angeles. In Cuba, an encounter with a purebred long-haired dachshund produced Oigame (listen to me), Digame (tell me),

Besame (kiss me), and Buggerme. They were adorable. Moments before giving Buggerme to the wife of the Israeli ambassador in Havana, my wife changed its name to Buscame (look for me). Mamouna's nymphomaniacal inclinations and our resistance to having her spayed led to her one major humiliation. In the incredibly well-equipped pet accessory section of Les Galeries Lafayette in Paris, I purchased a canine chastity belt. Of course Mamouna, who understood what it was for, didn't like it, and the family was usually too embarrassed to apply it. The result was another litter: Shadrach, Meshach, Abednego, and Gladys. The last puppy, born in London in a posh area near the King's Road, was Britannia Aphrodisia.

The final gift from Leopold was a handwritten sheet entitled "Advice for John." Part One was a list of influential expatriates living in Ciudad Trujillo divided into those who could be trusted and those who could not. The list of unreliables, subtitled Trujillistas, included the names of about fifteen of the leading business executives and other well-placed foreign personalities in the capital. As I recall, Otto was in this category. The list of who could be trusted was much shorter. It included Naescher, Bernstein, the manager of the Canadian nickel mine, Falconbridge Dominicana, the Israeli honorary consul, a Spanish car dealer, and Anna Maria Swartz, a charming and much-married professional photographer. Part Two concluded with advice that I suspect is unusual for the Canadian diplomatic service: "Never pay a girl more than $5. Dominicans pay $3." (Remember, this was 1960.)

∾ ∾ ∾

Darkness at Noon

Generalissimo Trujillo was the dictator of the Dominican Republic from 1930 to 1961. From an impoverished, chaotic, and heavily indebted political swamp, he dragged the country into the twentieth century. However, the price paid in basic human rights and freedoms was enormous – at the time, the highest in the entire hemisphere. Trujillo's efficiency in transforming the economy was matched by his efficiency as a tyrant. For me, as a very green diplomat, this was a major cultural shock. This chapter tells a small part of that story.

The oncoming car had skidded to a halt. I had jammed my brake on, but I kept sliding until I crunched into his fender and headlamp. Indignantly I threw open the car door and clambered out to demand in bad Spanish why the stupid driver was on the wrong side of the road. Three men, now outside their car, began shouting at me and pointing to a sign some thirty metres behind me. Visible in the arc of a street light at the intersection was a sign I had missed that said, "No entry – One-way street." One of the men, presumably the owner, stepped forward to examine the damage. Glancing at the front of my car, he sucked in his breath and barked at his companions. I could not understand what they said, but all three leapt into their car. The driver backed up, changed gear, and swung away from me.

What the hell was going on? I was totally in the wrong, but these people were not only rushing away from the accident, but in their haste would not even stop to straighten out the fender that was scraping the tread off the front tire and would soon destroy it. I ran after them for a short distance, shouting "Stop!" But the only effect was to accelerate the car and increase the tearing noise as the fender peeled off more bits of rubber.

I walked back to my car, mystified and unnerved. It was December 1960, and I was in the third week of my first diplomatic posting overseas. I climbed back into my car and attempted, unsuccessfully, to assure my two Canadian guests, one of whom was my mother, that everything was all right. I had picked them up at the airport and we were entering Ciudad Trujillo (formerly and subsequently Santo Domingo) when the accident occurred.

Next morning, at the embassy, I told Josefina, one of the locally engaged staff, what had happened. "Why," I asked, "did they drive away when it was clearly my fault?"

"Perhaps they saw your licence plate," said Josefina.

"Yes, they could have...but, my licence plate?"

"That would be enough," she said. "Your diplomatic plate is green – the same colour as the plates given to senior government officers. Look, let's go to the landing." We left the office and stood by the elevator. "When you've been here longer you will understand." She looked at me. "But then maybe you won't. There are a lot of foreigners here who don't want to understand.... At least you know why we can't talk about this in the office."

"Sure. The phones are bugged."

"And maybe the walls or the light fixtures – or maybe me. It's almost certain that one member of the embassy staff has been recruited by the secret police."

"Come on, Josefina..."

"You think I'm paranoid. What about the men in the car you crashed last night? You've just explained that it was your fault, but they ran away as if you were death itself. In a way they thought you were. It was dark, they couldn't see you very well. But they could see your plates and they were petrified. Anybody with green plates, except for diplomats, owes his position to Trujillo."

"Sure, but a fender-bender...?"

"Listen, their minds were racing with what might happen to them: they could be beaten up...shot on the spot...arrested. Terrible things happen here."

I went back to my office and sat down. This foolish accident was stripping away the remnants of my comfortable Canadian norms. A nightmare was taking their place. Those banana-brains in Ottawa had sent me to a tropical version of Arthur Koestler's *Darkness at Noon*. I was beginning to recognize that above the level of the *campesino* (peasant farmer), the principal beneficiary of the regime, the entire country was quivering with fear. The dictator's name was not mentioned, even in a neutral context, lest the maid, the telephone, or the microphone in the wall report potential conspiracy, or, more likely, the absence of the obligatory degree of respect. Megalomania had become a magnetic force. Everyone bent toward the dictator, and obsequiousness was an art form. Anything less than a superlative was an offence.

My friend Bernstein generally referred to Trujillo as "scrotums" – a term which secret police listeners were unlikely to understand. Two nights before, I was dining with him at Vesuvios, a popular Italian restaurant on the *malecón*, the seaside boulevard. While we were talking he put a finger to his lips. "Hear that?" he said. There was no traffic on the *malecón*, but a low "put-put" sound was approaching, like that of a single-cylinder lawn mower on low. It was, in fact, a Volkswagen Beetle being driven so slowly it was easy to see the people inside. "SIM," whispered Bernstein. "Scrotums is taking his constitutional a few blocks away, so the whole area is closed to traffic and patrolled by the secret police." The SIM (*Servicio de Inteligencia Militar*) in the Beetle were dressed in sports shirts and dark glasses. The slow beat of the engine had become their signature tune, transmitting fear within its audible radius.

As we left, Bernstein pointed to a large brass plaque on the wall of the restaurant. It read *"En esta casa Trujillo es el jefe"* (In this house Trujillo is the chief), and bore a portrait in relief of the great man. "Every Dominican," he said, still whispering, "from the lower middle class up, has to buy one of these damned things for their home and for their place of business. They're not cheap…and guess where the money goes?"

Ciudad Trujillo was not what I had in mind in high school when the first notion of a career in external affairs entered my head. My interest in service overseas had something to do with travel and perhaps also with grey, grim Toronto and chafing at what I perceived to be a school devoted to the recycling of affluent Torontonians and their affluence. The school, Upper Canada College, was posh and expensive and my recently divorced parents could only afford it because my mother, a teacher at a neighbouring girl's school, had negotiated a bursary. I was an indifferent student. I didn't like the school, and the school principal returned the favour.

The clouds parted at Queen's University where I discovered the joys of learning, pubs, co-eds, juvenile mischief, and summers spent at sea with the Naval Reserve. If the RCMP had been more alert or, more probably, had not shown good judgment, some of the mischief could have been my undoing. Deep in the Cold War, at the time of Senator McCarthy's 'commie' witch hunts, three of us planted a Soviet flag on the Kingston city hall (formerly the parliament buildings of newly unified Upper and Lower Canada). Our goal, which was to caricature the absurdities of East/West polarization, was not wholly successful. There was a howl of outrage that 'reds' had infiltrated the university and many of the burghers of Kingston demanded that the university be closed. We tried to dampen the worst suspicions by having one of our number, a theologian, interviewed on the fledgling local TV station. For anonymity he wore a paper bag over his head.

The following year, the leader of these conspiracies (now a retired judge of the Ontario Superior Court), organized the 'recovery' by stealth of the long-lost thirteen colonies. Eighteen of us in four cars crossed into northern New York State late at night and raised 1776 vintage Union Jacks on flag poles in front of municipal buildings, armouries and high schools (George III's flags have one less cross than the current version). Ingeniously designed by an engineer colleague, a tiny pin caused the flags to jam at the top of the poles. They had to be removed by fire engine ladders and steeple jacks. Fastened at the base of each pole was a placard which, upon deploring the "ignorance and arrogance" that led the colonies to forsake "the all-sheltering arms of his Britannic Majesty," proclaimed Colonel George Washington of the Virginia Militia to be "a scoundrel, traitor, rebel without cause." This ignited a short but very satisfying media storm, including an item in the *London Times*. With a few exceptions – the two schools that had to hire steeple jacks – the American reaction was good-humoured.

From Queen's I went to Trinity College, Cambridge (which in the mid-fifties was still delightfully, if uncomfortably, frozen in the Middle

Ages). From there it was off to External Affairs in Ottawa and from External Affairs to Ciudad Trujillo. Not, I thought, a natural trajectory.

I soon found that I could not send objective reports to the foreign ministry in Ottawa about the political culture in the Dominican Republic. It certainly wasn't for lack of material. If I were to report factually, my superiors in Ottawa would think my brain had baked in the sun.

An example of this problem, intimately connected to my work because a number of Canadians were involved, was the honours crisis. Local honours, both old and newly coined, were heaped upon Trujillo, as were foreign decorations. He had acquired just about every splendid, fawning title that could be squeezed out of a small country. He was by law *Benefactor de la Nación, Padre de la Patria Nueva, Generalissimo...* . Well-paid hagiographers projected his heroic image in illustrated volumes to the United States and to every corner of the Iberian world. Only one national prize eluded him: *Benefactor de la Iglesia* (church). The unexpected difficulties he found in obtaining this title made it all the more coveted. The Church had rules about this sort of thing. Every bishop in the country had to agree before this honour could be conferred. Most came quickly into line, including the archbishop of the oldest archdiocese in the hemisphere. But two held out. Thomas Reilly, an American, who was the bishop of San Juan de la Maguana, and Francisco Panal, a Spaniard, who was bishop of La Vega, resolved that they could not become accessories to this obscenity. Perceiving the recalcitrant prelates as a threat to both his ego and his authority, Trujillo gave a free hand to Johnny Abbes, head of the SIM, to intimidate them into submission. Prostitutes danced in the cathedral in La Vega. Reilly was burned out of his residence in San Juan de la Maguana and took refuge in a convent in Ciudad Trujillo.

The campaign against the bishops escalated into high farce. Radio Caribe, the mouthpiece of the SIM, announced that a prize would be offered for the best prose or poem in thirty-five words or less that successfully encapsulated the "treacherous and immoral character" of the two bishops. As an exercise of black-humoured irreverence, Ian Keith of

Falconbridge and I composed limericks that we recited to a small and discreet group of expatriates.

Parish priests and nuns also came under the surveillance of the secret police and of spies within their congregations. Most of the country's thirty or so Canadian priests and nuns failed to demonstrate adequate enthusiasm for the living beatification of the dictator. In this perilous setting, Father O'Connor of the Scarboro Order committed a capital crime. To the horror of his parishioners, O'Connor condemned the Generalissimo for his blasphemous presumption. One step ahead of the SIM and at considerable risk to themselves, two Scarboro priests bundled him into a car, whisked him to the airport, gave him a false name, and placed him on the next Pan American flight.

Many members of religious orders received threats. Some were injured, some burned out of their homes. Almost all learned of their supposed apostasy, as did thousands of citizens within listening range, from the same secret police-operated radio station that was reciting scurrilous jingles about the two bishops. A typical news item would report that Sisters of the Grey Nuns in Yamasa "had neglected to inform their students about the extraordinary contributions of the Benefactor to educational development"; or Father X "is believed to have devoted the proceeds of his collection plate to support the retail liquor trade"; or, more piquantly, "Parishioners in Bani will be shocked to learn that Father Y was spotted last night sneaking out of the back door of Doña Rosa's brothel."

When this happened I would take the battered official Chevrolet, drive to the parish concerned, fix a small Canadian flag to the standard on the fender, and motor around until I was sure the SIM had registered my presence and guessed the reason for it. There was really little else I could do. An official complaint to the government would be ignored, and anyway I couldn't be certain that my boss, who liked Trujillo, would approve. In any event, this was an agreeable duty. I met most of the Canadian priests and nuns, and often sat on their verandas, rocking with them in the warm night air, drinking rum or coffee. Some remain good friends to this day.

Two months into my posting in Ciudad Trujillo and I was beginning to think like Leopold. It was early evening. The sun had splashed down at speed, as it does in the tropics, and I was sitting having a drink with my friend Donald from the British Embassy. We were on his balcony looking out to sea and the remnants of an apricot sunset. The conversation unfolded something like this:

"Donald, I've been thinking."

"Never a good sign. What about?"

"Someone should do the old man."

"Trujillo?"

"Yes, of course, Trujillo."

"What do you mean?"

"Someone should kill him."

"Yes, someone probably will. So?"

"So it's not going to happen soon. He's too well protected."

"That's right. About six different secret police organizations. When they're not watching the citizens, they're watching each other."

"Meanwhile he goes on killing and turning this godforsaken country into some sort of tropical *Animal Farm*. You know about the Mirabel sisters?"

"Yes, I know. Raped, garroted, and pushed over a cliff in their own car. The stupid bastards thought they could make it look like an accident."

"And you know why?"

"Yes, because Minerva told the old man that she wouldn't go to bed with him. And she, Patria, and Delores had the guts – or maybe the stupidity – to plot against him."

"Somebody should kill the son of a bitch."

"Yes, you said that. But who? Who's going to get close enough?"

"Me."

"You!"

"Yeah, me. Nobody suspects a diplomat. Nobody searches a diplomat. There's at least one of those bloody awful state ceremonies every two weeks. The boss is sick, so I go. I'm not in the front row, but I'm pretty close."

"Jesus Christ! You're serious."

"Last week at the Te Deum in the cathedral, I thought about how easy it would be. I was less than fifteen feet from him…and you know I've got that Browning automatic."

"You're completely mad. And what do you suppose would happen to you?"

"Yeah, there is that. But Donald, do you know how many people he's murdered?"

"Approximately, yes. The embassy tries to keeps track. But for Christ's sake don't even think about anything so stupid."

We had another drink. Donald had been around. He had been one of Montgomery's desert rats in North Africa. He said that he would not repeat our conversation, as it reflected badly on my sanity. I went home to dinner and bed. A few weeks later at a ceremony in the National Palace I mulled over ballistics and an unobstructed shot. However, I was beginning to recognize that this was nothing more than adolescent bravado. And, as Donald had said, someone was going to do it. A few months later a small gang of patriotic assassins did. Curiously, fate had determined that I would be the only diplomat near the shootout when it happened.

On the morning of May 30, 1961, Radio Caribe accused Father McNabb, a Scarboro priest, of passing drugs to adolescents. Father McNabb and two other priests lived in Haina. That evening I set off for Haina along with Gordon Bruce, a friend visiting from Ottawa, and Mamouna. I followed the usual pattern, and we were invited in by Father McNabb and his colleagues. McNabb was unshaken and in his usual ebullient form. After rum and plantain chips we left to return to the city.

I recall that night vividly. A stiff breeze was blowing onshore. Shadows galloped along the highway as puffs of cloud flew past a full moon. Tall spumes of spray glittered in the bright silver light. Eight kilometres from the capital we were stopped by the SIM – two agents and their ominous Volkswagen. Submachine guns poked through both open front windows. Mamouna snapped at the barrel of one until restrained by Gordon. Another car was just visible at the verge of the road. We identified ourselves and were questioned and released.

Nearing the outskirts of town, we were startled by a cavalcade of Mercedes and Cadillacs moving west at high speed. Bursts of gunfire echoed throughout the city. Something dramatically out of the ordinary had happened. What it was I learned early the next morning from a British colleague. Trujillo had been killed in a gun battle very shortly before we arrived at the scene. It was his Chevrolet that we had seen on the coast side of the road, peppered with holes. His chauffeur was lying wounded about

Generalissimo Rafael Trujillo (1936)

thirty feet away, still undiscovered. Trujillo was gone. He had been stuffed in the trunk of one of the gunmen's cars.

The almost indescribably bizarre funeral a few days later remains one of the classic events of my career.

∾ ∾ ∾

The Dictator's Sarcophagus

In the spring of 1961, President Kennedy was visiting President de Gaulle in France. At 2:00 P.M. Dominican time, May 31, Pierre Salinger, Kennedy's press secretary, released the news of Trujillo's assassination to the press in Paris. This was almost three hours before the Dominican announcement.

The blunder by Salinger embarrassed the American government, and ignited the first suspicions that the United States was involved in the assassination. Radio Caribe, the voice of the SIM, made the official statement in the late afternoon of May 31. The following morning, newspaper headlines proclaimed, "*Vilmente Asesinado Cae el Benefactor de la Patria*" (The Benefactor of the Country Falls, the Victim of a Vile Assassination). Melancholy classics played on all radio stations, and funeral arrangements began. The corpse had been found in the trunk of a car belonging to one of the assassins.

Early on June 2, Ernie McCullough, the Canadian chargé d'affaires, joined the other eight members of the miniscule diplomatic corps in the National Palace to express condolences. Sanctions by the Organization of American States, imposed as a result of Trujillo's attempted assassination of President Romulo Betancourt of Venezuela, had closed most diplomatic missions the previous year.

At 9:30 that morning, when he returned home, Ernie called me. "John, Ambassador Logroño [the chief of protocol] has just told me the funeral will be in San Cristobal this afternoon. I'm not feeling well and would like you to go. A sad, tragic business." He was genuinely distressed. "By the way," he said, "dress is morning suit."

Morning suit! How in blazes was I going to find a tailcoat, vest, and striped trousers in two hours, in a tightly shut Ciudad Trujillo? A suit was in the end obtained through friends at the American Consulate General. By noon I was in the ancient official car en route to San Cristobal and almost lost in the folds of Matt Ortwein's morning suit. Matt was the consulate's administrative officer and much larger than I.

"Nice fit," giggled Balthazar, the Jamaican/Dominican chauffeur and apprentice brothel keeper.

San Cristobal was in pandemonium. Trujillo was venerated as a semi-deity. The country's impoverished and superstitious rural community knew that he had improved the quality of their lives. The dictator had developed markets for their crops, and built roads, courthouses, and schools – as well as torture chambers and a forest of statues to himself. About two thousand semi-hysterical *campesinos* had encircled the church. Between the *campesinos* and the church stretched a ring of several hundred heavily armed troops. Inside, the congregation was armed to the teeth – senators with holsters strapped to their striped pants, generals and admirals with an assortment of high-powered weapons. One of Trujillo's brothers, Arismendi, in the dress uniform of a three-star general, carried a sub-machine gun down the aisle to his place at the front of the church. As far as I could determine, almost the only people in the entire church without guns were the clergy and the diplomatic corps. President Balaguer was also unarmed. A dripping, overcast sky accentuated the gloom inside the church, but did not deter many of the congregation, especially those in uniform, from wearing dark glasses – a standard accessory for police-state apparatchiks.

Tension was palpable. The assassination had taken place less than three days before. Some assassins had already been captured and killed. There was enormous apprehension that surviving plotters would see the gathering in San Cristobal of all the senior figures and family of the regime as an irresistible opportunity for a coup de grâce. I had no way of knowing this at the time, but one of the key plotters, General "Pupo" Roman, the head of the army, was in the church. Trujillo's body had been taken to Roman's door as proof that the first stage of the conspiracy had succeeded. But Roman had vacillated, and the plan to take over the government with US support collapsed. Already a suspect, he was arrested three days later, tortured by Trujillo's son, Ramfis, and killed. A photograph taken during the funeral shows Colonel Estevez Leon, a Trujillo in-law and a SIM associate, glaring venomously at the general.

Two soldiers pushed a priest aside and clattered up the pulpit, searching for bombs. A car backfired and two hundred mourners clutched their weapons. We waited. Those with guns fidgeted with them. Unexpectedly, the cries of the *campesinos* rose in volume. Faintly and then loudly the beat of an engine grew in intensity. The crowd screamed. Inside, we had no idea what was happening and trembled with fear.

Balthazar described the scene as we drove back to the capital. The *campesinos* had watched, amazed, as a helicopter hovered above the churchyard. Over the heads of the crowd a hatch opened, and a huge coffin was slowly winched down to a waiting gurney. The *campesinos* shuffled and howled. The wailing grew louder and louder. The Generalissimo's coffin swinging in the air was a moment of unbearable, transcendent mystery for the dazed and credulous mourners below.

President Balaguer delivered an elegant, tremulously pitched eulogy. Troops fired saluting volleys. No one inside returned the fire. The service concluded.

Days later I was telling a friend at the American consulate about the funeral. It's so long ago that I can't recall with any certainty who it was, but I think it was Joe Fandino.

"But didn't you know?" said Joe. "Trujillo wasn't there."

"What do you mean he wasn't there? It was his funeral."

"Sure. But Doña Maria [the widow] wasn't taking any chances. She was afraid the plotters might get hold of the body and hang it from a lamppost like Mussolini. They found another body – not difficult for them – and put it in the coffin."

"And so where was Trujillo?"

"The widow and Ramfis decided to leave him somewhere safe. They put him in a freezer."

"In a freezer?"

"Yes." Joe paused. "The Benefactor's sarcophagus is a freezer at San Isidro."[1]

෮ ෮ ෮

"Down with Those who Rise"

It was the old man's iron will, ruthlessness, and immense political and micro-management skills that had kept oiling the million wheels of oppression and fear. A few months after the assassination, small cracks began to appear in the control system. People were shot and tortured as before, and the killers included Ramfis, Trujillo's creepy playboy son, but the Trujillo family and the senior apparatchiks were incapable of keeping the stopper tightly in place. Anti-government demonstrations became more frequent and more violent. A last attempt to shore up the family dictatorship was defeated by brilliantly timed American gunboat diplomacy.[2] The subsequent power vacuum set off a series of coup d'états and attempted coup d'états, culminating in civil conflict and the 1965 invasion of the country by US Marines. The episodes below offer a glimpse of embassy life during the strained and curious times before the country dissolved into civil war.

Charlie Hodge was the senior economic officer at the US embassy[3] and father of my then girlfriend Penny. Charlie had recently imported a new car and was worried about its safety in the deteriorating environment. One day he came to me with a proposition.

"John, the rioting downtown is increasingly intense and, as you know, we've become targets. The mob doesn't know whose side the Canadians are on, so they leave you alone."

"That's more or less right, but how can I help?"

"Well," said Charlie "I've imported a new car. It has diplomatic plates and once these bastards figure out that it belongs to an American, it may not last long. Your car isn't targeted because it's covered with Canadian flags."

"You want to trade cars?"

"Yeah, that's it. As a US diplomat I wouldn't feel right about putting Canadian flags on my car."

"But, if the car you are using already has the flags…"

"Exactly."

We made the change – it was supposed to be only for the latest crisis, and Charlie's car, an MG Magnette, was more fun to drive than my base model Vauxhall and I had no compunction about plastering it with Canadian flags. This was 1961 and the flag was the Red Ensign – a Union Jack in the top corner and the Canadian coat of arms in the opposite bottom corner.

I pasted flags on the doors, the trunk, the hood and on the roof. The flag on the roof was important because some of the rioters stationed themselves on the flat tops of the downtown buildings from which they would hurl broken bits of masonry upon police, military or any other vehicles belonging to the enemy or their assumed collaborators. At street level a much favoured missile was a jagged chunk of cast iron – taken from manhole covers that had been lifted from their moorings and smashed. Inevitably, the demonstrators were joined by young hoodlums or *tigres* whose motivations were not so much political as a libertine attachment to anarchy, pursued under what they supposed was a noble banner.

The Canadian embassy occupied the third floor of the Edificio Copelo[4] on Calle El Conde. In quiet times this was a good location – convenient for business and government offices. From the summer of 1961 and for the next four years until it was moved it was a terrible location. El Conde became the main thoroughfare for demonstrations and collision points for the attempts by the secret police (in the early days), the police and the military to subdue the demonstrators.

In one sense only was the embassy well situated at this time. We had a ringside view of the action. From our third-floor windows we could see up and down El Conde and the shifting fortunes of the contestants – demonstrators advancing often only to reverse as security forces and sometimes tanks marched or clanked toward them. After a few encounters the police and soldiers began to use tear gas, a development for which we were unprepared. As clouds of gas filled El Conde, our air conditioners sucked them into our offices to the irritation of everyone, especially the locally engaged staff, who kept warning us to stay clear of the windows..

When they weren't marching or confronting the security forces, the demonstrators were busy painting graffiti on every available space. The walls and shutters at the entrance to the Edificio Copelo were a good example. After six months there was virtually no vacant space on which to spray another slogan. From a distance some of them could be mistaken for canvasses by Riopelle. In many colours they exclaimed "up!" or "long live!" such and such a party or insurrectionary movement or "down with!" the government, the Americans or other villain of choice. They tended to be so boringly repetitive that while there was still space on our wall, some wag had written in red paint "*Abajo los que suben!*" (Down with those who rise!) – a pertinent commentary on a disintegrating political system.

Meanwhile the arrangement with Charlie worked well. Both cars survived, whereas a colleague's did not. Clark Leith, the assistant trade commissioner and only other officer in the embassy, had purchased a new Chevrolet Impala. The car arrived in late November. One morning in early December, with no sign of civil agitation, Clark parked his car on Sanchez, the street that intersected El Conde beside the embassy. Fatally, the Impala, Clark's first new car, glowed with new paint unblemished by paper flags.

The city was still quiet at about eleven o'clock when Clark drove off to the airport with Balthazar in the official embassy vehicle. His mission was to exchange diplomatic bags with the courier from External Affairs. By noon a demonstration, including an assortment of *tigres*, was moving down El Conde. A few shop windows caught un-shuttered were broken. As I watched, a young *tigre* with a club was looking at the green licence plate on Clark's Impala—the same colour as the plates on government

Domincan citizen hanging Trujillo in effigy.

Dominican being held at gunpoint in Calle el Conde.

vehicles. He began bashing the rear window of the car with his club. Perhaps because I was feeling guilty that I had not rushed out with paper flags at the first sign of disturbance, my next move was foolhardy. I ran out of the office into the street, hollering at the *tigre* to stop. "*Este es un carro Canadiense!*" He paid no attention. We fought briefly after which he took off down the street – not because I had won the fight, which was inconclusive. But, by this time he had tossed a burning torch through the broken window. I ran to the *farmacia* only two doors away, pounded at the door, shouting that I needed a bucket of water. A very nervous pharmacist opened the door a crack through which I explained my need and the urgency. He said that he was sorry and that he did not wish to become involved. After more loud palaver on my part, I was given some water, but by this time it was too little and too late.

According to word on the street, picked up by our cleaner, the *tigre* who had set fire to Clark's car, was now threatening to have me killed for trying to thwart his patriotic duty. Friends, who knew the dynamics of the town better than I, put this down to macho bluster.

The car was still burning when Clark returned.

Although insured, the coverage had a clause excluding damage by riot, war, or insurrection. Clark wrote to Ottawa seeking reimbursement for the car and shipping costs. At the same time I wrote a note to the Dominican foreign ministry, specifying the costs, seeking reimbursement and referring grandly to state responsibility for diplomatic property. Ottawa (the Trade Commissioner Service) wrote back saying that they would cover the replacement cost of the Chevrolet, but not the shipping. Within a few days of this answer, I was asked to call at the foreign ministry, a former residence of the dictator. No reason was given for the request. On arrival at his office, Nadal, the deputy chief of protocol, handed me a thick envelope. "This is for the car. Please be so good as to count it." Astonished, I opened the envelope which was stuffed with cash. I emptied the contents onto the desk and began to count. I counted something like $2800 or the equivalent in convertible pesos (about $20,000 today) which was the amount originally requested, covering both replacement cost and shipping. But why was there no accompanying note and why had Nadal made it clear that a receipt from me was not expected? I could only speculate that while they were able to honour their obligations for a few cars, they wished to avoid a written precedent that might force their hand if they were asked to pay for

Dominican Republic 23

the rebuilding of someone's embassy. Farfetched? Perhaps. If there was a better explanation, I couldn't think of it.

Returning to the embassy, I went to Clark's office. Stroking the lump in my jacket I said, "How do you feel about a Greek island vacation?"

Of course, we reported the whole story to Ottawa, indicating that Clark would return the government cheque. For a short time we wondered if we had done the right thing. Ottawa agreed that the cheque be returned, but that as they had determined that $2500 would be adequate compensation, we were instructed to return roughly $250 to the Dominican foreign ministry. We argued that this would leave Clark out of pocket and the Dominicans completely mystified. Eventually Ottawa agreed.

∾ ∾ ∾

Navidad con Libertad

The leader of the opposition vanguard, probing for political space, was an elderly patriot, Don Viriato Fiallo. He formed the first post-Trujillo non-clandestine opposition party, the Union Civica. He cautiously organized and proselytized, and although he was harassed and threatened, he survived. In early November he decided the time was right to pry open the lid. A political rally was to be held, and, for maximum symbolic impact, the small Parque Independencia, in the heart of the city, was chosen as its site. To everyone's astonishment, about two thousand people arrived. So did the SIM and several small military aircraft, which swooped over the crowd, dropping leaflets that warned of reprisals to be taken against those who disturbed the "honour, safety, and stability of the Dominican family." The secret police waved their guns and shouted at people to disperse. Some left, but most nervously held their ground, and no shots were fired.

I stood at the back of the crowd and listened as Fiallo began to speak. He must have said something about liberty, for the crowd began to chant "*libertad*," at first haltingly, then firmly, stretching out the three syllables louder and louder. They paused, Fiallo spoke, and the chanting resumed. This time it was "*Navidad con libertad!*" The military aircraft still flew overhead and the loose ring of secret police remained at the edge of the park.

Fiallo finished speaking to a tumultuous roar of *"Navidad con liber-tad!"* Tears ran down the cheeks of the people around me, and a lump grew in my own throat. As the last *"Libertad!"* subsided, someone at the front of the crowd began to sing the national anthem. The anthem had been sung every day during the dictatorship, but not like this. Today it was transfigured by courage and the scent of freedom. The crowd sang, knowing that their voices rang as they never had in the last thirty-one years. That afternoon a part of the nation rediscovered its soul.

∾ ∾ ∾

Meatballs, Moose Piss, and the National Day

Ernie McCullough, my boss at the embassy, had been evacuated as a result of a heart attack. Ottawa had shown no inclination to replace him in a country still quivering with the political convulsions set off by the assassination of the dictator. This had little to do with confidence in the remaining two officers, Clark Leith[5] and me, and a lot to do with the low priority assigned unstable tropical backwaters by the Department of External Affairs. Both Clark and I were twenty-six, and on the bottom rung of the foreign service career ladder, but, by reason of a couple of months' seniority, I was chargé d'affaires and host, with responsibilities I could not begin to imagine.

"Look at that!" said Clark. We both watched as an enormous bus marked "Fuerzas Armadas" drew up outside the Santo Domingo Country Club. It was the first of July, and Clark and I had arrived early to ensure that everything was ready for the Canada Day reception.

The bus offered the first inkling of things to come. The door opened and thirty-six musicians emerged. Two were carrying tubas. As a courtesy, the Dominican government provided embassies with a military or police band to play at National Day receptions. McVitie, the British ambassador, had warned me to insist on a very small band, and Longroño, the Dominican chief of protocol, had agreed – or so I thought.

"Bloody hell!" I said, looking at the tubas.

I walked inside to find Hilda, my maid. I had asked her to keep an eye on the club's kitchen. She looked at her feet and muttered, "Everything OK." It never occurred to me to ask Hilda why she appeared stressed.

The reason was Odo, the club's acting chef and the person responsible for producing the hors d'oeuvres. One canapé was to be meatballs, served with a spicy tomato dip. Hilda found that he was preparing trays of raw meatballs and setting them down on a window ledge exposed to the afternoon sun. Odo reacted badly to her remark that this was not a good idea. He picked up a meat cleaver, screamed, and lunged. Hilda escaped, but was still in a difficult position. If she did nothing, it was likely that salmonella or more virulent botulisms would be incubated in the guests. If she warned me and I took action, it was likely that Odo would do terrible, if not lethal, damage to her. In those days the Dominican courts dealt leniently with homicide in provocative circumstances, particularly if a woman was the provocative circumstance. In desperation Hilda devised a route out of her dilemma. Her plan was to collect each tray as soon as it was out of the oven, pretend she was heading for the reception rooms, and then dash around the corner to the trash bin.

Unaware of this impending disaster, Clark and I set off in search of the champagne. Before he left, Ernie McCullough had sold me his supply. He said it would be fine for me or whoever was going to give the July 1 reception. There were three bottles of Heidsieck and six cases of Ontario 'champagne'. Ernie was a supporter of Ontario wines well before they began to win prizes – and they hadn't won real prizes in 1962. One of our friends, who had lived in Sudbury and claimed to know, said it tasted like "carbonated moose piss." How would the French ambassador, the Papal nuncio, and many others react to sparkling *catawba*? It was too late to order champagne offshore and too expensive to buy it locally. Another friend, the owner of a bar and restaurant, suggested a solution. He said that the colder you chill wine, the harder it is to detect whether it is good or bad. By asking the country club to refrigerate the wine almost to the freezing point, we hoped to minimize embarrassment. Like the meatballs and the refrigerators, this plan was not working. The bottles were in galvanized tubs of water in which floated very small, rapidly melting blobs of ice.

"Damn," I said.

"Maybe we can get the waiters to serve the Heidsieck to the foreign minister and some of the ambassadors," Clark suggested.

"Maybe," I replied, thinking too late that it would have been an act of patriotism to remove the labels from the Canadian bottles.

The first guests soon arrived, to be greeted by Clark and me. Protocol required that while drink could be offered, the band could not play and food could not be served until the guest of honour arrived. The guest of honour was the foreign minister, and perhaps because I had by far the lowest rank of any head of mission, he was taking his time. I was nervous and worried about the speech I would have to deliver in my still modest Spanish. The band was neither nervous nor idle. Unable to play, they helped themselves to drink. Because of our other distractions, Clark and I had failed to realize that the musicians had become drunk. When, at last, the foreign minister arrived, they played the Dominican national anthem with unusual vigour – and the next anthem almost blew us off our feet. Subsequently, many Canadian guests remarked that they had never heard "O Canada" played with such enthusiasm.

According to custom, the band would play occasional pieces as background. If the party warmed up, they could be asked to play dance music. At this party, as soon as the speeches were over and the glasses of tepid champagne clinked, the band launched into an ear-crunching merengue. Dominican merengues are played loudly, even with four musicians, which is the usual number. A merengue played by thirty-six inebriated military musicians is an indelible experience.

In the thirteen months since Trujillo had been killed, there had been two failed coups d'état, one successful coup d'état, and a brief civil war that was snuffed out by American gunboat diplomacy. The ministers, the generals, the politicians, the businessmen, the mining engineers, the diplomats and their wives wanted to talk; some wanted to intrigue. However, conversation was impossible. I harangued and directed pianissimo gestures at the conductor, a portly army captain who had imbibed almost as much as his men, and I gave orders to the waiters to cut off their supply of drink. The band played softly, and conversation resumed. But not for long. The music soon shifted from gentle mambo back to frenetic merengue. I shouted at the fat conductor. He smiled and the decibels subsided; then the cycle repeated. Even by eccentric local standards, it was an unusual evening. Hardbitten ambassadors looked stunned. They and the foreign

minister were the first to leave. Shortly thereafter, and none too soon, the last guests had driven past the club's neatly spaced clumps of oleander to the coast road, and home. The ordeal was over.

Or was it? Next morning, I was dismayed to find that there was no one at the office when I arrived. I phoned Clark at home.

"What's going on?" I asked. "Everyone seems to be under the misguided impression that today is a holiday, including you."

"What are you saying?" rasped Clark. "Nobody's at the office?"

"Just me."

"Oh, God!" moaned Clark.

"What do you mean, 'Oh, God!'?"

"I mean that today is not a holiday. I feel like death, and if the others feel like me, you probably won't see them for a month."

"Son of a bitch!" I said, and my body temperature seemed to drop. "I'd better make some calls." I telephoned members of the staff and a few others. Without exception they had been sick during the night. The memory of my conversation with Hilda removed the last shred of hope that this sickness was unrelated to Canadian hospitality. I had been too busy and too tense to eat anything. I called Clark again.

"Do you know what we have done?"

"I can guess," he said.

"We've knocked out half the cabinet, the military command structure, the leaders of the business community, most of the diplomatic corps…and our friends."

"Well," he said, "look on the bright side."

"What bright side? This is a bloody disaster."

"At least," said Clark, "no one will remember the champagne."

(UBA

Whose Man in Havana?

In the fall of 1962 the Cuban missile crisis captured the attention of the world. I was still in the Dominican Republic, where the neighbouring waters were the scene of a test of wills between John Kennedy, who had to decide whether to follow through on his ultimatum that Soviet missile-bearing freighters should turn around, and Nikita Khrushchev, who had to decide whether to take Kennedy's ultimatum as a bluff, and order his freighters to proceed on course. These developments were much on our minds in Santo Domingo. But with coups d'état, counter-coups, and an election campaign, so much was going on in the streets around us that we were not as sensitive to the risks of nuclear extinction as we should have been. And, certainly, I had no premonition that I might be drawn into the fallout of the October Crisis.

In the spring of 1963 I received a telegram from External Affairs asking me to terminate my posting in the Dominican Republic as soon as possible and report to Ottawa for a briefing prior to a posting to Havana. The assignment was as attractive as it was unexpected. Fidel Castro had installed himself only four years before, Cuba was in social, political, and economic tumult, and the world was still reeling from its narrow escape from Armageddon. But getting away quickly was not so easy. In the miniscule embassy in Santo Domingo I was chargé d'affaires, and had been for a year – a ridiculous situation, because I was far too junior, but no one in Ottawa was clamouring to come to a country still quivering from the upheaval that followed the assassination of Generalissimo Trujillo. Because there was no replacement in sight, there was a lot to do, and I arrogantly thought I should do some of it before leaving. Besides, I wanted a holiday. A telegram was sent to External Affairs asking if I could delay taking up the posting. Surprisingly, if grudgingly, they agreed. Only when I arrived in Ottawa did I learn that the Havana posting was not a normal job.

At this distance in time, the background to the assignment may seem far-fetched. In April 1963 Lester Pearson defeated John Diefenbaker to become prime minister. President Kennedy had quietly rejoiced at the change in Ottawa. He and John Diefenbaker disliked each other. There were incentives on both the Canadian and American sides to ensure that the relationship was on a more solid footing. Although the Canadian armed forces had discreetly co-operated with the United States during the missile crisis, Diefenbaker had denied the Americans the full collaboration that Douglas Harkness, the minister of defence, had sought and that most NATO countries had already provided. For two days the prime minister had stalled placing Canadian forces on full alert. In the most authoritative chronicle of Canadian involvement (and non-involvement) in the crisis, Commander Peter Haydon noted that by October 24 most NATO countries were supportive of the Kennedy response. He wrote that the principal exception was Canada, whose "refusal to endorse Kennedy's diplomacy deeply upset the Americans."[1] On this day the *Globe and Mail* editorialized that the policy of "sitting on the fence [was] unthinkable." The *New York Times* had said much the same thing the day before. Bobby Kennedy's needle was sharper: "Canada offers all aid short of help."

The first meeting between President Kennedy and the new prime minister took place at the president's family compound in Hyannis Port on May 10 and 11. The official agenda for the Hyannis Port meeting covered the gamut of US–Canada relations (trade, security, fish) and included the acutely sensitive issue of US nuclear weapons on Canadian soil (a topic on which Kennedy and Pearson came to agreement). The conversation included Cuba, and the president's desire to see Canada in the OAS. On the latter issue, Pearson responded that the time was not right to join the organization.

JFK and PM Pearson at Hyannis Port in May 1963.

According to the declassified summary report of these meetings, and dated May 15, under the heading "Latin America," we learn that "the President expressed warm appreciation for Canadian assistance in the field of intelligence."[2]

Jim McCardle, who was at that time head of the Defence Liaison (2) Division, which dealt with security and intelligence for External Affairs, confided to me and to our ambassador in Havana that Pearson had confirmed with the president a recently established arrangement whereby an officer at the Canadian Embassy in Havana would respond to American intelligence "tasking" on Soviet military and naval activities in Cuba.

Kennedy and Khrushchev had fully understood that the world was teetering on the edge of an abyss. They had stood down their respective hawks – advisors, mostly military, in both the Kremlin and Washington who had pressed for a pre-emptive first strike. They had agreed on a solution. So, if the crisis was over, why would the Americans make a highly unusual request to Canada for intelligence support? Canada did not have (nor does it have now) a separate foreign intelligence service.

A month after the crisis, the Kennedy administration was fairly confident that Khrushchev had withdrawn all nuclear weapons from Cuba. Intense overhead photo reconnaissance by the US Navy and Air Force continued, but the level of trust in Soviet assurances was understandably low. The Americans could not be totally certain that all "offensive" as opposed to "defensive" weapons encompassed in the deal with Khrushchev had been recalled. Khrushchev had accepted Kennedy's condition that the withdrawal of aggressive missiles and their nuclear warheads would be verified by United Nations inspectors. Fidel Castro had vetoed the arrangement as an abuse of Cuban sovereignty.

Apprehension in Washington resurfaced in November 1962, when aerial photography revealed the presence of mobile "battlefield" tactical weapons. Called Lunas by the Russians and FROGS by NATO, these weapons had a maximum range of fifty miles, and nuclear capability. Some had been deployed near the US base at Guantánamo, a posture that some in Washington did not regard as defensive. According to David Coleman in his book *The Fourteenth Day*, Defense Secretary Robert McNamara referred to the potential use of Luna missiles as "the most dangerous element of the entire episode." Coleman adds that "detecting and identifying Luna missiles proved a challenge for US intelligence."[3] The Luna issue persisted. In February 1963 Richard Helms, the CIA's director of operations, informed a congressional subcommittee that although there was no evidence that Luna nuclear warheads were based in Cuba at that time, he "could not rule out" their presence. There was also concern about the estimated twenty-four operational surface-to-air missile (SAM) bases on the island, and the estimated sixteen Komar-class guided missile patrol boats. It was evident that Washington felt the need for more eyes on the ground. By this time there was also concern that Cuban counter-intelligence (the infamous G-2) had rounded up large numbers of CIA agents on the island, thus intensifying the requirement for more ground-level information.

In the half-century that has passed since the dramatic events of October 1962, a remarkable accumulation of data has been released for public and particularly academic scrutiny from both sides of the divide. David Coleman's recent research, especially previously unexamined presidential tapes, offers a much-improved understanding of the anxieties in Washington which continued after the main lines of the Kennedy/ Khrushchev deal had been reached on October 28 and which, in turn,

helps to explain why the United States would have sought 'non-profes-
sional' Canadian assistance with ground-level intelligence in Cuba. In
addition to the Lunas, Coleman cites: continuing uncertainty about the
withdrawal of all nuclear warheads; evidence that Soviet and American
interpretations of the weapons withdrawal agreement were not identical;
the presence of FKR missiles (a Cruise-type short-range missile) which,
like the Lunas, could be fitted with nuclear warheads; plans to establish
Soviet submarine bases; and concern that Ill-28 bombers (capable of carrying 12-kiloton nuclear bombs) had not been crated and shipped. In
November 1962, Anastas Mikoyan, Khrushchev's deputy, had been sent to
Havana to mollify an incensed Cuban leader. Instead, as Coleman quotes
him, Mikoyan found that "Castro's famed revolutionary passion was becoming worryingly apocalyptic."[4]

These were the central concerns. There were others. With his own vision kindled by success in Cuba, Castro was actively promoting armed
revolution elsewhere in Latin America. Priority targets were Venezuela,
Guatemala, and Colombia.

Another element that may have influenced the American request was
the fact, evident at Hyannis Port, that the US president, senior officers in
the State Department, and the CIA, had been impressed by the timeli-
ness and quality of the reporting from Canada's small Havana embassy
in the months both preceding and following the crisis. On its own initiative Ottawa had encouraged the embassy to undertake surveillance of the
loading and offloading of missile-shaped crates in the ports of Mariel and
Havana.

So, why me? After two and a half years in the Dominican Republic, I
had Spanish. Another factor influencing my selection might have been my
status as a reserve officer in the Royal Canadian Navy. I never found out.

In any event, the cogs in the East Block of Parliament Hill, where most
of External Affairs was then located, began to move. When it was agreed
that my assignment could be delayed, another junior officer was found to
perform the role on a temporary basis. Selected was the ebullient and delightfully eccentric George Cowley, who had just returned from a posting
in Japan. (Before joining the foreign service he had spent an adventurous
time selling encyclopedias in Africa.)

After several months in Cuba, George returned in time to share with
me his newly acquired trade secrets. We spent an afternoon in Zellers,

where George selected plaid shirts, khaki pants, and tennis shoes of a style that more or less resembled those worn by Soviet soldiers in Cuba. Officially Moscow said that the only Russians stationed in Cuba were a few service attachés at their embassy, but in fact in 1963 the number of soldiers was close to 30,000, and, to preserve the fiction, none were in uniform. Officially the Russians called their troops "agricultural experts." Unofficially they referred to them as "checkered shirts." George's advice, which I resolutely followed, was that I should camouflage myself. With my new wardrobe, and information on what and whom to expect, I was almost ready for Havana.

The last step was a visit to Washington, and then Langley, Virginia, where briefings at CIA headquarters were arranged for me. I should explain. What Mr. Pearson had confirmed was primarily an American enterprise. Specific taskings were to originate at Langley, and they were passed to the Canadian embassy intelligence liaison office in Washington, who passed them to DL(2) Division in the East Block. From the East Block, the messages were transmitted by special cipher machine to the embassy in Havana. The same laundering process was followed in the reverse direction, sometimes via the US embassy in Ottawa. Less urgent reporting from Havana was sent by diplomatic bag under cover of a letter.

At the conclusion of my briefings in Langley the senior CIA officer thanked me for taking on this assignment, then added, "We have a little gift for you," whereupon he produced a small, sophisticated camera with telescopic lenses. (Zoom lenses were not yet in common use.) I should not have been surprised, but I was. My mind raced – raced about what would happen to me if I was caught with incriminating film, either by the Soviets or the Cubans. It seemed to me that the chances of being caught lurking around Soviet military installations in a look-alike Russian plaid shirt were not insignificant. The Americans could certainly not protect me, nor would I want them to. The Canadians, who enjoyed remarkably good bilateral relations with the Cuban government and who would have insisted on my diplomatic immunity, would have been acutely embarrassed. While a niggle about being ungracious to my hosts also ran through my head, I politely declined.[5]

Now the Americans were surprised. "But how will you give us the detail we need about guidance and other electronic equipment? Configuration is essential for recognition!"

"Ah," I said, "I sketch. I will send you sketches." Expressions of dismay appeared. My interlocutors were no doubt thinking dark thoughts about secret agents in Havana sending back drawings of the inner workings of vacuum cleaners, as in Graham Greene's classic spy novel *Our Man in Havana*. According to my reflections at the time, film taken with a telescopic lens would identify me as a professional agent, while a captor might consider sketches to be amateurish, and therefore less blatantly incriminating. So sketching is what I did.

To my surprise, and thanks to intrepid research by Access to Information officers in Foreign Affairs and by Library and Archives Canada, I have been able to track down these sketches. Even better, they had been declassified, along with many of my reports. Several of these sketches are included in this chapter. At the time I was unaware of the extra steps taken by DL(2) Division to conceal the fact that (a) this reporting was taking place, and (b) all of these reports were shared with the CIA. The covering letters from Havana were marked "Secret" and addressed to the head of DL(2) Division. On arrival in Ottawa, they had been stamped not only "Canadian Eyes Only" – anomalous in the circumstances – but "Protect Source," as well as "Ottawa Only," a designation I had never heard of. It sounds like overkill, but it was clearly intended to restrict access as much as possible for this out-of-character clandestine mission. It may have been that the abundance of security classifications was also intended to provide protection for me. Possibly, but I doubt it. As far as I can recall, the potential hazards of the job were never discussed.

Several of my reports, including a telegram describing Soviet shipping movements and cargo, were found by my friend, Professor Don Munton, in the declassified archives of the John F. Kennedy library in Boston. Their source was clearly the Canadian embassy in Havana, and the CIA had sent them, along with other briefing material, to the White House.

Getting into Havana in the early sixties was a roundabout operation. Every country in the hemisphere had broken relations with Cuba except for Mexico and Canada. One route was from Moscow, with a fuelling stop in Gander, for the enormous long-range Tupolev 114s and Antonovs.

However, Aeroflot discouraged non-approved passengers. The route for most Canadians was by Cubana Airlines out of Mexico City on aging Bristol Britannias.

When I arrived in Havana, I was not taken, as I expected, to one of the infamously louche downtown hotels, but driven directly to my new residence in the once upper-bourgeois suburb of Cubanacan. There was no need to go to a hotel. My new home was fully equipped; it included a maid, Pura, and Blackie, a large dog of mixed breeding. It was explained to me that the owner, Mr. William Skilton, had mentioned to his friend the Canadian ambassador that he and his family would be leaving Cuba, and as soon as the unpleasantness with Fidel Castro came to an end they would return. In the meantime, the house and maid would be available to the Canadian embassy. Like many others, Mr. Skilton expected to return within a few months. George Kidd, the ambassador, had said, "Right, Graham's coming. That's where we will put him."

The house was called *Los Venaditos*, after the life-sized sculpture of a deer and fawn that stood on a small island on the street outside. It was a very comfortable, largish bungalow with a pale pink exterior. Inside, it was as if the family had just left for the weekend. The furnishings, the wall decorations, the plates, the utensils – everything was in place. A pipe hung in a pipe rack above an ashtray. Skilton was an American and the owner of a small factory, and he and his family had left with their suitcases for a short stay in Florida. Somehow they had managed to leave without attracting the suspicions of the Cuban authorities, who would normally have expropriated the house and its contents as they had done with those of all my neighbours. The surrounding houses had been seized and converted into boarding houses for *becados* and *becadas* – students from the countryside. One well-protected mansion nearby was occupied by young men from central Africa who were being given "specialized" military training.

The Cuban foreign ministry was given my address. I was married halfway through my posting, and Judy and I lived openly in Los Venaditos. Again, I should explain. All Canadian members of the embassy took turns travelling to Mexico City to exchange diplomatic bags with the regular diplomatic courier and to shop for goods not available in Havana. In the course of my trips, I met and pursued Judy, who was on her first posting at the embassy in Mexico City as secretary to the ambassador. For some reason of bureaucratic incompetence, the Cuban government never realized

Canada and the world as seen by Cuban cartoonists in the mid sixties.

that we should not have been living in Venaditos and that I should have been renting authorized accommodation from the Cuban state. While the Skiltons did not request payment, I paid them from my bank account in Canada. This arrangement was improper in Cuban terms and unconventional in embassy terms. I was learning that there were many things about this posting that were unconventional.

On the northern edge of Cubanacan was the Havana country club and golf course. Recently 'acquired' by the state, it was being transformed at Fidel's command into a cluster of schools for ballet, theatre, and the plastic arts. The design had been awarded to a genial acquaintance, Ricardo Porro. One of Cuba's most creative architects, Porro explained that his design had "erotic dimensions." Carefully moulded cupolas and other female and male parts were incorporated into the architecture. Art in Cuba was aesthetically uninhibited and bore no relation to the 'socialist realism' of the Soviet model. Political cartoons in the newspapers and poster cartoons, while anti-Yankee and pro-Fidel, were brilliant and eventually became collector's items. (I nicked a couple from telephone poles.) Porro was given the commission to design the Cuban pavilion at EXPO 67 in Montreal. However, his imagination soared beyond his budget and he was replaced.

Once on the ground in Havana my job was to identify Soviet weapons, electronic detection and communications systems, and, to the extent possible, the movement of Soviet troops and equipment. US naval and air force photo reconnaissance aircraft, high-flying U2s, low level Crusaders, and 101s provided the locations and rough configurations of Soviet military installations, but not enough detail. The coordinates were routed to me through Ottawa, and with this information plotted on a map, I would set off in my car, almost invariably on back roads, and drive as close as I could to the perimeter of the site in question – not too close, but close enough to sketch the equipment and make notes. Sometimes the camp was too well hidden, or the approach road would have alerted even the most gullible of Soviet guards to my intentions. Back at the embassy, I would attempt to identify the equipment by referring to a NATO manual of Soviet weapons and communications systems. The report, plus the sketches, would be sent by diplomatic bag. The sketches depicted SAM, Cruise (FKR), and Komar missiles sheathed in canvas – or, in the case of the Komars, partially so. I did not spot a Luna. The bag left once every fortnight to Ottawa via my romance route to Mexico City – a rather lengthy process for information that was potentially sensitive. However, in most cases a summary of the findings, and especially anything possibly significant, would be dispatched by the new dedicated cipher machine.

SAMs (also called SA-2 by NATO) were an intelligence priority from the outset of the crisis and throughout my period in Havana. Tensions, already near the tipping point, escalated on October 27, 1962, when a Soviet unit fired two SAMs at an overflying U-2 reconnaissance aircraft, destroying it and killing the USAF pilot, Major Rudolf Anderson. As previously noted, hawks in Moscow and Washington, and Fidel Castro in Havana, were urging pre-emptive nuclear strikes, and that danger was removed only on the following day, when the "unofficial" proposal from Kennedy to withdraw Jupiter missiles from Turkey in exchange for the removal of the nuclear missiles from Cuba received a positive response from Khrushchev. Conscious that delays in the transmission and decrypting of messages between the two capitals, which could take up to ten hours, were playing into the hands of the hawks, the Soviet leader ordered his reply to Kennedy to be broadcast openly from Radio Moscow. The prospect of reciprocal nuclear attacks never again reached the hair-trigger point of that week, but sabre-, SAM- and Luna-rattling did not come to an end.

Castro never accepted the Kennedy/Khrushchev deal. He may have begun to suspect that the primary objective of Khrushchev's bold move was not to protect the Cuban revolution, but to shift the strategic balance so that he could force the Western powers (the US, the UK, and France) out of Berlin.[6] In any event, as Mikoyan discovered, Castro felt betrayed. He complained to the Russians and fulminated loudly at the Americans. In April 1964, on the occasion of the third anniversary of his defeat of the CIA-organized invasion of the Bay of Pigs, Castro declaimed, "There are limits to prudence and limits to calm. There are limits beyond which one must not go – and these limits are being dangerously abused." In the same ominously hyperbolic tone he went on, "The Cuban people are not prepared to tolerate indefinitely the penetrations of the Marines [he was referring to Guantánamo] or stand idly by while their air space is being violated...and rather than a miserable peace, it is a hundred times better to have the dignified peace of the grave." It was a longer way of saying, "*Patria o Muerte*."

Nine days later, on April 28, 1964, the Cuban foreign minister, Raul Roa, delivered a letter to UN Secretary General U Thant protesting that six hundred American spy planes had overflown Cuba since the missile crisis, and that this represented "the arbitrary, provocative, illegal, and ir-responsible conduct of the USA, a country that has sent trained saboteurs into Cuba to subvert the Socialist order, destroy the property of the people, and commit murder."

At the time the British embassy in Havana called these statements "unexpectedly pugnacious." The Canadian embassy regarded them as more serious than posturing. In a telegram of April 21, following Castro's Bay of Pigs speech, the embassy said that "there would seem to be clear threats to attempt to shoot down US planes." At this time the Cubans did not control the SAM system, but they did use conventional anti-aircraft weapons (unsuccessfully) against low-flying reconnaissance aircraft such as the Crusaders flown by the US Navy or the Voodoos flown by the US Air Force. However, by the spring of 1964 there was mounting anxiety in Washington that Cuban pressure to take over the SAM system from the Soviet military might succeed. If this happened, the threat of escalation would instantly become more acute.

Unsurprisingly, the American reaction was firm. The State Department pointed out that it regarded the overflights as necessary in order to avoid

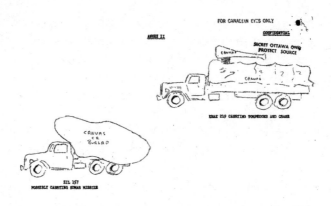

the deception used against them in 1962, warning that if Castro does shoot down an overflying aircraft, "another Cuban crisis could erupt immediately." In a statement issued on April 20, 1964, Dick Philips, the State Department spokesman, explained that "overflights are a substitute for the onsite inspection agreed to by the Soviets in October 1962, but which Fidel Castro refused to permit."

Against this background, it was understood that many of my taskings related to SAM missile sites. One long night sticks vividly in my memory. Air reconnaissance had reported that a Soviet base, probably a SAM missile unit, was packing up, either for redeployment within Cuba or for shipment back to Russia. The Soviet army moved its installations by night to avoid overhead detection. I was given the coordinates of the base and asked to scout the roads in an eastern radius to determine where the convoy was headed and what it contained. I was instructed to be in the target area, about a two-hour drive from Havana, by midnight.

Just before midnight I was driving along a secondary highway when I saw the dimmed lights of a line of trucks approaching. A long convoy of jeeps, large vans, trucks, and articulated trucks was moving eastward – all recognizably Soviet vehicles. Bingo! I had my quarry.

I drew up at the side of the road and opened my notebook. By then more than half the convoy had passed and the balance were moving too quickly for more than sporadic notes and inscrutable doodles. When the convoy had moved past I waited perhaps five minutes, turned my Volkswagen Beetle around, and headed off in pursuit. Apart from the Russians and

SECRET OTTAWA ONLY
PROTECT SOURCE

CANADIAN EYES ONLY

FOR CANADIAN EYES ONLY

ANNEX II   CONFIDENTIAL
                SECRET OTTAWA ONLY
                PROTECT SOURCE

THE TOP CONFIGURATION FROM THIS
SIDE IS NOT RECALLED

CANVAS COVER

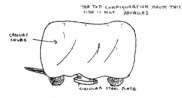

CIRCULAR STEEL PLATE

LEFT HAND SIDE VIEW.

ANNEX II

000702

FLEXIBLE WIRE ANTENNAE

ANTENNA MAST

GUY LINES

JUNG OR ALUMINUM BASE

ANTENNA

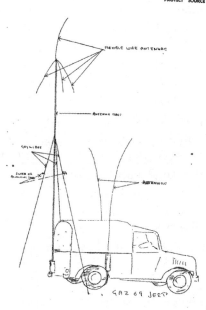

GAZ 69 JEEP

000690

Rear view.

Side view.

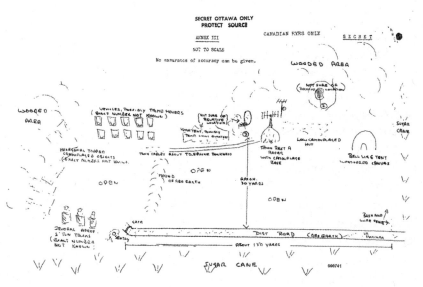

WOODED AREA

WOODED AREA

NOT SURE OF RELATIVE LOCATION

VEHICLES, POSSIBLY PRIME MOVERS
(EXACT NUMBER NOT KNOWN)

NOT SURE OF RELATIVE LOCATION

KHAKI TENT, POSSIBLY TEAM LIVING QUARTERS

SEDAN REST A RADAR WITH CAMOUFLAGE BASE

LOW CAMOUFLAGED HUT

SUGAR CANE

HEXAGONAL TOPPED CAMOUFLAGED OBJECTS
(EXACT NUMBER NOT KNOWN)

THIN CABLES ABOUT TELEPHONE THICKNESS

BELL LIKE TENT
WEATHERED CANVAS

OPEN

MOUND OF RED EARTH

OPEN

APPROX 30 YARDS

OPEN

BUSH AND WIRE FENCE

SEVERAL ABOUT 5 TON TRUCKS
(EXACT NUMBER NOT KNOWN)

SENTRY

GATE

DIRT ROAD (RED EARTH)

LA PACIANA

ABOUT 180 YARDS

SUGAR CANE

000741

myself, there was no traffic on the road. It was very dark; there was no moon, or at most a crescent. I overtook the vehicles slowly, two or three at a time. With my notebook beside me, I jotted down short descriptions of the vehicles and did rough sketches of the shapes of the loads. Of particular interest were the forty-foot-long canvas-shrouded canister shapes with pointed noses – almost certainly SAMs. To double-check on shapes and numbers, I drove on until I was about five miles beyond the convoy and parked, fairly well hidden by trees at the side of the road. I waited there until I saw the tail of the last flatbed, lit by a single blue light.

Perhaps I should have followed the convoy to the new destination, but this would have been pushing my luck. As it was, I found it curious that on a lonely country road in the middle of the night, no security vehicle peeled off to stop me and ask questions. Language problems, or perhaps orders to stay clear of the natives. There also appeared to be virtually no Soviet collaboration with the Cuban army or even with G-2, the Cuban intelligence service. Cuban motorcycle outriders would have been more alert to persons and vehicles that did not reasonably fit the setting. Apart from a brash moment when an embassy colleague and I were stopped from entering the secure communications area of one of the ancient Spanish fortifications in Havana Harbour (we excused ourselves as bungling tourists), I was never stopped in the course of these operations. Soviet bases, at least the ones that I observed, were lightly guarded, and almost exclusively by Soviet soldiers, who were not encouraged to fraternize with Cubans. (The Cuban soldiers wore uniforms.) I assume that luck also played a role.

My Zellers imitation Soviet sports shirts probably helped as well. My hair was fair, so to the Cubans I looked like a Russian soldier or an Eastern Bloc technician. My wife and I were sometimes greeted coldly by Cuban citizens as *Rusas* or *Czecas*. In the street in Holguin one afternoon, three Cuban men held their noses as they walked past me. I had been driving for a long time and was probably trailing fragrance, but I suspect that the gesture was more political than olfactory. Cubans, even many loyal Castro Cubans, did not care for the Russians and their East Bloc colleagues who came as technicians. A secondary factor may have been that in those days soap was not as important a feature of daily Soviet routine as it was for the scrupulously hygienic Cubans.

Several times I was accompanied by Vaughan Johnson, the embassy administrator and a sergeant in the Canadian Army Reserve. On one

Fidel Castro, Graham, and Ambassador Mayrand.

occasion the road took us within about twenty metres of a camp fence. Vans with electronic gadgetry were readily visible inside. However, there was no shrubbery or other cover nearby, and a drive-past at a non-suspicious speed did not afford enough time to sketch the parade of masts and swiveling hardware. It was broad daylight, and repeated drive-bys were out of the question. In the end we stopped within good viewing distance and changed a non-flat tire – probably Vaughan's idea.

When I arrived, the Canadian ambassador was George Kidd. As already mentioned, the reports that he and his first secretary, Dwight Fulford, sent to Ottawa during and after the October Crisis were highly regarded in Ottawa and Washington. At the Hyannis Port meeting, President Kennedy had singled out Canadian reporting for appreciation. Dwight and Barbara Fulford operated a ménage. On each of my frequent visits to their home I was amazed by the profusion of kids and dogs parading in and out of the doors and ground-floor windows. Some of the kids and most of the dogs did not belong to them. On weekends, this hodgepodge was packed into their station wagon along with picnic supplies for a day at the beach. The Fulfords were known to our French colleagues as *le cirque ambulant.*

I have mentioned Vaughan; there was also Gaby Warren, the third secretary, whose official activities were largely consular (two Canadians had been arrested, caught red-handed importing explosives for the CIA).[7] Gaby's *unofficial* activities were consumed by plunging into the incredibly rich Cuban musical scene and (to the chagrin of External Affairs) the hot pursuit of a beautiful Cuban girl. Gaby was exquisitely vulnerable to elaborate April Fool concoctions.[8] There were two delightful secretaries, Mavis Edmonds and Dorothy Lewis. The communicator who punched out my telegrams was George Franklin. He and I had a ten-dollar bet as to who would kill the greater number of tarantulas in our respective homes by the time one of us had to leave. George won, 5 to 4. One of mine was nesting in a slipper. The local staff were splendid; many of them suffered acutely when friends and close relations were arrested. I recall one young woman particularly. Her husband had been arrested shortly after their marriage and her anguish was never far from the surface.

The security guards, all former soldiers, formed another branch of the embassy family. They exasperated the Ottawa security people in DL(2) by consorting with Cuban chorus girls. One, a transplanted Cockney, admitted to us that his popularity had a lot to do with his access to nylons and other goodies not available in Cuba's austere, nationalized economy. As a British soldier, this fellow had been captured at Dunkirk and had spent the rest of the war in a German prisoner of war camp. He was, he told us, catching up.

The embassy was awash with courtship. In addition to Gaby's and mine, the genial and dry-humoured Chuck Svoboda, Gaby's replacement, married Lisa, the slim, attractive daughter of a Havana-based Swedish diplomat. Chuck was the only athletic-looking member of our motley crew.

For a young foreign service officer it was a fascinating environment. Everyone worked hard, but in Havana in those days the standard of diplomatic revelry was high, the zest of diplomatic party life being a function of both political isolation and local drama. There were swimming parties, and a Roman toga ball. I held several scavenger hunts, with points for commandeering a Soviet jeep (extra points if it contained Russians), a diplomatic bag (extra points if it was Russian one),[9] a Hungarian bus, and an electric toothbrush (almost non-existent in Havana at that time). One item, which spoke of change in Canada, was points for the best design of a Canadian flag.[10] A special bonus was offered to anyone who managed to obtain an authenticated hair from Che Guevara's beard. Che was in Havana at this point, but this bonus was not collected. The scavenger list may have been politically dodgy, but spirits were high and uninhibited. Shortly before my arrival, Gaby and George Cowley had convened a masquerade party at which each guest was invited to dress as his or her favourite sin. One diplomat, overdosed on bravado, came as Fidel Castro. These festivities invariably concluded in a cloud of ambrosial cigar smoke.

The Cuban system tolerated social intercourse between Western diplomats and citizens. Many of our friends were among the disenchanted and through them we obtained a picture of some of the challenges faced by ordinary Cubans. The food industries, large farms and food transport, along with much else, had been nationalized. The result was instant chaos and acute rationing. For example, bananas or tomatoes might be so plentiful in one part of the country that they would be left to rot, while in most other regions they would be unobtainable. Belts were worn (and are still worn) tight. However, some citizens found imaginative ways of beating the system – or at least a part of it. A Cuban favorite is *lechon* or pig roasted on a spit and its absence from the menu was intensely felt. Our friend, Carlos Agostini, a violinist at the National Symphony Orchestra, overcame the *lechon* problem. He and his wife, Maria Victoria, kept a pig, partitioned from view, on the roof of their downtown apartment building. This practice was illegal for a number of reasons, hygiene being only one. A constant challenge for the Agostini family was to avoid detection by the 'Committee for the Defense of the Revolution' (CDR), a neighbourhood snoop organization dedicated to reporting not just counter-revolutionary activities, but 'non-revolutionary' norms such as the length of a skirt (too short) or the length of male hair (too long). Another friend, Haydée Scull, did a flourishing and risky trade with the sale of hilarious lampoons of revolutionary excess, often featuring the CDR, beautifully executed in framed and painted relief sculptures.

At diplomatic functions the currency of conversation was too often rumour. In an environment of fear and rigorous censorship there were few reliable facts and those few were generally of little interest to our respective foreign ministries. The atmosphere was oppressive, although less insidiously suffocating than that in Ciudad Trujillo before the dictator's assassination. Enveloped in this fog, we made the best of it. At the time of my arrival a popular topic was whether Fidel was a full-blown

Marxist/Leninist or still the radical socialist depicted in the late fifties by New York Times correspondent Herbert Matthews. It was soon clear that he had jettisoned any 'liberal' precepts – an understanding that shifted the debate to whether he had ever had any. Discussion was non-stop on the fluctuations of Soviet/Cuban relations. A burning issue which consumed the diplomatic community for many months was the location of Che Guevara. Che had disappeared from sight and the latest rumours and alleged sightings were dissected by my colleagues and, of course, by me. Before long the subject had passed out of the zone of serious discourse and had become a suitable target for mischief – or so it seemed to me. Toward the end of a well-lubricated dinner party and in this mildly irresponsible state of mind, I was asked by a colleague from a non-aligned country if I had any fresh information on Che. In what I thought was a jocular tone, I replied, "Perhaps he has taken refuge in the Canadian embassy." Inevitably this rumour bounced back. The denials of the ambassador[11] (from whom I had hidden the provenance of the rumour) and the embassy staff were not always convincing.

Even with "control" in Langley there were occasional attempts to lighten the correspondence. In February 1964 a request was received by the usual channel to report on an "unidentified construction" near the village of Lombillo. A potentially suspicious configuration of concrete shapes in concentric ovals had been spotted by aerial surveillance. Interest was intensified as a result of the presence of Soviet tanks and an armoured car at the perimeter. Following a reconnaissance visit, I reported that the construction was almost complete, and that "a large herd of cows was observed feeding from the mysterious concentric troughs." The letter concluded, "Perhaps we should mention that according to local tradition it is our prerogative to develop ominous shapes resembling vacuum cleaners."

Of course I was not the only embassy-based intelligence agent working in Cuba after the October crisis. How many of us were there? I could not be sure. I was authorized to make myself known to one. X was brilliant and altogether remarkable. He gave parties at which he might compose Monty Python-like lyrics for pet, soap, and lingerie commercials that he sang to his own accompaniment on the piano, while Jacinto, his major-domo, kept the guests sustained with a steady stream of rum and gin-based cocktails.

One sticky afternoon I watched while the devoted Jacinto rolled up his pant legs, placed a gin and tonic on his tray, and delivered it to X, who was resting in his chair at the shallow end of his pool. This was the same pool into which Judy and I introduced a freshly caught five-foot-long marlin, which by then was dead. This fish, stuffed, now hangs in Vaughan Johnson's house in Ottawa. X's eccentric panache and Y, his beautiful wife, a former ballerina, inspired such mischief. On Y's birthday, we arranged to send her a magenta-coloured bidet filled with flowers. On another occasion I left on their verandah a home-made chastity belt, cut from an old tin tea chest and trimmed with foam rubber.

From time to time we did "joint operations." X was a professional and I admired his aplomb, but I did not participate in most of his activities, nor did he tell me about them. Those we conducted together were fairly straightforward – travelling to Cuban ports to check who or what was being offloaded from or loaded onto Soviet freighters or passenger ships.

By November 1963 the United States had blacklisted 187 ships for defying the US embargo on trading with Cuba, of which 56 were British, 54 Greek, 34 Lebanese, 10 Italian, and 8 Polish. Most of the non–Soviet Bloc vessels were the dregs of the sea. An embassy letter of November 7 describes them as "tired, rust-encrusted, with railings askew and cluttered decks – many looking like refugees from a Conrad novel," and observed that "at a time of over-supply of merchant shipping, it would seem that these aged tramps have little to lose by engaging in the Cuban trade." By contrast, the Soviet merchant ships appeared to be mostly of post-war construction and well maintained. Unlike X, who already spoke Russian, I had to learn the Cyrillic alphabet so that I could identify these ships.

In the course of our joint ventures, X and I developed a stress-relief therapy. On the way home we would find a quiet beach or a shaded glen and spread a picnic blanket. X would open a box from which he removed two small crystal goblets. From the same box he would take a thermos containing pre-mixed martinis. My contribution was a jar of olives.

Cuba was, of course, a dictatorship. But what sort of dictatorship? There were heartbreaking brutalities and breath-taking stupidities, but grim as they were, they could not be compared with the vicious barbarity of Trujillo's tyranny next door. Michael Arkus, a friend and the Reuters correspondent at that time in Havana, wrote "Despite ... the purges, limits on freedom and other restrictions, you never got the feeling that you were living in the oppressive, grey Kafkaesque police state that existed in other Communist countries in Europe or China – certainly not the atrocious hell conjured up in the counter-revolutionary propaganda from the Miami exiles." Arkus concluded that Cuba was "Leninism lite."[12] If you had to be born in a Latin American slum and if your parents understood the options and had some choice about where that would be, the chances are they would choose Cuba. Unlike the rest of Latin America, it had brought health care, education, and potentially a ladder to the bottom layers. If the alternative was illiteracy, disease, and an early death, they would look at the price as more than tolerable. However, for much of the large middle class, which was significantly larger than the Castro spin had cast it, the revolution was a disaster. And many of the disenchanted had been early supporters of Castro.

When the mission was over I sometimes wondered whether I had reported anything significant in that acutely nervous Cold War context. I don't know – Langley never told me – but I doubt it. I suspect that the real value of this mission had been its contributions to a basic intelligence task, which was the removal of question marks about the distribution of Soviet forces, the identity of their weapons and equipment, their combat readiness, and the existence or non-existence of collaboration with the Cuban army. One trivial example was the time we demystified "curious poles" as recently planted trees. Were Cubans operating SAMs? Were Soviet forces and equipment coming or going? Many others as well as myself were adding to the "big picture" that was being examined on a twenty-four hour basis at Langley and at the National Security Council in the White House. Whatever dark places the CIA had been and would go, this operation made sense. These were the years when many thousands of families were building nuclear fallout shelters in their basements or under their backyards.

There was another benefit. The operation was worth at least one brownie point in the overall relationship with the United States.

In the fall of 1964 my clandestine work came to an end. I replaced Dwight Fulford as number two in the embassy with a focus on political and economic reporting. My CIA work was taken on by Alan McLaine, who arrived with his wife Tudy and three small daughters, known to us affectionately as the frogs.

The towering event of the next twelve months was Hurricane Flora. The storm struck Cuba at seven o'clock in the morning, October 2, 1964 – the worst hurricane in Cuban history, and the sixth worst ever recorded in the Atlantic region. Reaching wind speeds of 230 kph, it cut a swath through Haiti, leaving five thousand dead. It came ashore in Cuba 30 km east of Guantánamo in Oriente Province, heading in a northwesterly direction. However, 80 km inland, and hedged in by a neighbouring pressure system and the Escambray mountains, it veered and began the first of several devastating loops. North of Santiago it turned 360 degrees, then moved east until it was just west of Santa Cruz, where it turned 200 degrees. On October 8 it headed inland, then left the island a few miles west of Cabo Lucrecia on the northwest coast. Flora savaged eastern Cuba for an unprecedented four days. Wind velocity slowed over the land; it was the rain that did the damage. In Santiago over 80 inches, or 2,000 mm, fell. Valleys and plains filled with water and huge segments of Cuban livestock and agriculture were laid waste. Despite a well-organized early warning, seventeen hundred Cubans died.

Ottawa was planning to airlift emergency assistance, and needed first-hand reports. Two of us drove east from Havana: Gaby into Camaguey, and me through other areas of Camaguey and into Oriente. Driving deep into the devastated area was a nightmare. For mile after mile flotsam hung from telephone wires, and even from the tops of the poles. Large swatches of both provinces stank of death and putrefaction.

Although I am writing about events that took place fifty years ago, I can still recall the almost adolescent thrill of most of these adventures. As a child, much of the fiction I was nurtured on included *Boys' Own* and the novels of G.A. Henty. Published in the decade before the First World War and handed down to me by my father, these swashbuckling adventures could stir the adrenalin of a child of the thirties and forties. Both personally and professionally, these were very good times. But they were not all good.

Hurricane Flora was appalling, but the worst single day was November 22, 1963. I was in the outskirts of Havana on my way back from an overnight mission in eastern Cuba. The car radio was on, and the program was interrupted to announce the assassination of President Kennedy in Dallas. I was desolated. My mind had magnified and undoubtedly exaggerated the link between the president and my assignment, but I always believed that he had been involved in moving the wheels that had taken me to Cuba.

UNITED KINGDOM

The Thames, Bunnies, and Bicycles

Our posting to London in the fall of 1967 came as a total surprise and proved in most ways to be a total joy. As a political officer I covered the beginning of the 'troubles' in Northern Ireland and spent many nights in the much-bombed Europa Hotel in Belfast while visiting British army officers, Catholic priests, and Ulster politicians. Two years into the posting and as a consequence of major government cutbacks I became the high commission's temporary press, cultural, and public affairs officer with access to fresh vistas on British society – for which experience I was highly motivated but inadequately prepared. This chapter focuses on incidents involving the cast in Canada House. It opens with our setting on the Thames.

5 Petyt Place was our first home in London and the one which received our sons Gywn and Peter soon after they were born. It stands at the end of a tiny cul-de-sac in Chelsea. All five houses look out over Cheyne Walk onto the Thames with a view of the Albert Bridge to the east and the Battersea Bridge to the west. Until 1941 this perspective had been blocked by another row of houses. Blown up during the blitz, they had been replaced by a sunken garden and a bronze nude. At the head of the street is Chelsea Old Church – heavily damaged by the same blockbuster, but restored. It is also known as the Church of Sir Thomas More, Henry VIII's martyred lord

Battersea Bridge at Chelsea.

chancellor, canonized by the Catholic Church as St. Thomas More and vilified by Protestants as a brutal persecutor.

Judy had found this jewel, and the rent was affordable because London property values were stagnant and in 1967 the Canadian dollar was strong against the pound. The sixties also meant that the Thames was still a vibrant commercial artery. Enchanting even in fog, the view from our sitting room windows was alive with barges and tugs. It was not difficult to understand the attraction of the Thames and especially the textures of brick and water in the late afternoon sun to people like Caneletto, Turner, and Monet. The only flaw in this idyll was the foul smell when the wind blew down the river from one of London's industrial parks. The Borough Council explained that it was the result of the cracking of juniper berries at the gin distillery in Wandsworth. As in other places, we were lucky in our timing. Soon after our departure the barges disappeared and the prices skyrocketed. Number 5 was eventually bought by one of the heirs to the Max Factor cosmetics fortune.

Petyt Place was only about a twenty-five-minute bicycle ride to my office in Canada House on Trafalgar Square. Succumbing to the milieu,

I purchased an ancient Raleigh bicycle, to which I attached an even older carbide lamp. Crushed lumps of carbide, obtained at the flea market where I bought the lamp, were placed in the central compartment of the lamp. Above was another compartment for water. With a gentle twist of the valve water drips onto the carbide and produces acetylene gas.[1] The flea market salesman assured me that the process was straightforward. It wasn't. In the evening my plan was to ignite the lamp in the marble foyer of Canada House to escape the wind outside on Cockspur Street. The water valve had to be turned with precision. Too much or too little water meant no ignition. However, through trial and much error I found that the most important skill was timing the match to the gas. Just like a barbeque, a few seconds too many and there is an explosion. One large explosion in the foyer broke the glass in my lamp. Arrival by bike was much easier than departure. Hauling the bicycle up the High Commission steps, I walked it into the main elevator, emblazoned in brass with Canada's coat of arms. As the elevator ascended, I perched on the saddle so that when the doors opened I peddled past the high commissioner's office along to my office at the end of the corridor – tooting my ooga horn at the open doors of my colleagues. Fortunately, as he was not an early morning person, I never ran into the high commissioner on this stretch.

For four years of our time in London the high commissioner was Charles Ritchie. One of Canada's most accomplished diplomats and its most celebrated diarist,[2] Mr. Ritchie was a beaky, thin-faced man with a miniature moustache and a mid-Atlantic accent. Elegant and sophisticated, he swam through London's royal and aristocratic waters like a seal and somehow managed this performance without affectation. His natural ability, independence of mind, and scalpel wit generated a magnetism for those of us close enough to feel his warmth. Our respect was in no way dimmed by his reluctance to accept the condescension with which Canadians were still sometimes treated by our hosts.

To the uninitiated a summons to Mr. Ritchie's office was an intimidating experience. His door and most importantly his privacy were discreetly protected by his secretary, Betty Burgess. That door opened onto a space the size of a ballroom hung with a colossal crystal chandelier, eighteenth- and nineteenth-century royal and equestrian portraits and carpeted with one of the two largest Persian rugs in England – the mate is in Windsor Castle.[3] Past the floor-to-ceiling windows that looked out onto the fountains of Trafalgar Square and Nelson's monument, his huge antique desk was at the far end – a hike of perhaps seventy feet. Many years before, someone informed the then high commissioner that the only office in Europe more opulent than his belonged to Benito Mussolini.[4] Mr. Ritchie was uncomfortable with the imperial splendour of this office, but equally concerned that no modern architectural vandalism should despoil it.[5]

The high commissioner's hospitality often extended to his staff. Late one morning I was invited by Mr. Ritchie to join him and his other guest, John Halstead, then an assistant under-secretary in External Affairs, for lunch at the Travellers Club nearby on Pall Mall. After drinks the three of us headed for the washroom, a cavernous chamber fitted with enormous enamel urinals. Mr. Halstead and I went from the urinals to the washbasins to wash our hands. Mr. Ritchie proceeded directly upstairs from the urinal to the dining room. When the two of us joined him at the table, a slight frisson of embarrassment hung in the air. Mr. Ritchie looked at us and remarked dryly, "I don't know about you two, but my privates are generally cleaner than my hands."

The much smaller but still majestic office next to the high commissioner's was occupied by the deputy high commissioner. Two of the same tall windows looked out on Trafalgar Square – the other two on Cockspur Street. My recollection of this office is very clear because for two years (1981-83) it was mine, although with a more modest title than deputy high commissioner.[6] The desk with an approximately six feet by six perimeter was another gorgeous antique from the Larkin collection, and did service sometimes in the evening as a bar for small receptions. In the late sixties the occupant was Louis Rogers, a smart, practical, world-weary, often dyspeptic diplomat, possessed of a mordant sense of humour.

Suffering neither fools nor foolishness, on this particular afternoon he was vexed by request from one of his junior officers for authorization to spend representational funds on membership in the newly established Playboy Club on Park Lane. The arrival of the first bunny club in London had caused a stir among traditionally buttoned-up Englishmen.

Before completing this account, it may be useful to explain the role played by gentlemen's clubs in London. This institution began to replace coffee houses toward the end of the eighteenth century as places where aristocrats and professional men could meet for food, drink, politics, business, socializing, and gambling. Their importance, their gambling facilities and their numbers

have declined in the present century, but in the 1960s they were an integral part of London life and the conduits of much business and professional intercourse. For diplomats in London, a club was an essential professional tool.[7]

On this occasion, the culprit, Terry Bacon, was summoned to Louis's office. According to Terry, the conversation went something like this:

Rogers: "Bacon, what the hell do you think you are doing? If you expect me to sign off on this thing so that you and your friends can goggle at inflated breasts at government expense, you are out of your mind."

Bacon: "Yes, well – it's not quite like that. My most important contacts are people in key jobs in the Ministry of Defence and the Foreign Office. They are very busy, our colleagues in other embassies are chasing them and I can rarely get them out to lunch or to my home or even on the phone. That means I can't do my job as I should."

Rogers: "So?"

Bacon: "I guarantee that if I invite these guys to the Playboy Club, they will come."

Rogers: "I'll sign."

Bacon was right. No-one refused.

JAPAN

Sake and the Advancement of Cultural Diplomacy

Following two years as speech writer to Mitchell Sharp, the secretary of state for external affairs, I became head of the Academic Relations division. This was a sleepy section of the department which was, by no stretch of the imagination, at the centre of Canada's foreign policy. However, it had advantages. There were agreeable colleagues in neighbouring divisions who let me have funds that they could not spend. In Patrick Reid I had an exceptional director general who had the rare ability of making good ideas happen. Together, with a tiny but first class staff, we developed Canadian Studies Abroad as a new dimension of Canadian cultural foreign policy – an initiative which became one of the department's most cost-effective programs.[1] This story traces the unconventional beginnings of Canadian Studies in Japan.

Anyone who thinks Canadian diplomats are a collection of nerds and dandies has never met the late Dick Gorham. Of Dick's many strengths, several stand out. He was a superb diplomat, a delightful and considerate person. He had the most extensive repertoire of semi-obscene stories of anyone I have ever met. A former boxer, he could and did drink bigger and tougher characters under the table. And he spoke fluent, idiomatic Japanese. Not understanding a word, I observed this last skill near the end of a pub crawl in Tokyo.

Dick was minister, or number two, at the Canadian embassy in Tokyo. I was in Tokyo with an ambitious and modestly funded plan to establish Canadian Studies in Japanese universities. Following a visit to a university on the outskirts of Tokyo, Dick proposed an evening of quiet carousing. Joining us was Jack Dirksen, the embassy third secretary, assigned by Dick to be my interpreter. Our final bar was Dick's favorite – a tiny place with paper walls and Dick's own bottle of Suntory whiskey on the shelf. The proprietor welcomed Dick and placed the Suntory on our table. It was Dick's because the bottle bore his character in Japanese script on the label. By the time the Suntory was demolished and a jug of sake was partially emptied, an argument had erupted between Dick and Jack about an obscure point of Japanese grammar. The argument, which was in Japanese with occasional asides to me in English, grew in intensity. The bar's literate clientele were evidently fascinated by the debate and not least that it was being conducted in their language by two *gaijin* (foreigners). There were five; each one took sides and joined the debate. The jug was soon emptied and it was time to leave. But no syntactic consensus had been achieved and the debate broke out again on the subway platform. To my astonishment, two travellers standing nearby, caught the drift of the argument and offered their points of view. This was an augury of interesting times ahead.

Two days later Jack and I took the bullet train to Kyoto where we were hoping to promote the concept of Canadian Studies to one of Japan's most prestigious universities. Graciously received, we were invited to lunch with a vice president and two academics at the university's private restaurant. The dining room was traditional. The windows were set low as everyone dined on cushions in the *seiza* (kneeling) position. Through the windows we could see a beautifully manicured formal garden complete with stone water basins and stone lanterns. Course after course was served by geisha in kimonos who seemed to float around us in a perambulating version of the seiza (modified lotus position). And, of course, sake was served.

Following lunch Jack and I returned to our hotel – selected by Dick, it was a traditional Japanese inn, featuring very thin reed mattresses. An essential part of the Canadian Studies plan was to have three basic texts, one on the Canadian economy by Ian Drummond, a digest of Canadian history by Ken McNaught, and another on Canadian political governance by John Saywell, translated and published in Japanese. For this purpose we had invited a Kyoto publisher for tea. External Affairs would subsidize, but his firm would have to take on the project and eventual distribution. Because the inn was seriously traditional, tea was served to us seated in the seiza position. Unaccustomed to being folded under my knees, my leg muscles were in rebellion. However, the tea and discussion went well – so well that the publisher invited us both to dine with him that evening in his private restaurant.

While not as posh as the university restaurant, it was elegant and totally Japanese, which meant, of course, that dining was again in the seiza position. It was a lovely dinner, but attempting to anaesthetize my legs, I drank large quantities of sake. Unaccountably, this did not prevent our host from suggesting that, after dinner, we should head to his private bar for more drink. This establishment was nearby and turned out to be a karaoke bar, but this was early karaoke, which involved only a microphone, which was passed from cubicle to cubicle, and a public address system – no interactive technology. Mercifully, the seating was Western and we settled in to enjoy the noises from the other cubicles and to absorb more sake, not realizing that as guests we would be expected to perform. A bit shaken by the arrival of the microphone, it was decided that Jack would start. We were asked to sing something Canadian and Jack sang an ancient and hopefully now forgotten folksong, "When the ice-worm nests again." The tune can charitably be called insipid and it received polite, tepid applause from the surrounding tables. My turn. My song repertoire was extremely thin and I was determined not to sing "Alouette." Gurgling with litres of sake, I heard myself saying "No, no, I will not sing a Canadian song, I will sing a Japanese song." This was translated by Jack and followed by loud intakes of breath and people saying (according to Jack) in reverend tones "Ohh! You sing Japanese!" In high school I had been in the chorus of Gilbert and Sullivan's Japanese spoof "the Mikado" and for some odd reason I could remember Gilbert's apparently faux Japanese lyrics. With only a moment of sober thought I would have realized that singing an elaborately phony Japanese song in a real Japanese bar full of partially inebriated Japanese citizens could result in my being torn to pieces or at the very least terminating any chance that our host would publish the Canadian texts. In the absence of sober thought I belted out:

Miya Sama, mia sama
On n'm-ma no mayé ni
Pira-Pira suru no wa
Nan gia na
Toko tonyaré tonjaré na.

As I had been taught in the chorus, I followed immediately with a repetition of the verse. What happened next? To my surprise and confusion, I brought the house down – and incidentally saved the publication of the Canadian texts. Loud applause from all corners of the bar. Why was there such an undeserved happy ending? I didn't find the answer until nearly forty years later when doing some minor research for this chapter. Google then informed me that Gilbert had actually lifted the words from an ancient Japanese military marching song.

GUYANA

Caviar and Christmas Trees

Near the end of a full year which the family spent in Quebec City, enjoying a superb public service program with the over the top name of 'perfectionnement biculturel' and the excitement of the René Lévesque election, External Affairs advised that Haiti would be our next assignment. The post was to be upgraded from chargé d'affaires to ambassador. However, a new under secretary decided that Graham did not sound sufficiently French for Haitian sensibilities – although Creole is as distinct from French as Spanish is from Portuguese. The next plan was to appoint me as consul general in Boston, but that was vetoed at cabinet by Jean Chretien, then minister of Trade and Commerce, because my CV showed insufficient trade experience (this was true). Ten months later we were posted to Guyana and no superior objected. As when I was posted to the Dominican Republic eighteen years earlier, I groaned when I learned my destination. But like my Dominican experience, it soon proved to be eccentric and exhilarating. I was going as high commissioner. Judy, our three children and I arrived in Georgetown in October 1978.

Peter Houliston, the development officer at the high commission, and I were knee-deep in the water on the Guyanese side of the Takutu River and pointed toward Brazil when Diane stopped us. She asked if we were wearing tight bathing suits.

"Tight bathing suits?"

"Yes, tight bathing suits."

"But why?"

"Well, there's this fish…."

The Takutu is a minor tributary of the Amazon and home to the piranha – but not the aggressive, voracious variety, unless you happen to be bleeding. There were sting rays, but if you were careful you could avoid stepping on them. There were electric eels, too, but they were further up the river. A bathing suit, tight or not, wasn't much use against these hazards.

Diane explained, "There is a small, orifice-seeking fish…" We swam, and arrived intact (and illegally), on the Brazilian shore.

Diane McTurk had been the elegant public relations director of the Savoy Hotel in London, but at this time she was a formidable, elegant cattle rancher. We had spent a day trying in vain to set up a short-range communications network to protect the local ranchers from Brazilian rustlers. Peter and I were thwarted by a nervous Guyanese minister who had informed the small local police detachment that our authority to distribute the radios had been withdrawn. The minister had been afraid that non-existent anti-government rebels would use the system for their own destabilizing purposes.

Guyana was not seen as a plum posting. Georgetown, the capital, is about six degrees north of the equator, and while the city is on the Atlantic, it is washed not by a turquoise sea but by a three-mile-wide band of brown silt swept up from the Amazon delta. It had been dyked by successive Dutch, French, and British colonial governments, and at high tide it was below sea level. It possessed a mouldering charm and delightful people. At that time the country was ruled by Forbes Burnham, an engaging rogue who practiced a destructive, cosmetic Marxism. His personal standard as prime minister bore a palm tree girdled by an alligator against a purple background. On special occasions he wore purple open-necked tropical suits, or "jack-suits." We called him "the Purple Alligator." His officials called me "Comrade High Commissioner."

Some of his qualities, together with the isolation of the country, had attracted Jim Jones, who had established a religious community in a remote jungle corner of the country. Jones had developed Russian as well as Guyanese connections – and a minor Canadian connection. Every fortnight he sent a team to the capital for provisions and films for his outdoor theatre. One member came regularly to the Canadian high commission to borrow films from our library. Perhaps *Wheat Farming in Saskatchewan* or the National Film Board favourite *How to Build an Igloo* had the desired disorienting impact on his flock.

The Russian connection was different. Bishop Jones, as he called himself, was cultivating the Soviet embassy, because his Guyanese welcome was wearing thin and he hoped to move his community to the Soviet Union, where alienation from his homeland, the United States, would be complete. For their part, the Russians had no intention of letting Jones or his people anywhere near the Soviet Union. They cultivated Jones to learn why the cult rebelled against the American way of life, hoping to exploit this rich vein of anti-American publicity.

A group of about six of Jones's trusted associates attended the Soviet National Day reception, which was where my wife and I ran into them. They told us about their experiment to establish a greed-free multiracial religious colony. They did not seem stressed out and certainly not suicidal. As we discovered later, that impression was also shared by Vladimir, the Russian ambassador (whose wife had squeezed toothpaste on the arm of his white diplomatic uniform to hide the ravages of green mould).

Two weeks later Jones's bodyguards killed US Congressman Leo Ryan. He had travelled by bush plane to Jonestown with the idea of investigating this controversial colony and identifying children and others alleged to have been taken into the community against their will. The deeply paranoid Jones, fearing retaliation and, above all, the end of the group's cherished privacy, called upon most, and coerced others, to commit suicide. Over nine hundred died from drinking Kool-Aid spiked with cyanide.

Among those few who survived were two of Jones's lieutenants. They and one other, who did not survive, were instructed by Jones to deliver three suitcases full of US cash to the Soviet embassy. The suitcases never made it.

Jonestown cast a dark cloud over our lives in Guyana, but Judy and I did not hold the bizarre Jonestown connection against the Russian ambassador. In fact, we quite liked him and his wife, Helena. About a year after the Jonestown tragedy (and before the Soviet invasion of Afghanistan, at which time we were told by Ottawa not to consort with the Russians),

Canadian High Commission, Georgetown.

Vladimir, the ambassador, took me aside at a cocktail party and asked if I could obtain a Christmas tree from Canada.

"A Christmas tree?" I asked.

"Yes – but of course we do not believe in God. My wife, myself, and staff, we miss real pine tree. But especially smell. We will pay."

Vladimir drove (or rather his chauffeur drove) a Lincoln Continental, and Helena told us that he loved to buy his suits in New York. Vladimir could pay – but in the end that wasn't necessary.

A Canadian company was doing seismic work in the interior, not far from the Takutu River. They agreed to bring trees from Canada in their chartered aircraft. They brought fourteen trees – for hospitals, old people's homes, themselves, the Soviet embassy, and one for the Canadian Residence. They were free. However, there was one snag. The plane was arriving from Canada at the end of November. Given the Guyanese climate, by Christmas Day there would be no needles and no scent. Even the Russians wanted them for that date.

The problem was solved by a friend who ran the state fisheries company and to whom I promised a tree. The trees were stored in his freezers and retrieved for distribution the morning of December 23. That afternoon Judy rang me at the office to say that the tree had thawed out, that it looked splendid, and that the whole house smelled of fish – and did I remember that we were having the staff Christmas party that night?

Vladimir didn't seem to mind the smell, or if he did he didn't say anything. On Christmas morning the Lincoln arrived outside the residence bearing a large box of assorted vodkas, Georgian champagne, and caviar.

∾ ∾ ∾

The Phantom Saboteur

Peter Ustinov, Lawrence Durrell, and others found the Cold War players an irresistible target for comic satire. In most cases they fictionalized the bizarre reality. In Georgetown fiction was unnecessary.

I didn't set out to sabotage the North Korean propaganda campaign in Guyana, nor, of course, were there any instructions from Ottawa to do so. The fatuous claims of successful human engineering and the unctuous adulation heaped on the Supreme Leader, Kim Il Sung, were more than sufficiently counter-productive on their own without any help from Western librettists. What happened was the result of boredom and the mischievous pleasure of playing a game with a determined adversary. However, making sense of the absurd requires a few lines of context.

Too small and too isolated, Guyana was never an important pawn in the Cold War. Nevertheless, so intense was the East/West engagement that both sides invested heavily in unlikely and usually unrewarding places. Guyana offered an example of how zealous political courtship, initially by the United States and Britain and then by the Soviet Union and China, could produce disappointing and occasionally bizarre results.

In the early 1960s Washington and London became increasingly alarmed that Guyana was shifting to the East. Their solution was to find and then tutor a local leader sympathetic to their goals. They selected Forbes Burnham, an ambitious Guyanese politician and alleged moderate. The plan involved instruction by the CIA and Britain's MI6 on how to manipulate elections. With his new skills Burnham was able to overcome the numerical voting advantage of his Marxist opponent and became prime minister, whereupon he turned his back on his Western benefactors to embrace the 'Socialist' suitors. Through the seventies and until his death in 1985 he had become part of the Non-Aligned Movement and an 'associate' member of the Communist Bloc. The sugar and bauxite industries were nationalized and other economically disruptive policies were implemented. Although Burnham was too fond of the material benefits of Capitalism to become a fully disciplined Marxist Leninist, Moscow was not going to ignore a gift horse in South America – even though this gift horse was walled in by rainforest with no road connection with any of its Latin American neighbours. The Russians established a huge embassy with more space, more staff and more luxurious cars than the US embassy. Nations such as Libya, East Germany, China, Yugoslavia, and North Korea soon set up missions in Georgetown. Political nomenclature changed. The nation became a 'Cooperative Republic' and correct social intercourse began with the salutation 'comrade' as in 'Comrade Minister' or in my case 'Comrade High Commissioner'. Disenchanted Guyanese called the culture "So-So Socialism" and composed a calypso with that as the central lyric.

Like my colleagues in most parts of the world, I spent an annoyingly disproportionate amount of time sitting in the antechambers of ministers or senior officials, waiting for the door to open. In Georgetown these rooms tended to be on the frowsy side as befitted old wooden buildings being slowly consumed by termites and dry rot. Basically furnished, they always contained a coffee table or a credenza piled high with magazines and brochures. But unlike other waiting rooms there were no *National Geographics* or *Homes and Gardens* – not even *Time Magazine*. There were usually some Guyanese government pamphlets, but most of the reading comprised embassy handouts supplied by Georgetown's exotically varied diplomatic community. It was not long before I realized that the North Korean embassy's publications with images of the Supreme Leader were almost invariably to be found at the top of the heap. It seemed unlikely that this arrangement reflected the interests of waiting-room visitors and was more likely the result of direct intervention by some minor North Korean apparatchik. "Ah hah," I thought. Why not use the waiting time constructively by taking all the North Korean propaganda, stuffing it at the bottom of the pile, and replacing it on the top with *Forbes* and other material from the Capitalist and wicked West.

The Phantom Saboteur.

2014   JWG

Over the next several weeks I tackled my self-appointed task in four or five ministry waiting rooms, thinking that for each antechamber this would be a one-time event. I was mistaken. Occasionally, within as short a time as a week, I would return to the ministry to find that I was looking at Kim Il Sung's face on the top of the coffee table. The Supreme Leader had resurfaced and I had underestimated my adversary. It was obviously the routine responsibility of a third secretary or perhaps more senior member of the embassy to do the rounds of all of the principal government offices, to add new material, but primarily to ensure that coffee table reading was 'correctly' configured.

Surprised but stimulated by the challenge, I continued this Cold War skirmish and often wondered whether the 'credenza crisis' had been drawn to the attention of Pyongyang and whether the embassy ever identified the phantom saboteur.

∾∾∾

Alcide

Travel into the interior of Guyana, especially by road and small boat, was one of the joys of this posting. Except along the coast there were very few roads, and those few were rough logging roads through rain forest and over small mountain ranges. A tough four-wheel-drive vehicle (in my case a long-wheelbase Land Rover) and lots of provisions, including rum, were essential. Genial companions also helped. This is the story of two such journeys.

I had never before met anyone who wore three pairs of trousers at the same time. As one pair began to rot and let in more light and bugs, a better pair was slipped over them. This did not mean that the outside pair was in good shape – it was through its holes that the remains of the other trousers were visible. But they were fairly clean, and for Alcide it was obviously a convenient arrangement that gave him three times as many pockets. Alcide was a pork knocker – a Guyanese term for prospector.

He led me and a friend, John Cary, up a stream to pan for grains of gold and the very ordinary-looking pebbles that might be diamonds. In some of Guyana's rivers gold and diamonds are mined together.

Alcide was seventy-five, bright, lean, crinkled, and mahogany-coloured. He stepped easily from stone to stone. With a nimble swishing motion the sand left the pan, leaving only grains of gold, or nothing. We found nothing, and after a while sat down on some boulders to rest. John asked Alcide if he had any gold to sell. Alcide reached into a pocket of his furthest inside trousers and drew out a plastic envelope. He showed us some small strips of pounded metal. John selected what he thought a goldsmith could use to make earrings for his wife. Alcide chose another pocket, brought out and assembled a jeweller's scales. The gold was weighed and John paid cash. Bewitched, I asked Alcide if he had any diamonds. He reached into another pocket and brought out several Vicks VapoRub phials. He emptied them one by one onto separate sheets of paper. Most of the stones were industrial grade. All were uncut, but one phial contained gem-grade stones. I selected one with a crude marquise shape. Alcide pulled out another set of weights for diamonds. Mine was about half a carat.

"How much will that cost?"

Alcide calculated and said, "1,820 Guyanese dollars." This was a little more than $200 US at the time.

"I don't have enough cash. I don't suppose that a cheque is any good to you?"

"Cheque is fine."

Judy, who was back at the camp, seemed pleased; if she thought I'd been had, she didn't say so – unlike Mr. De Silva, a jeweller back in Georgetown. "You've bought a diamond from a wild black man in the jungle. You don't know a rough diamond from a cough drop. It's probably quartz." He looked at it closely.

"Hmmph. You're lucky. But it's almost certainly flawed, and a poor colour." He placed it under a jeweller's microscope.

"Um, well,…you're lucky. It's clear and a good colour. Let's see about the weight."

The weight coincided exactly with Alcide's measurement. De Silva conceded that I had paid a fair price. I floated out of the store pleased with myself and pleased with Alcide.

Alcide had been a pork knocker on the Potaro River for fifty years. His home was at Waratuk Falls. If his scattered holdings and his leases of gold- and diamond-bearing shoreline within a twenty-mile radius of Waratuk had ever been assessed, they probably would have shown that he was at least a millionaire. Alcide would have been amazed and possibly disconcerted. His joys were the search for gold and diamonds, his few friends on the river, the exercise of his mind, the monthly visit of his girlfriend from downriver, and an almost untrammelled freedom.

His father and his grandfather lived well into their nineties in St. Lucia. He believed he would go on for close to a hundred years. As Alcide told it, his great-grandfather came to St. Lucia from Corsica, where he had known the young Bonaparte. His grandmother was born of the union between the Corsican and a Black slave.

We met again about a year later. I had been invited to join, as an unpaid gaffer, an English/Guyanese film crew heading up the Potaro to do a documentary on pork knockers. Alcide, with his strong, grizzled face and earthy anecdotes accompanied by bursts of warbling cackles, was given a leading role. We shot some film the first morning, but managed to drop one reel in the Potaro. Alcide invited several of us – Joey, Eric, Chan, and me – to his shack on the riverbank for cucumber sandwiches. The thin soil supported cucumbers and not much else. Outside the shack was a clay oven where he baked his bread. When we entered the main room, Chan, who is a veterinarian, noticed a set of clean precision instruments.

"What are these?" asked Chan.

"Ah," said Alcide, "I do a bit of dentistry."

In another corner of the house was another, larger set of surgical instruments, different from the first, and one or two medical books.

"Ah, well, I do a bit of doctoring."

Another pork knocker, who had joined us, explained that the nearest certified physician and dentist were a day and half away and that as far as he was concerned – and that went for anyone else scattered along this reach of the Potaro – Alcide was a successful dentist, homeopathic GP, and surgeon.

After lunch, at our insistence, Alcide entertained us with some tunes on his fiddle.

Late that afternoon, when there was a breeze and it was cool in the shade, I walked with Alcide into the forest. I carried a small tape recorder with the idea of capturing his observations. His knowledge of flora and fauna surpassed that of the local Amerindians with whom, for a time, he had been an apprentice. The sap of that tree was used in the preparation of an infusion against fever; the leaves of that vine could be used against another fever; pounded and boiled, the bark of that tree would become a poultice. There was a multitude of aphrodisiacs. He identified herbs and leaves that could be used for spider, scorpion, and snake bites. There was very little that grew or moved on its own that Alcide could not identify.

In the evening we sat by the shore drinking rum, listening to stories of the Potaro, and looking at the water. It had been stained the colour of iodine by the roots in its path. In the distance was the steady roar of Kaietur Falls, where the river dropped eight hundred feet.

On my return to Georgetown I tried to persuade government botanists and other specialists to visit Alcide and record this extraordinary and possibly valuable accumulation of knowledge. There was interest, but no action.

I remained in touch with Alcide through mutual friends and looked forward to seeing him when the time came for the screening of the completed documentary, entitled *Men of Gold*. We had sent word ahead that we would be coming to Mahdia, the only substantial village near the Potaro,

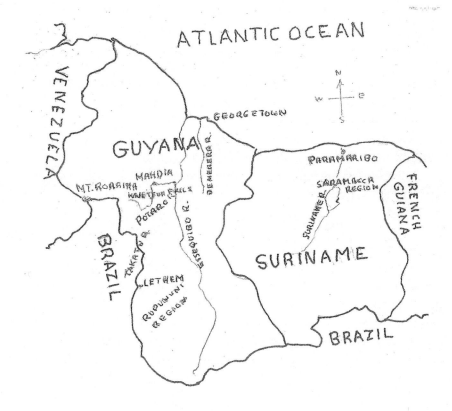

and the only one accessible to those who had taken part in the filming. After a night camping in hammocks in the rain forest, we bounced into the village with a projector and a generator that were strapped onto a mattress in the back of our Land Rover.

Mahdia consisted of a few rows of shacks, including a ramshackle guest house where we were to stay, a small schoolhouse, a remarkable concentration of gold and diamond dealers, a profusion of bars, a psychedelic disco, and several brothels. There was also a government office presided over by Oscar, the befuddled district commissioner. Oscar had agreed to make arrangements to show the film – but he hadn't done so. To make amends, he had us circle the community while he hung out the side of our Land Rover shouting, "Flim show! Flim show! Alcide and the boys! Eight o'clock in the schoolhouse!"

In the meantime preparations were not going well. The entire community was descending on the schoolhouse, which was too small, and the generator had not survived the long timber trail. Eventually we negotiated a spacious room with chairs and benches behind D'Aguiar's Gold and Diamond Emporium and Bar. This soon filled to overflowing. D'Aguiar lent us a generator, but there were still technical problems.

This was not a quiet suburban audience. It had high expectations, and as the wait lengthened the crowd became loud and restless. Eric and I were wrestling with the equipment when Joey came up to us.

"Man," he whispered, "this is a rough crowd, and they've been soaking up D'Aguiar's rum. Look, the Land Rover is outside, and it's switched on. Pretend we're going for some tools and make a run for it."

"Easy, Joey," said Eric, who was tightening a connection. "She'll work." She did, and none too soon.

The show was a double feature. It began with a National Film Board animated film about the fatal sexual mishaps of a postman. This was a good appetizer, but it was the main course that transfixed the audience. It was about them and their way of life. They had never seen themselves on a screen before, and every time one of them appeared there were loud screams and coarse suggestions. When the star performer appeared, shouts went up: "Alcide! Alcide!"

These shouts, though, were louder, and different from the others. Alcide wasn't there. We had learned only when we arrived in Mahdia that he had died three weeks before – long before his one hundred years.

♋ ♋ ♋

Three-Piece

Apart from the inexpressibly horrible drama of the murders and mass suicide at Jonestown shortly after we arrived, Guyana was definitely not on any international beaten path. This did not mean that life was dull. Far from it. Three-Piece is one illustration.

It was about 9:00 A.M. and already hot outside. Strong Guyanese coffee had not yet stoked my metabolism when the telephone rang. It was Astrubal Pinto de Ullysea, the short, urbane Brazilian ambassador.

"John," he said, "my country has been insulted by one of your banks." His voice rose. "And I have been personally irrespected."

"You have been what?"

"Listen to me. You know Chester Hinkson, the manager of the Bank of Nova Scotia?"

"Yes, of course. You mean Three-Piece," I said, trying, unsuccessfully, to lighten the conversation.

"Hinkson, Three-Piece, whatever – *coño*! He should be chopped into small pieces!"

"Good God! What has he done?"

"He has been attempting deliberately to destroy the decorum of my embassy...to prevent us from working...to detricate our dignity. You know, the embassy is up against the wall of the bank. One week ago he placed loudspeakers by this wall – the wall of my office – and turned on his disgusting music. Yesterday afternoon, he pushed them to the top."

"You mean full volume?"

"*Si*, full volume. It was terrible, unspeakable. It was outrageous! Of course, I went immediately to the bank and insisted on speaking to Hinkson."

"Did Hinkson apologize?"

"Apologize! I was received rudely and told to leave. As Canadian high commissioner, you must speak to Hinkson."

On the surface there appeared to be a dichotomy between the conservative appearance of Hinkson, or Three-Piece, and his behaviour. Three-Piece almost invariably wore a three-piece suit. Elsewhere this would have been unremarkable for a bank manager. In Guyana, though, he was unique. Not even Vladimir, the Soviet ambassador, who liked to parade his Brooks Brothers suits, would wear a vest in Guyana's Turkish-bath climate. Apart from Three-Piece and the Soviet ambassador, almost no one wore a jacket. Apart from these two and George, the American ambassador, almost no one wore a tie. The custom that Three-Piece regularly defied had been set by President Burnham, and was one of the few sound policies imposed by this leader on a much-abused and increasingly impoverished nation.

As Astrubal and the entire Brazilian embassy had learned, Three-Piece was a jazz and reggae fanatic. He had been a musician in his native St. Lucia. His corpuscles were syncopated with jazz and West Indian rhythms. Three-Piece was also our neighbour in Bel-Air Gardens, separated from us only by Mr. and Mrs. Greathead, and Laura, their thirty-four-year-old parrot. When his wife was away, Three-Piece gave parties. They were the best parties on our side of town. The outdoor amplifiers outboomed the tree frogs until about 4:00 A.M. and antagonized all those who were not invited.

Before I could collect my thoughts and call Three-Piece, the phone rang again. It was Three-Piece calling me.

"John, how well do you know the Brazilian ambassador?"

"Pretty well. Why?"

"Man, you will not believe this…" He paused. "The little shrimp is a fucking maniac!"

"What do you mean?"

"You know – well, you wouldn't know. To perk up the staff I set up a recreation room in one of the empty offices upstairs. We use my tapes. Yesterday, after work, about six of us were relaxing and listening to music when the little bugger bursts in. You know we share a wall with the embassy."

"Yes, I know."

"We were playing Bob Marley when he came in. Man, he got red in the face and started to shout. I turned the machine off and told him that if he was going to insult me in front of my staff he could get the hell out. The little bugger gets more red in the face, reaches into his pocket, takes out this bloody great pistol, and points it at me. Imagine! A pistol in my own bank!"

Two days later, Astrubal and Three-Piece met in my office. Three-Piece said that he would move the recreation room, and Astrubal apologized. Soon after, Three-Piece invited Judy and me to his next party.

Maynard

The role of the locally engaged staff in a diplomatic mission is often underrated. Usually they are conscientious and loyal. This is especially the case in isolated hardship posts. In Georgetown we were very fortunate, but sometimes the good staff members

brought with them their idiosyncrasies. This was the case with
Maynard.

Maynard's obsession was automobiles: large, sleek, flamboyant automobiles. He also liked girls, including his ex-wife. Girls were drawn to his dark Apollonian features, effervescent personality, and high-status job. Mostly, he regarded my wife and me with tolerant affection; at times, with ill-concealed indignation. He shared his warm heart and appetite for life with all of us, but cars had a place by themselves. Up to the time of our arrival in Georgetown, this had proved to be a happy union between addiction and vocation. Maynard was the high commissioner's chauffeur.

One of the great moments in his life came when my predecessor inveigled the Canadian government into purchasing, as the official vehicle, one of the largest cars then manufactured in Canada, a Ford Brougham LTD. While down-market from the Cadillacs and Mercedes favoured by the Soviet, North Korean, Libyan, East German, and Chinese ambassadors, it was extravagantly out of proportion to Georgetown's miniscule status on the Canadian diplomatic landscape. Maynard was ecstatic.

That this behemoth was black in a country whose proximity to the equator meant that the sun seemed suspended directly overhead for most of the day was unimportant. Nor did it greatly matter to Maynard that the automatic windows were jammed shut. This had happened when the car had been dropped from the dockyard crane on arrival in Georgetown. Body damage was repaired, but not the windows. This would not have been a problem if the air conditioning had functioned. It seldom did. Without air conditioning and with rear windows that someone had managed to pry open a mere three inches, the official car was a mobile sauna. I cursed my predecessor every time we slithered out of the car like steamed catfish for some official function. Our diplomatic colleagues must have thought that there was something wrong with our metabolisms. Maynard never complained.

Futile efforts to fix the air conditioning and the windows kept the car regularly in the garage. Premature wearing of the brake pads also laid it up for long periods while spares were ordered from Miami or New York. Whenever he was on some errand by himself, Maynard drove like a Brazilian taxi driver, scorching to a stop and then catapulting forward when the offending pedestrian, bicycle, or draught animal no longer blocked his trajectory.

Garaging of the Ford was a reprieve for Judy and me, but it was purgatory for Maynard. Stripped of his polished black status machine, he was reduced to chauffeuring our personal car. Status was a simple equation for Georgetown drivers. It rose and fell with the glamour and pretension of the car, and had very little to do with the clout or nationality of the employer. Judged by that test, my wife and I placed a crushing weight on Maynard's ego. Our car was an elderly Volvo station wagon that bore the corrosive marks of many Canadian winters. Any association with this clapped-out ruin was deeply painful for Maynard. In order to avoid the scorn of his colleagues he would wear sun glasses with large lenses and slump invisibly behind the steering wheel whenever the car was stationary.

In a very short time Maynard became part of our lives and a friend to our children. He was our first guide to the city, to the roads that run along the sea wall, and to the ebullient eccentricity of the colonial administrators who had given names to the coastal villages (particularly the British and French, but some Dutch as well): Onverwaght, Jacoba Willemina, Sans Souci, Le Repentir, Recess, Golden Fleece, Adventure, Perseverance, Now or Never, Catherine's Lust, and Paradise. (Although it would give more piquancy to the nomenclature, I don't think the villages actually stand in that geographical sequence.) He would take us inland to the red water creeks and Amerindian settlements at the edge of the rain forest, imparting along the way his views on the mores of Guyanese society, its joys and shortcomings. I hadn't realized how important he had become until he was dead.

We had been in Guyana for just over a year when Rafeek Khan, a friend of Maynard's, phoned me at home on a sticky Saturday afternoon. Maynard had taken his ex-wife for a fast run on his motorcycle. A car had approached in the wrong lane. He had braked and skidded in an attempt to avoid it, but he was killed. His ex-wife broke two ribs and a collarbone. The death and its terrible stupidity stunned me. Devastated, I went outside and lowered the flag to half-mast – a gesture that, I discovered later, is normally reserved for heads of state. I spoke to Rafeek again and to one of Maynard's sisters and was told that in keeping with tropical custom, the funeral was to take place the next afternoon in the village where his mother lived.

The following day Judy, Rafeek, Rafeek's wife, and I set out in the office Land Rover. The village was about an hour's bouncing ride along a road deeply rutted by trucks, ox carts, and the rainy season. We parked by a flame tree at the edge of the village and walked to the tiny house with a tin roof where Maynard's mother and a large extended family lived. It was easy to find. Prayer flags sprouted from the front garden and those of its neighbours. The house overflowed with villagers, and from its centre came a terrible keening noise. About a dozen women, all relatives, pressed against the coffin, wailing, and endlessly repeating Maynard's name. This was an East Indian village, and our first Hindu funeral. Light was failing and lamps and candles had been lit. The stilts on which the house was built creaked with the overload. There had been rain earlier in the day, and the sweet, musky smell of the mud united with the incense to envelope the crowd.

No one seemed to be in charge, but the bedlam subsided and we were received by Maynard's mother. She drew a breath, dried her face, and explained that everyone had arrived and it was time for me to give the eulogy. This was not the moment to express surprise, and there wasn't time to even think about what I should say. We squeezed through layers of mourners and past the candles until my waist was touching the open coffin. I looked down. There was a rising murmur of grief, and my throat was constricting. With difficulty I began to speak.

∾ ∾ ∾

"Will the Dynamite Explode if I..."

Travel by road from the coast to the Brazilian border was not possible in the seventies and eighties. It is now feasible in the dry season, and a bridge has been built across the Takatu river that connects Guyana to the Brazilian highway system. At the time of this story, the logging roads ran only half the distance. All travel to the distant interior was by air. Usually, it was uneventful.

"Sorry, the Islander is on the fritz," said the airport manager. "You OK with a single-engine?" I had arranged a lift from Ogle Airport near Georgetown to Lethem on the Brazilian border with CEFIL, a Canadian company doing seismic tests for oil in the Rupununi district on the

Brazilian border.[1] CEFIL had chartered a twin-engine Islander and invited me for the ride because I had an aid-related chore in the Rupununi. The high commission's policy, like that of CEFIL, was to overfly the rainforest only in twin-engine aircraft. When a plane disappears beneath the forest canopy it is difficult to find, even with emergency radio signals.

My visit wasn't urgent but, ill-advisedly, I agreed. The manager introduced me to George Grandsault, the pilot, who was loading trays of soda pop into his five-passenger Cessna. I clambered into the co-pilot's seat and attached headphones, and then we were off – but not, I learned through the headphones, directly to the Rupununi. George explained, "We're going to Bartica to pick up more stuff."

Bartica is a rough and scruffy centre for gold and diamond mining and possesses the remains of a cement runway built when Guyana was still a British colony. It is only a twenty-minute flight from Ogle. We crossed the Demerara River and then turned left at the Essequibo, one of the great rivers of South America. The old cement was no longer smooth, and the Cessna bumped along toward a pile of boxes upon which sat six soldiers armed with First World War–vintage rifles.

"What's this?" I ask George.

"I meant to tell you. We're taking a load of dynamite to the Rupununi for CEFIL."

"It's a hell of a lot."

"Yeah," says George.

The dynamite and other explosives had been stored in a Guyana government magazine near Bartica under the control of the Guyana Defence Force. With the passenger seats removed, the soldiers shifted the cargo into the plane. I expressed concern to George about the number of boxes being loaded aboard this small aircraft.

"No big ting," said George – a Guyanese expression.

The last box was loaded and George and I were taking our places in the cockpit when the sergeant said to George, "I'm going too."

"Forget it," said George. "There isn't room."

"Make room. My orders are to accompany the dynamite."

"You mean," said George, "that if we start dumping this stuff over the president's residence, you'll shoot us?"

"You got it," said the sergeant, and he sat on two boxes behind us with a Sten gun, a weapon from the Second World War that resembles the plumbing for a small sink.

If I'd had any sense at all, I would have got out of the plane, but I experienced a sort of horrible fascination with the improbable sequence of events. George turned on the ignition, and we bounced along to the far end of the long runway, which ends at the bank of the Essequibo. When we were almost at the end George pulled back on the stick and we began to lift. Immediately I heard a "bleep, bleep" noise in my headphones.

"What's that?"

"It's the stall warning indicator."

"Stall warning! What does that mean exactly?"

"It means that we're within three knots of losing lift."

"Jesus! You mean falling. Let's start chucking these boxes now!"

"Don't get excited. We'll be fine."

Fortunately, there were no tall trees at the end of the runway. We cleared some bushes and the bleeping continued. George banked, so that our ascent was over the Essequibo and its golden sandbars. After what seemed a very long time, George lowered the nose and the bleeping stopped. My breathing returned to normal and I looked down at the rain forest. Popular fiction, as far back as William Henry Hudson's *Green Mansions*, from the beginning of the last century, depicts the tropical forest as oppressively uniform – "wall to wall" emerald green. Not so the Guyana forest. From 1,500 feet it is a tapestry of many shades of green, occasional flashes of rust, and the bright yellow blossoms of the Wallaba tree. Almost all are hardwoods with such a high density that they sink in water, and there as many as twenty-five species to the acre. The range of colour has seasonal changes, but at this time the canopy is a subdued version of early fall in the Laurentians – surprisingly beautiful.

My contemplation of the forest was broken by George. "Will the dynamite explode if I transmit on my radio?"

"You're asking me!?"

"Yeah. We may be OK, because we're not carrying the caps, but I'm not sure, and I have to talk to Lethem."

"I'll see what it says on the boxes." I swivelled in my seat to examine one of the boxes that were piled beside the sergeant. "It says don't hit with a hammer or expose to flame or sparks. Nothing about radio transmissions."

George switched on the transmitter and asked for Lethem. Lethem didn't respond, but the pilot of the twin-engine Guyana Sugar Corporation plane did. He was flying from the Rupununi to Ogle. They bantered and he asked George about his destination. George explained, adding, "The Canadian high commissioner is with me."

"The high commissioner? He must be out of his mind to fly with you."

POSTSCRIPT

Seven months later, George, five passengers, and his Cessna disappeared on a flight to view the strangely sculpted top of Mount Roraima. This is an immense *tepui*, or mesa, where the boundaries of Brazil, Venezuela, and Guyana join. The setting for Arthur Conan Doyle's famous novel *Lost World*, it was the fictional home for dinosaurs, protected through the millennia by the sheer walls of the mesa. The passengers were British engineers and the wives of two of them. The engineers were in Guyana to work on the sea defences (much of the coast is below sea level at high tide). Neither the plane nor anyone in it was ever seen again.

᪣ ᪣ ᪣

The State Funeral of the Honourable Linden Forbes Burnham August 9, 1985

I was in Ottawa at the time of President Burnham's death, and, as director general for the area, I accompanied the Canadian delegation to the funeral. We flew in a Government Challenger, and picked up West Indian prime ministers en route.

"Albert, there's somebody under the coffin."

"Yeah, Chief, it's a Russian technician."

"A Russian technician?"

"Yeah, man, dis is one crazy funeral."

"What in the name of God is a Russian technician doing under the president's coffin?"

"Yeah, well de choke and rob artists that thief de whole country, dey go to de cabinet and say dey want de old bastard preserved like Lenin. De technician and some oder fellas, dey fly in and pump him full of plenty Russian embalming stuff."

"It better be good. It's ninety-five out there and the humidity's the same."

"Yeah, dis ain't Red Square, man. And it don't help dat dey bury him first."

"Bury him first?"

"Chief, dey had a family funeral. In dis climate dat's de custom – within twenty-four hours of croakin. Dis jamboree we got now in de stadium was supposed to be a memorial service. Den de Russians give in – dey are really pissed now – but dey come and de fellas have to dig de old man up."

"Son of a bitch! A resurrection!"

"Yeah, everybody say de Father of our Nation is change to a Mummy."

"Where did they bury him?"

"Out by de Seven Ponds in de National Park. Chief, you gotta know where dey dump Queen Victoria when Burnham move her from out in front de Parliament. Dat's de place."

"There is someone else under the coffin."

"Yeah, Chief, dey got all kinds of tubes and bottles under de gurney – and if dey don't work, de old bastard gonna cook up like an iguana."

"The national flags are supposed to camouflage all that stuff?

"Yeah."

"Who's that with the trumpet?"

"Haslin, Haslin Paris, governor of de Central Bank and friend of de old man. He gonna belt out some Purcell and maybe de Last Post...Viola's idea."

"Jesus...there's his daughter Sally. She looks awful. But I don't see Herb, the son-in-law."

"Yeah, well, you won't."

"What do you mean?"

"Chief, you know de old man make that smartass Herb minister of health when he come back from Cuba with that quicky degree?"

"Yes, I remember."

"Yeah, well de old man take sick with his throat. And Doc Jones, he want to scrape her down with a local anaesthetic. Mistress Viola say, 'No way! Fly Forbes to Miami in de presidential plane.' Somebody say de plane is broke. Herb, he tell de old man, 'No big ting.' He bring in a pair of Cuban doctors… and dey do it in Georgetown Hospital."

"Georgetown Hospital! That termite palace – rats, and no running water past the first floor?"

"Yeah, Chief, you know how dey are. Dos lizard brains will do damn near anything for a socialist success."

"And…?"

"And, yeh dos Cuban clowns, dey forget to check his heart…and it turn out to be enlarged. Dey gas him up good…and poof! De old bugger is bowled – middle stump."

"Jesus!"

SURINAME

Clothes Make the Man

Although based in Georgetown, I was also non-resident ambassador to neighbouring Suriname, to which I made periodic visits. Content with local autonomy and the advantages of Dutch social services, the Surinamese had resisted pressures for full independence from a Netherlands government anxious to shed colonial trappings. Sovereignty was reluctantly embraced in 1975; the celebration of its fourth anniversary is described in this chapter.

"Where are the trousers for my dinner jacket?" I asked Judy, as I rummaged in my suitcase.

"When you called from Port-of-Spain you said, 'Pack my dinner jacket.' I packed your dinner jacket."

An hour before, we had arrived at the Hotel Torarica in Paramaribo, the small, very tropical capital of Suriname.

"You didn't pack my trousers?"

"You didn't ask for trousers."

"Dinner jacket means jacket and trousers. Do you expect me to present myself to the President in a tuxedo top and beige slacks?"

"Lower your voice. Perhaps you can rent or borrow them."

"In downtown Paramaribo, with half an hour before this bloody fandango at the palace begins? You must be joking."

Without Judy's practical guidance, my professional career as a diplomat would have been an unbroken chain of gaffes and disasters. This was an exception to the norm.

"Why don't you try the maître d'?"

A brilliant idea. Eric, the maître d', presided over the hotel dining room in a tuxedo, and he was about my size. I called the dining room. Eric expressed sympathy, but said he was sorry. He had two sets of dress clothes. One was at the cleaners, and he was wearing the other one on the job. I put the phone down and glared at my wife. Then the phone rang. It was Eric. He had decided that the president's annual Independence Day reception took precedence over the needs of his dining room. The clothes would be sent up as soon as he could get away from the dining room. Ten minutes later a waiter arrived bearing Eric's dress clothes.

Eric was my height, but he was younger and slimmer and wore his clothes in a form-fitting crooner cut. The jacket was snug but wearable. The pants were amazing. It was like putting on a pair of gabardine tights. With a lot of careful tugging I could get them on, but could not move the fly above half-mast.

Judy agreed to go on ahead to the palace. As she left I said, "For God's sake, don't tell anyone what has happened."

I lowered the cummerbund so that it covered most of the exposed triangle of underwear and completed dressing. As I stepped gingerly into the hall I found that my mobility was restricted. It was clear that a difficult evening lay ahead. To avoid bursting Eric's seams it was necessary to go down a small set of stairs slowly, and sideways. God knows what I looked like. I reassured myself that by the time I arrived, the receiving line would be over and I could slink quietly out onto the badly lit palace balcony and pretend normality. The taxi was another ordeal. It was impossible to sit down comfortably. I wedged myself against the floor with my feet and against the back of the seat with my shoulders, using the forward edge of the seat as a fulcrum for my thighs.

At the stately old wooden palace, the former residence of the Dutch governors, I was able to manoeuvre crabwise up the steps. Navigating cautiously into the ballroom, I was alarmed to see the president and Mrs. Ferrier still in position at the head of the receiving line. By the time I began to advance into the ballroom there were no other guests sheltering me from the direct line of sight of the host and hostess. I pulled my trousers upward, pushed my cummerbund downward, and minced self-consciously across the ballroom floor. It may have been all the constriction below my waist that loosened my reasoning. Maybe, I thought, as I drew painfully close to my destination, they still think I'm the Soviet ambassador. Ten months before, to the colossal irritation of the real thing, Surinamese protocol gazetted me as the Soviet ambassador, and the real Soviet ambassador, with the improbable name of Romanov, as the Canadian. The Soviets had just invaded Afghanistan. Could I, with my spandex tuxedo and a thick Russian accent, do terrible mischief to Soviet standing in this country? A marginally saner part of my mind prevailed. This train of thought, it said, is more likely to lead to unemployment.

The president smiled politely and took my hand. Mrs. Ferrier remarked that she had spoken to my wife. If they had noticed my distress, which was probable, they were magnanimous.

With as much haste as my trousers would permit, I fled to the shadows and the other guests on the balcony. Just beyond was a dark jungle of branches where the president's howler monkeys practiced acrobatics by day. Judy was talking to a group of friends. As I came up to them, instead of looking me in the eye, they were staring fixedly at my trousers and smiling.

"So much for state secrets," I said.

"Hrr, hrr, hrr…," giggled the entire group, including my wife.

Ulrich, a Belgian entomologist and long-term resident of Paramaribo, raised his head.

"Umm…I experienced a…uh…similar sartorial crisis," he said. He went on in his precise English, "I had been living in Suriname for about six years when I received an invitation from the Dutch ambassador to attend a black-tie dinner. You know Mad Max? He was the ambassador then."

None of us did.

"Well, he was something of an amateur botanist, and he invited me to a formal dinner. When I removed my dress clothes from the cupboard, I found that that they had been attacked by moths. Most of the holes were small, but there were three large ones in the trouser legs – one the size of an English crown. As with you, this unfortunate discovery was made the night of the party. Patching was out of the question. What to do? Then it occurred to me. I applied black shoe polish to my legs. He glanced at my unusual midsection arrangements. "Umm…unlike your situation, no one noticed the subterfuge."

Conversation drifted away from personal embarrassment. The sound of tree frogs and the faintly ripe fragrance of tropical compost rose from the marsh at the near side of the Suriname River. The pinching around my loins was becoming sedated by champagne, and, comforted by the dark, I began to relax. Judy and I were among the last to leave.

Back at the hotel, we stood talking to friends in the lobby when a waiter appeared. "Ambassador," he said, "the maître d' presents his compliments and asked me to ask you about the pants and jacket."

"My God!" With all the trauma and the champagne, I had forgotten Eric. I had promised to come back quickly so that he could return in uniform to the dining room. Self-conscious again, I tugged on my cummerbund and exited carefully to our room. A few minutes later I was in the kitchen. Eric was wearing jeans and a T-shirt and an expression that varied between exasperation and professional composure. He was given his tuxedo, my apologies, and a large tip.

෴ ෴ ෴

Jewels of the Forest

Suriname, like Guyana but more so, had a thinly populated interior largely untrammelled by the modern world. There were virtually no roads. Catching a glimpse of the rich cultures still flourishing beyond the small capital of Paramaribo required connections. I was lucky to have had one.

She was wearing a traditional Saramacca sarong, a broad-banded plaid of yellow, red, and black, and brass rings at her ankles. Tattoos in sacred patterns marked her belly and her breasts. At the request of my guide, interpreter, and friend, she was tying my hair into a series of stooks. This improbable event was recorded in a photograph that has long since disappeared.

This and the other photographs taken on a journey to Saramacca villages on the upper reaches of the Suriname River were an unexpected challenge. The Saramacca know the camera, but they dislike it. As in some isolated communities in other parts of the world, they believe that when the lens opens, it reaches out and takes a part of the soul. The Saramacca reacted to the camera with a mix of dismay and fear. Fortunately, along with my 35 mm I had brought an old Polaroid black and white, the kind that needed a fixative rubbed on the print twenty seconds after it extruded from the camera. By taking a picture of a tree, developing it, and passing the print to the villagers, I was able to exorcize the Polaroid, and by some mystery of association the 35 mm became acceptable too.

The coiffure came at the end of our trip and filled our time while we waited for the small Cessna to collect us. The airstrip had been cut from the rolling forest and was shaped like a novice ski jump, its grass and seedling cover periodically chopped back with machetes. The aircraft took us back to Paramaribo, the nation's capital, where our journey by road and by boat had begun two days before.

We had travelled by boat due south, deep into the rain forest. My purpose was to see the interior and visit the "Bush Negro," or "Maroon" communities. The Bush Negro are the descendants of slaves who had escaped from the Dutch in the seventeenth and succeeding centuries. Most of those who set off to form communities beyond the reach of the colonial power had been born in Africa, in the kingdom of Dahomey, on the gold and ivory coasts. They fled to the interior of Dutch Guiana, taking with them the languages, religions, tribal organization, and art forms of their homelands. Insulated by an immense forest, the resulting cultures offered a more authentic glimpse of some early central- and western-African societies than can be detected in Africa today. But my visit was not made to a culture frozen in time, nor certainly to any Amazonian version of *The Heart of Darkness*.

When we entered the upper Suriname River, most fragments of Western influence vanished behind our open boat, apart from the drone of the outboard motor and the sound of the occasional transistor radio on the shore. The green walls of the forest rose up on both banks. In between deluges of rain, which kept humidity at 100 percent and insects multiplying, the sun broke through the canopy and dappled the surface of the river. Somewhere out there there were caimans, snakes, piranhas, howler monkeys, tapirs, jaguars, parrots, and macaws, but apart from the insects, we saw few natural inhabitants.

Sporadic clearings revealed small villages and plots of cultivated land, usually sown with cassava, banana, or plantain. The wooden huts were thatched, many giving the impression of being freshly barbered. They were not what we would describe as single-family houses. The Saramacca practice a one-sided, sustainable polygamy. Under this arrangement, a Saramacca man may take more than one wife, as long as he can provide each with a home, tools, and sufficient land to support her and her children. In practice it is usually the medicine man or shaman who possesses the resources, and the resilience, for multiple wives.

From the river it was easy to distinguish traditional villages in which the shaman exercised enormous power from those communities that had converted to some form of Christianity. The traditional villages were marked by rustic arches of twisted bamboo that stood at each end to keep demons from entering.

Rapids eventually blocked further progress to the south. We stopped at the village of Djumo to rest, to explore, and to call on the headman, who received us dressed in a toga and loincloth. His assistant wore a chauffeur's cap, Western trousers, and an iron ring on his left bicep.

The man responsible for this expedition, as well as my hairdo and other embarrassments, was Jimmy Douglas, a Surinamer of mixed African and Scottish ancestry. A former district commissioner and chief of police, he was at that time the curator of the Fort Zeelandia Museum in Paramaribo. At the museum and at his home I had absorbed a lot of peanut soup and some knowledge of the six tribal communities of Bush Negroes and the Amerindians with whom they shared the forest – on non-amicable terms. The Dutch had not enslaved the Amerindians, and the latter had, in recompense, helped to recapture runaway slaves. The few who were caught were subject to some of the most ghoulish executions known to the history of slavery. Neither Jimmy's accounts nor the exhibits in his small museum had prepared me for the extraordinary richness of the Bush Negro, or, in this case, Saramacca, culture. It is suffused with art forms. Aside from textiles and tattoos, the medium is mostly wood: houses, chairs, canoes, paddles, kitchen implements, and winnowing trays. The artisans are not, as we would expect, master craftsmen and their apprentices, but most of the adult members of the community, who make their own canoes and tools and shape them according to the aesthetic principles of the culture.

When they crossed the Middle Passage from Africa, the original Saramacca must have brought with them a Muslim influence. Representational images are never seen. The art form is essentially three-dimensional. It is more elastic than geometric, but with a symmetrical discipline in the easy flow of its shapes. Some anthropologists disagree, but Jimmy believed that the force that invested beauty and a high standard in Saramacca art is contained in the spiritual significance of each carving.

For me, the most spectacularly impressive creation is the corial, or canoe. The gunwales are worked; the thwart is carved; bow and stern are extended into points and picked out with brass studs. The transformation from a hollowed tree trunk is sublime.

I was enchanted by my short visit to the Saramacca. Through Jimmy, I began to negotiate the shipment of a canoe to the Museum of Civilization in Ottawa. The project collapsed five months after our expedition when police sergeants, led by Desi Bouterse, launched a coup d'état and established their headquarters in Jimmy's museum.

POSTSCRIPT

Bouterse was sentenced in absentia by a Dutch court for drug trafficking and has been under indictment for the 1982 murder of fifteen opposition politicians. He was elected president of Suriname in 2010 in a relatively free election.

TRINIDAD AND TOBAGO

Me, Mick Jagger, Jungle Fever, and the Legion of Evil

Paul Laberge, my colleague in Trinidad, and his wife invited Judy and me to join them for Carnival in Port-of-Spain. Paul and I participated. The ladies watched and winced.

"Yes, it's true. I was in the same band as Mick Jagger...and we won a prize."

"Get serious, Dad. Mick Jagger's big-time," said my ten-year-old.

"Yeah. And Cuthbert knows more about music than you," said my eight-year-old. Cuthbert is our parrot.[1]

Judy joined the conversation. "That's right, Cuthbert can hold a tune."

"Hey, you're supposed to be on my side – and you were there."

"I stayed a safe distance from your capering," Judy replied.

"Why, Mum?" asked the ten-year-old.

"Because I prefer not to join your father when he is making a spectacle of himself."

"Dad, how did you get that weird sunburn?" enquired the eight-year-old. We were on the patio of our house in Georgetown, Guyana. I was wearing shorts, and slats of red skin were showing on my arms and legs.

"Good question," said Judy as she walked outside, leaving me to account for my activities to the children.

We were just back from Carnival. As it is in Brazil, the other great Mardi Gras Festival, the Trinidad Carnival has become a glittering expression of national culture as well as a release from a year's accumulation of stress. Calypso, soca, reggae, and the clear, bright syncopations of steel pans join with pungent lyrics, extravagant costumes, and thousands of barrels of beer and rum. This jangling, gurgling kaleidoscope pulses and surges over the streets, parks, and bars of Port-of-Spain, up the hills, and into the villages. In Canada, if you want to, you can ignore manias like the Super Bowl or the Stanley Cup. But Carnival is inescapable and marvellously indiscriminate. All ages, from five to eighty-five, dance. And if you don't have a partner you make do, holding a stick of sugar cane or a rum bottle.

The first practice sounds are heard in January. Day by day the volume grows, flaring with the first light of dawn on *Juvé* (from "*jour ouvert*"), the Monday before Ash Wednesday. The culmination is Shrove Tuesday, or Mardi Gras, the day when marching bands compete for the title of best band, best costume, best calypso. Everything stops at midnight, and the giddy, dehydrated revelers peel off their costumes and go home to bed almost too exhausted to remember why they are still wearing a smile.

The band contest is the main event of Carnival Tuesday. Design, fund-raising, composing, and recruiting can begin ten months earlier, but in most bands there is always room for latecomers, for whom the price of entry in those days might be a few dollars and help with last-minute preparations.

My friend Paul persuaded me to join a band, or "play mass," as this union with a demonic scrum is called.

"What do we have to do?" I asked, preparing to backpedal.

"Oh, you mean the preparations," said Paul. He led me toward a warehouse on French Street that had become a volunteer sweat shop.

"They're behind schedule. We have to help complete the costumes."

"Does our band have a name?"

"Ah," said Paul, "it's called 'Jungle Fever.' It's being put together by Peter Minshall. Last year he did 'Danse Macabre' and almost won. The bands are divided into sections, and each one has a different costume and a different name. In our band, for example, there's 'Scarlet Fever,' 'Yellow Fever,' and 'Maljo, the Evil Eye.'"

"And what's our section called?" I asked, looking apprehensively inside the warehouse at a sea of iridescent fabric.

Graham 'jumping up'.

"Ours is called 'Delirium,'" said Paul, and he introduced me to the chief couturier and the mask designer as a new recruit.

We were set to work painting and stapling moulded masks representing witch doctors, tropical birds, and monkeys. After several hours our foreman told us that the work would be finished by the next shift, and that we should collect our masks and costumes. I had seen our masks – we had worked on several tall ochre-coloured heads with huge purple eyes and satanic smiles – but I had not seen our costumes.

"Here they are," said Paul, his hearty voice not quite disguising his unease. We stood in front of what appeared to be a psychedelic lingerie counter, glowing violet and lime green, and marked appropriately with a notice that said "Delirium."

"You think I'm going to wear this?" I said, picking up a pair of flimsy green panties neatly trimmed with violet.

"Come on," said Paul, pumping his voice with joie de vivre, "it's Carnival…you want blue serge? But…," he said, then paused, suspending the garment from his own fingers, "you may want to wear a jock strap."

"Hmm," I muttered. "Carnival's a great cover for crazy stuff, but I'm not doing drag. Look at this top."

Like the briefs, this was designed for the female anatomy: it featured a bare midriff and a modified halter top. The outfit was completed with stretch fabric bands for the elbows and knees in violet and lime green.

At this point even Paul was having second thoughts. But the Delirium leader, whose rum punch we were drinking out of paper cups, gave us a pep talk. He spoke about memorable experiences and team spirit. He introduced us to other members of the section. I shrugged my shoulders, and Paul told our leader we would be seeing him early Tuesday morning. As we turned to go, he called to us. "By the way, you know that Mick Jagger will be jumping up in 'Jungle Fever'?" (In the calypsonian jargon "jumping up" means dancing.)

Mick Jagger and the Rolling Stones reached far afield for inspiration, to many distant, exotic places, and often to Trinidad. He and Bianca (this was 1981) were at the reception given by the president that evening. Paul and I were there too, and our wives consented to join us, since we were not in costume.

"Are you sure you want to do this?" asked Judy. It was seven o'clock Tuesday morning and I was climbing morosely into my snug green and violet briefs. She was in bed, gazing at me with a mixture of amusement and astonishment. She had seen the costume, but she had not seen it on me.

"Right now, I'm sure I don't. But last night I promised Paul we'd do it together."

"Well, if you're going, stay away from photographers. Two Canadian high commissioners hopping around like alien transvestites would make the tabloids."

"Look," I said, peering at my reflection in the bedroom mirror. "My mother wouldn't recognize me."

"Good," said Judy. "Have a nice day."

And so we set off. It was clear and bright. Already warm. Delirium settled itself behind one of Minshall's mobile groups of steel pans. The pans were fixed in metal frames, which rolled on large castors. Canvas screens, also attached to the frames, protected the musicians from the sun while they beat out a rhythm to which we, unprotected, danced and sang.

> De Jungle is in our blood
> De fever is in our heads
> Jungle Fever is not new
> Jungle Fever, it's the beast in you
> As soon as Christmas done
> You feel it comin' on
> Awoo oowo oowo oowo oowo oowo oowo
> Jungle Fever, Jungle Fever

"Fever" was pronounced "fee-ver," with the syllables stretched out and accompanied by a contrapuntal movement of shoulders and pelvis.

Jungle Fever and its 1,800 members were wedged between Tribal Festival and the Legion of Evil. Behind the Legion of Evil was Munshie, the Mystical Pheasant. Somewhere ahead, or maybe behind, was Mick Jagger.

It required an effort to recollect that this was Shrove Tuesday, a date set aside by devout Catholics to have their confessions heard. The mood in Port-of-Spain was unfettered hedonism. The ritual was pagan, linked more to the vernal equinox than to the Christian calendar. And Bacchus and the local distillers were enjoying a good day. Drink was definitely an asset, but you had to strike the right balance, and maybe even the right octane, to fuel the system, to achieve an anaesthetic rather than a paralytic effect, and to remain on the same lunar plane with the swirling bodies around you. It also helped to be in peak physical condition. Paul and I were deficient on both scores, me much more so. At mid-afternoon the Jungle Fever band was not yet in the Savannah Park and past the judges' stand. The Carnival snake was over a mile long. Sections rear-ended each other, stalled, took pit stops, and misinterpreted the parade marshal's orders. The noise was thunderous, and my stamina was fraying. By just after six the judges had seen us and we were marching off the Savannah. I waved goodbye. Paul, on his third wind, went on gyrating.

I returned to Paul's house, stinging with too much sun, and collapsed in a comfortable chair with a cold beer. Judy came in soon after, exclaiming that she thought she had recognized me from the stands.

"How could you recognize me? There were two hundred of us, all wearing masks."

"I was right. I did recognize you," she said, looking down. "It's the black socks with the brown shoes."

An hour later Paul bounded in with the news that Jungle Fever had won. It was named best band of Carnival.

"Well," I sighed, turning toward Judy. "I can go back and tell the kids that I played in the same band with Mick Jagger and that the band was the best in Carnival."

"Yes," she said, "and explain how you got sunburned in horizontal stripes."

GRENADA

Pierre Trudeau and the Embarrassment of a Full-Scale
American War against a Very Small Island

*We returned from London in the late summer of 1983. The
Department of External Affairs was in the throes of major re-
structuring aimed at improved policy coordination. The trade,
political, economic, immigration and overseas cultural functions were clustered under geographical directors-general. I was
appointed director-general of the Caribbean/Central America
Bureau. Central America was awash with problems, but Grenada
was the first major crisis.*

It was about seven o'clock in the evening and I was still at my desk in
the Pearson Building in Ottawa when the telephone rang. The date was
October 24, 1983. At the other end was Jean-Pierre Juneau, counsellor at
the Canadian embassy in Washington. He and his colleague Jacques Roy,
the chargé d'affaires, had just returned from the State Department where
they had been informed that the United States would take "appropriate
action" to protect its nationals in Grenada and its strategic interests in
the Caribbean. They were told consideration was also being given to the
evacuation of Canadian nationals. Juneau added that the Americans had
provided no time line about when the "action" would take place nor anything on the form it would take. However, neither Jean-Pierre nor I had

any doubt about the intended "action." President Reagan had decided to invade Grenada.

Of all the islands of the British West Indies, Grenada (population 91,000, and producer of one third of the world's nutmeg) had the most chequered adolescence as a sovereign state. The prime minister at independence in 1974 was Sir Eric Gairy, a noxious eccentric who once lectured the United Nations General Assembly on UFOs. He let it be known on the island that his elevation to first minister was divinely inspired. More grievously, he organized the Mongoose Gang, a collection of local thugs, to suppress opposition to his government. His overthrow by force by Maurice Bishop in 1979 was welcomed by most of the citizens.

On October 12, four years later, Bishop and his government were overturned by a group of hard-line Marxist-Leninists. That Bishop was a soft Marxist and an ally of Fidel Castro gave the affair and its bloodletting a Bolshevik vs Menshevik colouration. The new junta, the Revolutionary Military Council, executed Bishop and thirteen others including cabinet ministers and union leaders. There was no evidence that Cuba or the Soviet Union were involved in the plotting, the outcome of which was a setback for both countries. Western intelligence agencies were taken by surprise and the unlikelihood of this drama was reinforced by evidence that the only combat-ready professional military unit on the island was a detachment of Cuban soldiers – invited to the island by Bishop. In fact, Castro publicly condemned the killings[1] and on the eve of the invasion had refused a Grenadian request for more troops.[2]

The Cuban soldiers had been dispatched to provide symbolic support for Bishop and protection for the completion of a new airport. Many of the construction workers were also Cuban and, as the invaders discovered, had military training and access to arms. As sabres began to rattle, Castro assigned a colonel with African combat experience to command the troops in Grenada. The airport was intended by the Russians and the Cubans to be a significant strategic asset.[3] With a runway length of 9,000 feet, it could accommodate the behemoth-like Antonov aircraft, thereby facilitating Russian, Cuban, and African air linkages – a facility which would spare the Soviets the awkwardness and restrictions associated with using Goose Bay and Gander as staging bases.

The governments in the Eastern Caribbean were understandably alarmed. They were exceedingly vulnerable. With the exception of a small military command in Barbados, their security forces comprised tiny contingents of modestly armed police constables, many on bicycles. On the other side of the Caribbean the Cold War had been rekindled by the success of the Sandinista revolution in Nicaragua and by American reaction to that success. With the exception of Costa Rica, Central America was becoming a battleground. In Washington the president, Ronald Reagan, was already known for a 'no more Cubas on my watch' mantra. Grenada was already on his radar. A few months earlier Bishop had referred to the "fascist clique in Washington" and had prophetically mentioned "the possibility of military intervention."[4] Reagan was still haunted by the hostage taking of American diplomats in Tehran four years earlier. The terrorist explosion in Beirut, which occurred two days before the invasion and killed 241 US Marines, dramatically reinforced the hard line.[5] At very high speed the Reagan government assembled a coalition of countries from the Eastern Caribbean, the Organization of Eastern Caribbean States (OECS) – St. Kitts, Antigua, Dominica, Saint Lucia, and Saint Vincent – plus Barbados and Jamaica to provide international cover and 'allied' participation in the invasion.[6] Its purpose was four-fold: the expulsion of the Cubans; the removal of the junta; the installation of a more congenial interim government; and the rescue of an estimated 600 American students at the St. George's School of Medicine, an offshore US college.

As the Pentagon planners quickly realized, these were not easily compatible objectives. The application of military force to accomplish the first three could precipitate hostage taking of the students while a diplomatic approach, which might liberate the students, would leave the Junta and the Cubans in place. Moreover, the completion of the airport would thwart American strategic objectives. Hawkish views were in the ascendancy in the Pentagon, the State Department and ultimately in the White House. It was decided that the only tactic capable of achieving all objectives was the use of overwhelming force. It was anticipated that the sheer weight of a combined military, naval, and air operation would intimidate defenders and minimize military and civilian casualties. By October 23, with the Beirut explosion ringing in his ears, President Reagan had authorized the use of a huge sledgehammer to crack the tiny Grenadian nut.

Given the US objectives, their obsession with rooting out Communism in the hemisphere, and the political winds blowing around the White House the Pentagon plan made some sense. However, it soon became apparent that it did not make sense to Prime Minister Trudeau – nor to many others. Talleyrand, if he had been around, would have warned Washington "*Surtout, pas de zéle.*"[7]

When I put the phone down after the Washington embassy call, I could not anticipate Trudeau's thinking. However, I did realize that the prime minister and the acting secretary of state for external affairs had to be informed as soon as possible. Marcel Massé, the undersecretary, was still in the building. I consulted with him and he agreed that I should speak to Jean-Luc Pepin, the minister of state for external relations, who we both assumed was the acting foreign minister in the absence of Allan MacEachen, who was in the Middle East at the time. Pepin was sound and approachable.[8] I called Pepin who asked me to join him in his office in the Centre Bloc. After a short briefing we discussed the line that he should take with the prime minister. Our primary concern was with the approximately eighty-five Canadians on the island. Many were semi-permanent residents, some were tourists scattered in beach hotels, five were Canadian University Services Organization volunteers and six were engaged on official Canadian aid projects.[9] They could not leave because all international flights had been cancelled. Specifically, the concern was that foreigners could be used as hostages to prevent any attempt by the Americans to take the island by force. The murder of Bishop and his colleagues left little doubt in our minds that the Junta would not be squeamish in its use of hostages.

For the previous week my staff and I, with the support of the high commissioners in Barbados and Port-of-Spain, had been attempting to charter aircraft to begin ferrying the Canadians out of Grenada. Identifying and alerting many of these Canadians had been done by Joe Knockaert, the consular officer from the high commission in Barbados, who had been on a duty visit to Grenada when the coup took place. The closest airport to Grenada with a small fleet of charter aircraft was in Barbados, but arrangements did not fall quickly into place. Tom Adams, the prime minister of Barbados cancelled our charter out of Barbados. We tried Piarco, the airport of Port-of-Spain, Trinidad, but again there were problems with clearances. The Trinidadian government was being skittish about any involvement with the Grenada crisis. This problem was finally resolved the afternoon of October 24 by Noble Power, the high commissioner in Barbados who telephoned several recalcitrant regional prime ministers.

But by the time the decision was passed to the air crew it was too late to fly. Pearls, the small Grenada airport, had no landing lights and shut down at 6 P.M. "OK," we said, "let them start the shuttle tomorrow morning."

That evening in his office Pepin agreed that our overriding priority should be our nationals and that we should obtain the authority of the prime minister to make immediate contact with the Americans to urge them to delay military action until all foreigners who wished to leave had been able to do so. At this point we were not aware of any of the detail of the American plan, nor how advanced it was. But even if Trudeau agreed, and we assumed he would, we were not sanguine that a call from the Canadian government, albeit with the idea of saving lives, would divert the US government from its timetable. Even so, we felt a powerful obligation to try.

Pepin called the Prime Minister's Office and was told that Trudeau was not immediately accessible. The minister insisted that the issue was important and should be brought urgently to the prime minister's attention. Pepin put the phone down and we waited. I can't recall precisely but it must have been about forty-five minutes before Trudeau called. The conversation was short and, as Pepin recounted, did not proceed as we had anticipated. The prime minister was evidently not pleased to be interrupted, especially by a minister with whom he was not on good terms. He didn't object to making a case with the Americans for time to evacuate stranded citizens, but did not accept the urgency. He would not agree to contacting the Americans that evening and concluded the conversation by saying "Send a telegram."

I sketched out a message along lines acceptable to Pepin, returned to my office, wrote out the telegram to the embassy in Washington in longhand, and delivered it to the Communications Centre for urgent delivery. It was then about 10 P.M. At the heart of this telegram were these passages:

> there is a possibility that your government might engage in a rescue operation of American and foreign nationals in Grenada in conjunction with member states of the OECS. We are grateful for your willingness to include Canadian nationals. However, we are most concerned that such an operation, if undertaken by force, could lead to panic and the taking of hostages with consequent real risk of bloodshed. As you know evacuation arrangements are

*already in train. We very much hope that nothing will be done
to jeopardize their success. We would appreciate your assurance
that no operation which might meet armed resistance will take
place while some groups of foreign nationals have been given the
opportunity to leave with the consent of the present Grenadian
authorities.*[10]

Even hypothetically, this telegram could not have produced action until early the following morning.

The following morning was pandemonium. It was immediately obvious that our labour the previous evening had not only been futile but unexpectedly embarrassing. The morning news programs were consumed with the invasion which had begun at dawn. A massive force had descended on Grenada – over twenty-six warships, including three aircraft carriers (*USS Independence*, *USS Guam* and *USS Saipan*) and a force of over 7,000 soldiers, including Seals and Marines.

A related news story was delivered by a CBC reporter who had joined a gaggle of journalists assembled early that morning on the lawn of Gerald Regan, the minister of state for foreign trade. The reporter had apparently consulted a press club list to learn who, in the absence of MacEachen (who was in Egypt), was the acting foreign minister. Fortunately for me, my egregious error in assuming it was Pepin, was shared by everyone consulted the night before including Marcel Massé and Pepin himself.[11] However, none of this was any comfort to the hapless Regan. Transparently ill-informed and unable to offer the press any sense of the government's reaction to the crisis and nothing about the safety of Canadians, he was driven off to his office in a towering rage.

Meanwhile, the prime minister summoned an emergency meeting in a board room in the Centre Block of Parliament. Regan was there. So were Marcel Massé, senior officers from National Defence, a cluster of officials from the Prime Minister's Office and the Privy Council Office and myself. Pepin had not been invited.

The prime minister was in a foul mood. In a diary note I had scribbled uncharitably that his tie was at half mast and that his face had the "raddled look of someone who had spent the night on the tiles." One of his first questions was how a major American invasion force, involving the collaboration of seven Caribbean countries could be assaulting Grenada without the prior knowledge of the Canadian government. Surmising correctly that it would not be well received, I intervened to describe the telephone call from Washington and to mention the report given to him the previous evening by Pepin. I was treated to a cold prime ministerial harrumph.

This was Tuesday. Grenada had been a hot topic in the House of Commons on Monday and the previous week. Now and for the next week it was front and centre. That afternoon Brian Mulroney, leader of the Progressive Conservatives, demanded to know why we were not supporting our American ally and why we had not been informed in advance. Nettled, but still formidable on his feet, the prime minister retorted: "Madame Speaker, I think the answer to that is rather simple. These countries (the US and Caribbean partners) were determined to support an invasion. They know that Canada is not in the habit of supporting invasions of other countries."

On Thursday, Ed Broadbent, leader of the New Democratic Party, castigated the government for not informing the United States government earlier of its opposition to "a possible invasion." Trudeau's reply was not wholly accurate: "The first suspicion that an invasion might take place was Monday night. The moment I heard about it, I did ask for that message to be sent." The prime minister added that the government had previously taken "steps to ensure the safe evacuation, if need be, of Canadian nationals who were in Grenada."

As proposed by Massé, one of the decisions taken at the meeting with the prime minister was to establish a multi-departmental task force, chaired by me, which would meet once or twice daily. In the absence of an operations centre in the Department of External Affairs, the task force met in a conference room near my office.[12] Our small team soon discovered that servicing the process requirements of the task force, preparing minutes, distilling and circulating telegrams and other intelligence, and preparing agendas consumed most of our time, leaving little for the substantive issues including input on the formation of a new government in Grenada, the recruitment and training of a new constabulary to replace the wholly politicized and now defunct police force, and the evacuation of our citizens. For almost a month the Task Force was producing daily situation reports. Also it was increasingly impossible to ignore the widening conflict in Central America. And, of course, there were other demands: preparing draft answers to questions in the House, liaising with embassies, frequent daily contact with our high commission in Barbados, and helping the Press Office field the onslaught of questions – some embarrassing.

Underlying, and to a high degree, undermining our various action plans was the prime minister's take on the crisis. Unstated, but implicit in the board room was the depth of Trudeau's indignation with President Reagan. Perhaps correctly conjecturing that Trudeau would have opposed an invasion, neither Reagan nor George Shultz, his secretary of state, had spoken to Ottawa – leaving only that vague State Department signal, delivered at the eleventh hour. President Reagan and Prime Minister Trudeau did not care for each other, but it is not certain that personal chemistry was a factor in the decision to withhold information. Reagan did call his good friend Margaret Thatcher, but only at the last minute and not to consult. For once on the same wave-length with Trudeau, Thatcher was furious – a reaction that upset the Americans, who had strongly supported Thatcher in the British recovery of the Falkland Islands from Argentina two years before.[13]

Meanwhile in Grenada, the invasion was not proceeding either efficiently or bloodlessly. Codenamed Operation Urgent Fury, the invasion lacked "inter-operable communications." The naval command centre's radio system on the flagship, *USS Independence*, was not compatible with those of some of the military units causing delay, confusion, and worse. Even the one CIA agent, flown in two days before the invasion, could not transmit intelligence because the CIA's chartered yacht, which was to receive her intelligence reports, had been chased out of range by the US Navy.[14] Joe Knockaert, the Canadian high commission officer on the island, shook his head in disbelief when asked by a general and then by platoon commanders about roads and paths to move troops from point A to point B.[15] The invaders had landed without basic maps. Knockaert explained that maps of the island were available for sale at most local shops.

Friendly fire accounted for a number (unspecified) of the 19 Americans killed during the engagement and 116 wounded. Forty-five Grenadians were killed and 358 were wounded. The Cubans, including the armed construction workers, lost 25 with 59 wounded. The Pentagon's public report on Urgent Fury notes that its success was "marred by the consequences of inadequate time for planning, lack of tactical intelligence and problems with joint command and control."[16] The cast of the operation was studded with figures already or yet to emerge in fame or notoriety: George

H.W. Bush, Admiral John Poindexter, Caspar Weinberger, Oliver North, General (Stormin') Norman Schwartzkopf, and Robert McFarlane.

The good news was that no foreigners were held hostage. Six hundred US citizens, mostly medical students, were successfully evacuated along with 121 foreigners, including 29 Canadians. Many Canadians, largely the permanent residents, opted to stay put. However, the extrication of those Canadians who wanted to leave remained mired in a Catch-22.

The Grenada situation report from our operations centre, October 26, was explicit. "It is extraordinary and disquieting that the US authorities should manage to give us four conflicting reasons for their inability to provide clearance in the course of one day."[17]

In a story datelined October 27, Oakland Ross of the *Globe and Mail* described the final Canadian attempt to retrieve our nationals. He and other journalists were aboard a Hercules C-130 Canadian Forces aircraft. As the aircraft made its approach to Pearls airport, the pilot was informed that the Canadians had already been evacuated by the US Air Force and would be landing in Raleigh, North Carolina. However, when this aircraft arrived in Raleigh it was discovered that there were no Canadians on board. The Hercules returned to Trenton, Ontario, and the Canadians were eventually removed by another US aircraft.

Pentagon preparations for the invasion had been nourished by wishful thinking. State Department officials wrote that "in Western Europe, where US willingness to fight for European soil was questioned, such action might inspire confidence in the United States."[18] The international verdict did not support this thesis. The UN resolution condemning the United States for "flagrant violation of international law" was carried by 108 votes with 27 abstentions (including Canada's) to only 9 opposed (several Caribbean and Central American countries, Israel, and the United States).[19] Gerard Pelletier, long-time friend and colleague of Trudeau and at this moment ambassador to the UN, explained to the General Assembly that Canada was "not yet convinced that the invasion of Grenada was a legitimate exercise of the right of self-defence." The Pentagon report noted that "in Ottawa, spokesmen questioned the need and justification for US intervention, especially after the Canadian government had already announced plans to conduct the peaceful evacuation of its citizens."[20]

Ronald Reagan is reported to have dismissed the international criticism in the belief that opinion in the United States would back him up.

This perception proved to be correct. The president's popularity rose in the wake of the invasion and reinforced his determination to support right-wing military governments in Central America and the Contra forces in Nicaragua.

The crisis led to other long-term consequences. Post mortems on the many failings of Operation Urgent Fury were followed by the most radical changes to the structure of US combined operations since World War II. A lesser change, but one with immediate impact on my bureau, was the recognition that American knowledge of the English-speaking parts of the Caribbean was woefully inadequate and considerably inferior to that of the British Foreign Office and the Canadian Department of External Affairs. The US State Department proposed the creation of semi-annual American/British/Canadian meetings to share analyses and prognosticate about the Caribbean. The proposal represented some easing of tensions and both the U.K. and Canada were pleased to accept.[21]

Reaction in Grenada to the invasion was mixed. Relief that the murderous Junta had been removed and its most ardent supporters imprisoned was widespread, but was qualified by dismay at the heavy destruction in St. Georges, the capital, and especially by the toll of dead and wounded Grenadians. The Pentagon had deployed the 9th Psychological Operations Battalion, known as PSYOPS, to minimize negativity. When I visited the island many weeks later very few Grenadians were wearing the PSYOPS-produced T-shirts. One was emblazoned with crossed US and Grenadian flags with the caption "AMERICA THANK YOU FOR LIBERATING GRENADA TUESDAY 25 OCTOBER 1983." Another, under the heraldic arms of the 505th Airborne Infantry, bore the inscription "ON TO HAVANA."[22]

In Ottawa, the prime minister's indignation had not run its course. Allan Gotlieb, our ambassador in Washington, called on Langhorne A. Motley, the assistant secretary of state for Western Hemispheric Affairs to convey Trudeau's views on the invasion. Motley was a Reagan appointment, a former ambassador to Brazil and an Alaskan real estate developer. Described by Secretary of State Schultz as "a real scrapper,"[23] he had been one of the architects of Operation Urgent Fury. Motley and I met several times in the months following the Grenada crisis and it was Motley who described the meeting with our ambassador. Gotlieb apparently delivered his message forcefully. So forcefully, Motley told me, that he had never come "so close to punching out a foreign ambassador."

While vexed with Reagan, Trudeau was almost certainly more deeply distressed with his friends in the Caribbean who had formed the coalition. The prime minister's indignation shaped policy over the next month. Correctly interpreting this focus of Trudeau's anger, some top officials began concocting a revised Canada/Caribbean aid policy which would penalize those islands that had collaborated with the Americans. This bizarre policy drama rose to a point of absurdity with the suggestion that Grenada should also be deprived of some CIDA (Canadian International Development Agency) assistance – presumably for allowing itself to be invaded. John Robinson, my colleague in CIDA, and I were horrified. Helping to put Grenada back onto its feet with some sort of stable government and a responsible police force had become an urgent priority. But as we quickly learned, attempting to move past officials who were on the PM's wave length was difficult. At the time I had no evidence that Trudeau had condoned or was even aware of these machinations and so gave him the benefit of the doubt and privately blamed the officials.

Thirty-one years later a friend put me straight. In 1983 he had been working with the Privy Council Office and had been a note-taker on board the government aircraft that carried the prime minister and his team from Ottawa to the November 1983 meeting of the Commonwealth heads of government in New Delhi. In the course of a discussion of the draft for this chapter he told me that he had been present during a conversation between Trudeau and senior officials at which the prime minister instructed that development assistance to a number of Caribbean countries should be reduced. Fortunately, and soon after, reason began to prevail with the return of MacEachen from the Middle East.

But the question persisted. Why had Caribbean leaders failed to alert Trudeau?[24] After all, he had cultivated the Commonwealth Caribbean. He was on good, even warm terms, with most of the island leaders. He had seen them only a few months before and had bestowed upon them increased CIDA assistance. A rumour circulated that Dame Eugenia Charles, the prime minister of Dominica, had tried to call Ottawa, but had the wrong telephone number. This never seemed very credible. The facts, when they emerged two years later, offer a lesson on the importance of the idiosyncratic variable on the conduct and understanding of foreign policy.

In August 1985 I accompanied a minister of state in the new Mulroney government, who had been designated to represent Canada at the funeral of President Forbes Burnham of Guyana.[25] The minister had offered to pick up any prime minister from the Eastern Caribbean en route. Two had accepted, one of whom was Sir John Compton of St. Lucia. From St. Lucia to Georgetown, Guyana, I sat with Sir John.

Sir John had been one of two spokesmen for the Organization of Eastern Caribbean States (OECS) at the time of the invasion. I asked him about Dame Eugenia's wrong telephone number story. "Ah that!" he snorted. "All myth. But I will tell you – the real story is just as strange."

The Americans had insisted on total secrecy. However, given the special connection with Canada and particularly with the prime minister, it had been agreed among his colleagues of the OECS that Trudeau should be contacted and that he, Sir John, would speak to Trudeau or pass a message to him by safe hand. Sir John decided that the simplest way would be to telephone his friend Alan Roger, the Canadian high commissioner in Barbados who had been accredited to all of the OECS countries. Sir John called and was told by the receptionist that Mr. Roger had left Barbados on the conclusion of his posting. She asked if Sir John would like to speak to his successor. He said no and asked if he could speak to the head of the aid section. He had left for Canada. Sir John then asked to speak to the head of the political section. Same response. This person had also left the high commission. Asked again if he would like to speak to the new high commissioner, he threw up his hands metaphorically, while clutching the receiver and repeated "no." He was not prepared to discuss the most sensitive military strategy involving the Caribbean since the Napoleonic wars with someone he had never met. He put down the phone. Enveloped in the preparations for an invasion of which he was a titular partner, he abandoned the quest.

HAITI

Le Chien Est Mort

This incident occurred during an official visit to Haiti in 1986 with a colleague from the Canadian International Development Agency (CIDA) following the collapse of the government of Jean-Claude Duvalier and the end of twenty-nine years of dictatorship by father (Papa Doc) and son (Baby Doc).

The singing drew my attention. Two men digging a trench at the far end of a field were chanting as they swung their spades. I walked closer and recognized a Haitian rhythm, a powerful Vodou chorale. The two men sang with relish. I was about fifteen feet away when one of them picked up a dog that had lain hidden by a pile of dirt. He held the dog by its back legs and dropped it into the trench. There was a plop, but the dog made no noise.

I looked at the men. *"Le chien est mort?"*

Absorbed in work and song, they had not noticed my approach. Now they turned, and one of them paused and said to me with a broad smile, *"Oui, le chien est mort,"* whereupon both men began to chant again with renewed enthusiasm as they shovelled dirt into the shallow grave.

Recoiling from this macabre tableau, I hurried to the house where I was staying. This was my fourth day in Haiti, and only eight days after the flight of the last dictator, Jean-Claude Duvalier, or "Baby Doc." Propelled by international pressure and domestic unrest, he left for a gilded exile in the south of France with his beautiful and larcenous wife, who was soon to leave him. He left behind jubilation, shooting, and *déchoucage* – a Creole word that could mean anything from destroying the home of a hated, now impotent, enemy to dismembering him.

Commercial air service to Port-au-Prince from North America had not been restored. John Robinson and I arrived on the first plane from Santo Domingo, at the other end of the island of Hispaniola. He was the area director general for CIDA and I was his counterpart for External Affairs. An otherwise short and uneventful flight turned clamorous when the stewardess absent-mindedly announced to the mostly Haitian passengers that we had just landed at *"L'Aeroport International François Duvalier."*

Port-au-Prince had not changed since my last visit, when the previous dictator, Papa Doc, in whose memory the airport had been named, was still alive. Washed by a wide, turquoise, and tepid bay, the city sprawled in an exotic jumble at the foot of the mountains. Downtown Port-au-Prince resembled the New Orleans French Quarter, but reconstructed by Charles Addams and left in the sun to decay for a hundred years. Once-splendid, extravagant, tropical homes, designed for pleasure and off-shore zephyrs, had become the raddled ghosts of their past: most louvres were gone, the gingerbread and wrought iron broken, and the turreted roofs, sheathed in tin, were tilted and rusted. Inside they teemed with children, flies, and mosquitoes. Each room contained at least one family. Laundry left tinctures of colour against the weathered grey siding.

Closer to the sea, there was no worn architecture that spoke of a profligate, comfortable youth, only slums, perhaps the worst slums this side of Calcutta, slums whose stench extended beyond their line of sight.

We were staying above all this, in a lovely modern residence on the side of the mountain, shaded and cool at one thousand feet. The grave digging I had observed was about one kilometer from the house. Night was falling quickly, as it does in the tropics. From down below in the city came the occasional crack of gunfire, audible over the distant thrumming of drums. It had been foolhardy to stray so far by myself. I suppressed the urge to run.

Back in a secure and pleasant home, I sat down while a drink was poured. Less tense, and starting to feel that my jitters might have been a bit overblown, I gave my host and hostess a spare account of my adventures.

There was no comment until I concluded my story, and then Suzanne, wife of Tony Malone, the ambassador, asked, "What colour was the dog?"

"What do you mean, what colour was the dog?"

"Just tell me the colour."

"It was black."

"Ahh," said Suzanne. "They were burying the mayor."

"Burying the mayor?"

"Yes. Until last week, when he was thrown out, Dieudonné Duval was the mayor. He was a Duvalieriste and Tonton Macoute, feared and hated by the people. Somehow he escaped the *déchoucage* and disappeared. Mère Katrin, a *mambo*, or priestess, declared that she had used her sacred Vodou powers to transform Duval into a dog – a black dog. The gardener told me that no black dog is safe in all of Port-au-Prince."

(ENTRAL AMERICA AND COLOMBIA

Go by Boat: Travels with Allan MacEachen

*In the mid-1980s the conflicts in Central America and asso-
ciated human rights abuses had become the most heated topic
of Canadian foreign policy debate. This was my most active file
during my five years as director general for the region and involved frequent travel to Central America. All of these visits were
marked by traumatic and eccentric encounters. This visit was
with Allan MacEachen, then deputy prime minister and secretary of state for external affairs. It took place in April 1984.*

"Holy God! Have a look at that!"

John Noble, one of our team members, was looking through the per-
spex at the space toward which the helicopter was descending. The helicopter had five stars painted on the outside and the words *Presidente de
la Republica de Honduras.* Allan MacEachen, his small delegation, and
two journalists were being transported by helicopter from Palmerola, the
Honduran air force base, to the Tegucigalpa airport. This was because
the pilot had declined to squeeze our almost new Challenger between the
hunched shoulders of two mountains to land at the national airport. We
all craned our necks to see what our colleague was talking about.

Below, with rapidly increasing clarity, we could see a parade-ground
formation of three companies of soldiers in gorgeously vivid Napoleonic
uniforms, complete with gold piping, epaulettes, shakos, feathers, and

bandoliers. One company wore blue jackets, another raspberry red, and the last, white. They were cadets from the air force, army, and navy academies. In front of them was a small dais, and from it to a point on the airfield apron was stretched a long red carpet. We looked uncomfortably at each other. The agenda for the minister's visit to Honduras was supposed to begin an hour after we reached the hotel. We were dressed for tropical travel, not for a state occasion. Self-consciously, we clambered out of the helicopter onto the red carpet, where MacEachen was greeted by the foreign minister of Honduras and the chief of protocol.

As the foreign minister extended his hand, there was a thunderous detonation, then another, then another. On a grassy knoll, well behind the cadets, two howitzers were banging out the appropriate salvo – or whatever they thought was appropriate. It was unlikely that the Hondurans, or anyone, for that matter, knew the number of rounds required to greet a visiting deputy prime minister. This extravagant and unexpected welcome had been laid on at the express wish of President Sauzo. His chief of protocol much later told me that the president had wished to celebrate the first ever visit to Honduras of a Canadian foreign minister.

Everything was proceeding according to plan until about the ninth shot, at which point the blank shell misfired and a gout of flame flew out of the barrel, igniting the tall, dry grass around the artillery. The flames spread quickly, and there was a short period of pandemonium while soldiers, and eventually an airport fire truck, put out the fire.

Four days later, after full visits to Nicaragua and Costa Rica, the Challenger took off from San Jose. We were en route to Bogota and a meeting with President Betancur and his foreign minister.

The flight was an opportunity to relax. The trip through four countries of Central America had been the first major foray by a senior minister to the most neuralgic area of Canadian foreign policy at the time. The expedition had begun with a short visit to George Schultz in Washington. Schultz, who was then President Reagan's secretary of state, was an old friend of MacEachen's. Nevertheless, it was as tricky to explain why Nicaragua was a key part of the agenda, as it was to navigate the often impassioned presentations on the subject by presidents, foreign ministers, and generals. MacEachen managed this with insouciance, steering a path that endorsed neither the Sandinistas nor the Contras. The Canadian government's purpose was threefold:. to respond to growing pressure in Canada to engage positively with Central America; more specifically, to help find a way to stop hostilities; and to urge the demilitarization of the region by all parties, including the Soviet Union and the United States. In the end we earned the respect of almost all sides in Central America and a grudging, aggrieved tolerance by Washington, but had only limited success with militant, pro-Sandinista opinion in Canada. When Joe Clark succeeded MacEachen as secretary of state for external affairs, he took up this challenge with gradually increasing success – but that is another story. We were at the end of a stressful week, and four hours of flying time with drinks in hand would have been a welcome break.

Alas, this was not to be. About forty minutes out of San Jose the Challenger's pressure seal cracked. At 40,000 feet, we were approximately 11,000 feet higher than the peak of Mount Everest and were rapidly losing most of our oxygen. The pilot threw the plane into a steep dive, pressed his

Mayday transmission button, and pulled the lever for the release of oxygen masks. The cabin filled with a cloud of white vapour, which quickly dissipated. Masks deployed for the pilot, co-pilot, and navigator, and for MacEachen and three others sitting in armchairs in the first row of the passenger cabin. Several masks, including that for the steward, failed to release from their overhead compartments. Others deployed but provided no oxygen. The compartment above me had opened very slightly, and I probed with my fingernails until I was able to dislodge the mask. This was shared with a colleague with whom I was sitting on a sofa facing the side of the aircraft, and it was almost immediately shared also with two journalists who joined us from the chairs behind us. Suddenly alert to the problem of four passengers relying on one oxygen mask, Keith Bezanson from CIDA, who had a functioning mask and was just in front of me (or, given the pitch of the aircraft, just below me), gestured to me to sit on his lap and share his mask, thereby reducing the one-mask dependency on the sofa from four to three. Fortunately we were above jungle, not mountain, and levelled out at 3,000 feet. The plunge down seemed to have gone on for a long time, but in reality it must have been less than three minutes. When the trauma was over and we were safely at our new cruising altitude, someone shouted, "Let's have a drink!" and David MacDonald of the *Winnipeg Free Press* pulled out the bottle of rum he had purchased at the duty-free in San Jose.

"Wait a minute," he said. "There's an inch of rum missing – and the bottle has never been opened." We speculated on this and eventually concluded that alcohol had evaporated through the cork top.

"Minister," someone said, "if that happened to the rum, imagine what it's done to our brains."

As we approached Uplands Airport in Ottawa at the close of the expedition, an ode to our odyssey in calypso form was recited to MacEachen. A few verses from this vapid doggerel are set out below:

Canada send de big road show
To see dose countries down below.
De right, de centre, and – no compromise –
Include de people's paradise.

'Welcome to Colombia, Mr. MacEachen. How was your flight, sir?'

Cartoon by Franklin of the Globe and Mail.

De Opposition and de rest
Say dat dis be important test.
So off de delegation go
With Al MacEachen lead de show.

Den next we go to Bogota
To learn from President Betancau.
So off again our heroes flew,
But Challenger now drop de shoe.

De drop be fast and breathless too,
But minister know what to do.
And while he sit and show "sang froid,"
Bezanson kneel and pray to God.

And Claude, he cool and tall,
He phone his broker in Montreal.
He say, "Work fast and sell my share
In dat big firm called Canadair."

McDonald, de plume of de *Tribune*,
He look around de cabin room.
"Oh, Man," he grin and den he say,
"No problem wid de lead today."[1]

PANAMA

The General and Margot Fonteyn

My work as a regional director general was varied. It included formal protocol duties, such as attending state funerals of foreign heads of state, and briefing the governor general for the presentation of credentials by newly arrived ambassadors or high commissioners. In those days the official rig for a presentation was morning dress. I would change into this uniform at my office in the Pearson Building and then, weather permitting, cycle along Sussex Drive to Rideau Hall. Seated portentously in the back of the horse-drawn state landau, the envoy clattered up the drive, accompanied by RCMP outriders resplendent in scarlet uniforms and beribboned lances. It was a marvellous ritual, now sadly downgraded to a Cadillac and business attire. Another occasional duty was accompanying a minister or senior parliamentarian to the inauguration of a new head of state. These events sometimes offered unexpected entertainment. One such occasion was the inauguration of the president of Panama in 1984.

Although it was never clear that Nicolas Ardita Barletta had beaten his opponent freely and fairly, his inauguration was an important event. It was the first election in Panama after seventeen years of military rule, and also the first since Jimmy Carter had turned over ownership and administration of the Panama Canal to the Panamanians. Representing

Author en route to an official function.

the Canadian government at Barletta's inauguration was Chris Speyer, a Progressive Conservative parliamentarian from Cambridge, Ontario. I was there as his advisor, as was Chips Filleul, the non-resident Canadian ambassador, and Susan Howell, second secretary, based, with Chips, in San José, Costa Rica.

The inauguration ceremony took place in a vast convention hall in Panama City. Getting there was the second challenge we had to face – the first had been the discovery that Canada's official gift, an Inuit sculpture, had been stolen. The route to the convention centre funnelled into a narrow roadway that was soon choked with limousines and taxis entering from both directions. Horns were blaring. Drivers were shouting. The police had overlooked the need for a transport plan. Observing this chaos from our taxi, Chris opined that the colourful shambles "was worth the price of admission."

Inside the convention centre the thousand or so seats were slowly filling up. George Schultz, US Secretary of State and President Reagan's representative, walked in to subdued applause. A few minutes later Jimmy and Rosalyn Carter arrived to a tumultuous ovation from the Panamanians. Well past the appointed hour the hall was full, and the outgoing acting president and the members of the Supreme Court, all in white linen suits, had taken their seats on the stage. They left one chair empty for Barletta at the centre. There was a long pause, and then a short, frumpy-looking man with a pitted face and white uniform strode to the middle of the stage and nudged the man sitting beside the empty chair. This person rose, causing a sequential shuffle of rising, moving, and sitting that ended only when the junior judge at the end of the row was shuffled off the stage. It was musical chairs without music. I turned to Chips and whispered, "Who's the interloper?" He replied, "General Noriega wants everyone to know who is still running the country."

Barletta was (and is) a decent man. He resigned a year later, when he was unable to rein in the corruption in his administration. Chief among the villains was the same General Noriega. Subsequently imprisoned in the United States for narcotics trafficking,[1] Noriega was apparently responsible for manipulating enough votes to enable Barletta to squeak ahead of his opponent, Arnulfo Arias. Arias was a political eccentric on a grand scale and a Panamanian legend. In 1940 he ran and won the presidency on the National Socialist (i.e., Nazi) ticket. To no one's surprise, the Americans, who controlled the Canal and whose gunboat diplomacy had separated Panama from Colombia in 1903, conspired with the Panamanian military, and Arias was overthrown. Shifting his politics to a quasi-Marxist platform, Arias ran again in 1968 and won. Once more the United States and the Panamanian military were unhappy and Arias was quickly overthrown. On this occasion Arias presented himself as a candidate of the centre-left. Possibly, he should have won. There was never a serious investigation into whether he had been the victim of election fraud.

As the band played the Panamanian national anthem and the chief justice slipped the presidential sash over Barletta's shoulder, I murmured to Susan, "Now is the time to shout, 'Viva Arnulfo!'" She snorted quietly and rolled her eyes.

Two hours later we passed the bandoliered and handsomely uniformed guard at the presidential palace. Beyond the gate was an even more impressive formation. Standing perfectly erect in a pool, as if in honour of the occasion, were the presidential egrets. There were about a dozen birds, uniformly white and displaying a quiet dignity not always present that afternoon. Several stood on one leg, but that did not spoil the effect.

Inside the palace among a moving shoal of guests, we opened a conversation with an elegant woman who was standing beside an immaculately dressed gentleman in a wheelchair. We introduced ourselves, but I did not catch her name. She then introduced our small group to the man in the wheelchair, her husband, Roberto (Tito) Arias, a nephew of Arnulfo. It was then that I realized the lady was Dame Margot Fonteyn, one of my heroines during our time in London. Although not married until the mid-1950s, they had met in Cambridge in 1937, when Arias was a student and Fonteyn was dancing at a local theatre. The marriage was ill-starred. Arias was a charming, reckless political adventurer and philanderer. Fonteyn had been on the point of divorcing him when he was shot in a botched assassination attempt. According to contemporary reports, the would-be assassin was (a) the agent of a plot hatched by the Panamanian chief of police, (b) the husband of one of Arias's mistresses, or (c) both. A bullet penetrated his spine, leaving him a quadriplegic. Fonteyn abandoned the divorce and returned to Panama to devote most of her remaining years to the care of her husband.

Although we must have spoken for ten or fifteen minutes, I don't recall what we talked about. But I remember other details. Fonteyn ensured that the conversation was lively and pleasant, and that her husband, whose speech was limited, was always engaged. Louis Martinz, a long-time friend of both, is quoted as remarking, "Oh, my God, that woman is a saint. Yet she never makes herself look like one. Saints don't, you know."[2]

(ENTRAL AMERICA

Fireworks and Foreign Policy

Joe Clark was secretary of state for external affairs (foreign minister) for four of my five years as director general for the Caribbean and Central America. Several years after he had left active politics and I had left the foreign service I prepared a short paper at his request on what I thought Canada's engagement with Central America had achieved and how this had happened. The paper was also a case study on how a modest power can serve the international community and burnish its own image by hard slogging in a niche area and do so without burning bridges to a powerful and, at times, less principled partner. What follows is based on that paper and on further comments from Mr. Clark. This chapter, a bit like the piece on Grenada, strays from the book's intent, which was to be primarily anecdotal. If it is any comfort to the reader, the next and most succeeding chapters revert to the original plan.

Canada's Central America policies in the eighties did not produce spectacular results, nor were any of the breakthroughs the direct result of Canadian initiatives. However, Canadian diplomacy did contribute to the changing political environment in the region – reciprocal concessions that led to the end of civil war and the beginnings of a regulatory and peacekeeping framework – and they did this against the odds.[1] The odds were heavily stacked against an independent Canadian policy toward Central America, not only because of the usual prudence about unduly annoying Uncle Sam, but because this policy was being pursued simultaneously with the Mulroney government's primary foreign policy objective, which was the free trade agreement with the United States.

Moreover, a determined American position about the spread of 'more Cubas' in the hemisphere, while counterproductive was, in the Cold War context, at least understandable. Disagreement on Central America was inevitable. Expressing that disagreement, while containing it within the parameters of a 'we agree to disagree' policy, was a major achievement. Each side viewed the Central America conflicts through separate prisms. As set out in the Kissinger Commission of 1984 the US saw the issues in terms of the Cold War while Canada saw the roots of the conflict in poverty, hugely uneven distribution of wealth, and the failure of social justice, including the brutal oppression of the indigenous population of Guatemala. The intervention of outside powers, on both sides of the Cold War divide, only aggravated an already incendiary situation. Allan MacEachen, then secretary of state for external affairs, made the point clearly in a February 1984 speech: "In keeping with Canada's position against third-party intervention in Central America and the supply of armaments to opposing factions, we oppose continued military support for anti-Sandinista insurgents just as we oppose the promotion of, and support for, armed insurgency in El Salvador and Guatemala by outside powers."

In September 1986 and following an announcement that the US Congress had allocated $100 million for aid to the Contras, Joe Clark, MacEachen's successor, declared that "[this] decision runs counter to our position. Canada has constantly emphasized its firm belief that the countries of Central America must be free to seek their own solutions without interference from any outside source."[2] On top of sound policy, this was a useful reassertion of bipartisan consistency on Central America. In response to my notes, Clark clarified that "Part of the import of Mr. Mulroney's and my position was that it affirmed and extended a constructive interest in development and peace in Central America as being broadly Canadian, and not merely the product of one party. That was important beyond Central America."

In 1987 Clark welcomed the peace proposals presented by President Arias of Costa Rica, which fell "within the spirit and framework of the

Contadora (reconciliation) process"³ – the same proposals that the Reagan administration had vigorously attempted to torpedo.

Nicaragua and the 'Sandinista contamination' were issues about which Ronald Reagan held very strong views. My recollection is that George Shultz (secretary of state) was not enthusiastic about Canada's Central America policies. It is then remarkable that the government stuck to an independent course, and maybe just as remarkable, got away with it. It helped, of course, that from President Reagan's point of view Brian Mulroney was a big improvement on Pierre Trudeau. It also helped, as Joe Clark has written, that George Shultz "always understood that there were genuine differences between the two countries on several issues and saved his real concern for the questions he considered most important for our long-term relation."

Although the policy line was independent – sizable CIDA contributions for the Ortega government in Nicaragua, opposition to US support for the Contras,⁴ criticism of human rights abuses on all sides – it was framed so that it was not aggressively 'in your face' to Washington.

This caution played differently in much of Canada where a re-play of reaction to the Spanish civil war drama was taking place – but with significant differences:⁵ If we exclude the two world wars, never before or since has Canadian civil society become so exercised about a foreign policy issue. A parliamentary committee, mandated to sound public perceptions of foreign policy across the country was astonished to find that Central America topped Canadian concerns about apartheid in South Africa, nuclear disarmament, the Soviet Union and Eastern Europe. The Soviet/ Afghanistan conflict was low on the Canadian public's list of priorities.

Also, public opinion was unevenly divided. The most vociferous expressions favoured Nicaragua. It is useful to recall how this came about. The Spanish civil war mystique was a part of it. There was a strong emotional sympathy for impoverished Nicaragua battling not only against the wickedness of the Somozas and against corrupt and dangerous neighbours, but mostly because Nicaragua was the David to the American Goliath.

The media regularly reported butchering, and targeted assassination by government-linked military and vigilante death squads. They were generally accurate. It has since been verified that most of the killings in El Salvador and Guatemala were at the hands of death squads. Subsequent findings in Guatemala reveal that over 90 percent of the political murders in that country were committed by the military and associated right-wing death squads.

Although development assistance to Guatemala was suspended for several years because of the horrific scale of human rights abuses, and a number of statements made by Clark and others in government directed against these outrages, many in Canadian civil society and the parliamentary opposition attacked the government's response as pusillanimous. In the *Realpolitik* of the time it was far from that, but not surprisingly, there was little sensitivity to the government's predicament. One of the astonishing features of this period was the extent of the well-coordinated and impressively orchestrated campaign against the government's allegedly submissive pro-American position. The spectrum of organizations involved was truly ecumenical: the United Church, the Jesuits, the Mennonites, the Salvation Army... International assistance organizations such as Oxfam became deeply engaged in political advocacy. Many of them, especially the Toronto-based groups, developed very smooth and productive relations with the media and with parliament. The NDP was active in the campaign. It was often joined by Lloyd Axworthy, Warren Almand, and other Liberal members of parliament. The result was that the government was almost relentlessly attacked. We prepared mountains of draft statements and material for questions and answers in the House of Commons for MacEachen, Clark and often for prime ministers Trudeau and Mulroney.

One of our premises was that it was naive to suggest the Central American situation could be painted in black and white. The Sandinistas were authoritarian and responsible for a share of atrocities (albeit relatively small in relation to their neighbours), human rights abuses, denial of democratic rights and abuse of the indigenous peoples in the Atlantic region. Heavily armed with modern Soviet weapons and military aircraft, they were capable of destabilizing their neighbours. Delivery of these weapons was usually facilitated by the Cubans. The Sandinistas were backing insurrections in other parts of Central America with materiel and political support.

Canada was increasingly involved in pushing reform through diplomatic dialogue and CIDA projects. However, efforts supported by Canada, Scandinavia, and others to press the Guatemalans and the Salvadorans toward democratic systems met with only limited success. In 1984 the reformer, Napoleon Duarte, was elected president of El Salvador with moderately benign results. Two years later Vincente Cerezo, a putative reformer, was elected president of Guatemala, but was unable to exercise any authority over the military. Honduras already had a democratically elected government, but it was largely under the thumb of the heavily US-influenced military command.

We concluded that to side fully with Nicaragua by terminating CIDA programmes to El Salvador, Honduras, and Guatemala and diverting these resources to Nicaragua, as advocated by the churches, civil society, and many parliamentarians, would undermine the limited progress we were making with these governments. It would also remove (admittedly small) pressure points on democratic, human rights, and social issues. Besides, the poor and under-privileged in Guatemala, Honduras, and El Salvador had much the same appalling quality of life as most of the poor in Nicaragua. Why penalize them?

Moreover, picking one side would be fatally counterproductive to the efforts that we were making in concert with Latin America and the Contadora process to help create an environment in which cease-fires and reconciliation might be possible. Through much toil, including MacEachen's and Clark's meetings with the Central American presidents and senior ministers and with Mexican foreign minister Sepulveda, our policy of dealing openly and helping all of the countries of Central America (except for a three year suspension of Guatemala) was showing results. Canada had been accepted and recognized as a significant player in the peace process. In our view it would be irresponsible to squander the leverage that we had accumulated.[6]

On the basis of his personal engagement, Joe Clark offered another dimension:

> Canadian involvement in Central America was an important element of our bilateral relation with Mexico (who had also come to Canada, not the USA, for advice on how they might join GATT). My impression is that Sepulveda pressed his more influential colleagues to encourage us. Also, if my recollection is correct, that led to an invitation to me to join the annual "Rio Group" dinners of eight to ten hemispheric foreign ministers (including the USA) at the United Nations General Assembly. Those contacts had implications beyond Central America,

including a growing recognition by Latin governments that Canadian policy on important hemispheric issues could be independent from that of Washington, and a growing awareness in Ottawa that this was an appropriate time to take our seat at the OAS as a prominent part of an active commitment to multi-lateral political organizations, including the Commonwealth, la Francophonie, the United Nations, and leadership on environmental issues.

The Canadian government's insistence on not caving in to opposition pressures enabled us to play a supporting role in the peace process. Canada sent diplomatic and military teams to help devise the verification and control procedures.[7]

A lot of my time was spent in the media trenches. In those days external affairs officers could discuss and defend government policies on the radio, television programs, in speeches, and on the pages of newspapers. I also devoted time to one-on-one conversations with many of our opponents and media people. Sometimes this worked and sometimes not at all. Several friendships date from these skirmishes. In these days of distance and distrust between the government and the bureaucracy all of this may sound Pollyannaish, but at no time did I squirm under or protest political directives with which I was in fundamental disagreement.[8] Such disagreements did not exist. It helped immensely that I was part of the consultative dialogue.[9]

Was this the post-Pearsonian 'golden age' of Canadian diplomacy? Perhaps. It is a term that invites abuse and is best avoided, but seen from the second decade of the twenty-first century those years appear bathed in gilded light.

VENEZUELA, HAITI, AND THE DOMINICAN REPUBLIC

A Is for Aristide

In 1991 I was in Caracas as ambassador. The president of Venezuela was Carlos Andres Perez.[1] Although flawed and eventually impeached (probably unjustly), he was the most internationalist of all Latin American leaders at that time – more genuinely "Bolivarian" in leading Latin America and the Caribbean toward rational goals than Hugo Chavez, who attempted to bring him down in a failed coup d'état. This is a story of Perez's efforts to restore the glimmer of democracy in Haiti that began with President Aristide's election in December 1990, and of my own tangential engagement in this process.

Tuesday, September 30, 1991, had been a disaster. The Reverend Jean-Bertrand Aristide, who at thirty-seven had won the presidency of Haiti in elections supervised by the UN and the OAS, had crashed to the bottom of a roller-coaster week. Five days earlier he had made his debut at the United Nations General Assembly. He spoke of the usual things, "dignity" and "democracy," and impressed the UN delegates with his intelligence and compassion. On September 27 in Port-au-Prince, however, he gave a very different speech. What fuelled his lethal eloquence was mounting apprehension that the election he had won nine months earlier was threatened on three fronts: the wealthy bourgeoisie, hardline Duvalierists, and the Haitian army. In the preceding weeks, a number of Aristide's opponents had been "necklaced" by street crowds, a procedure in which a gasoline-soaked tire is slung on the shoulders of the victim and ignited. Another local term for this grisly form of execution is "*père Lebrun*," after the owner of a tire store. In this speech President Aristide referred directly to "*le supplice du collier*" (the torment of the necklace), and urged the crowd of militant supporters not to forget to give the enemy "what he deserves." He spoke of the value of the constitution, and then intoned with unmistakable menace:

"*Quel bel outil!*"
"*Quel bel instrument!*"
"*Quel bel appareil!*"

Four months earlier, and several months after Father Aristide had won the first authentically free and fair elections in Haitian history, the president of the Dominican Republic, the country next door, predicted a bloody conclusion to this experiment in democracy. There were other sanguinary forecasts. And they proved accurate. About midnight on September 29, a group of soldiers surrounded Aristide's private residence. Apparently alerted by telephone, the French ambassador extricated Aristide from his home and brought him to the presidential palace, where he left him under the protection of the presidential bodyguard. By 8:00 A.M. rebel troops encircled the palace. Aristide attempted to broadcast a message exhorting the Haitian people to "go out into the streets to save democracy." Through the morning there were reports of widening disturbances and revolt, and news, subsequently confirmed, that several politicians had been assassinated, including one shot in his jail cell.

In New York, the Haitian ambassador to the United Nations sought an emergency meeting of the Security Council to "consider the situation and its consequences for regional stability." A majority of the members, led by India and China, opposed action by the Security Council on the grounds that what was happening in Haiti was an internal matter. The Organization of American States responded with more vigour, and scheduled a meeting of foreign ministers for the following afternoon.

In Caracas there was rising concern, but little hard information. Bernie Dussault, the Canadian ambassador in Port-au-Prince, was unable to send telegrams out. Shooting in the streets kept him from his chancery.

I was anxious to find out how President Perez was reacting. Venezuelan relations with the Haitian government were close, and the president's office probably knew as much as anyone outside of Port-au-Prince, with the possible exception of the Americans. There is a special bond between Venezuela and Haiti that dates from the timely support given by President Pétion of the newly independent black republic to Simon Bolivar in his war of independence from Spain. Despite concern that Aristide might be a rudderless populist, the relationship had flowered anew between presidents Perez and Aristide. I knew that Perez and Beatrice Rangel, minister of the presidency and chief of staff, would be alarmed, and called for an appointment with Rangel. She would see me at two that afternoon, but cautioned that the meeting would have to be brief.

Beatrice had a long, rectangular office in the north wing of Miraflores Palace, facing Avenida Pastor, the main roadway outside the palace. I recall the juxtaposition because eight months later a rebel tank moving along Pastor raked the windows with heavy machine-gun fire. On that occasion President Perez used cunning and audacity to turn the tables on rebel troops (under Lt. Col. Hugo Chavez, who was subsequently imprisoned).

In the early afternoon of September 30 it seemed unlikely that I would learn anything. The office was bedlam. Senior military officers and civilian aides rushed in and out with paper and verbal messages. Worse, a phalanx of six telephones on Rangel's credenza pealed like an electric xylophone. Four were handled by two secretaries in the outer office. The fifth was a direct line to President Perez. The sixth seemed to be a line to military intelligence. I sat on her sofa sipping chamomile tea waiting for a break in the storm. When it came, the situation she described was bleak. Rebel soldiers surrounded the Haitian palace. No units of regular soldiers had emerged to defend Aristide.

I asked Rangel if I could tell her a story.

"Now? You must be mad!"

"Just listen, I'll compress it."

What follows is a fuller version of what I call the Dominican parable.

Just before dawn on November 16, 1961, a well-organized military coup had been launched in Ciudad Trujillo (soon to be returned to its original name of Santo Domingo). Six months earlier, the dictator, Generalissimo Trujillo, had been assassinated with a little help from the CIA, and now his less bright but equally villainous brothers were attempting to restore the family dictatorship with the wholehearted support of the Dominican army.

As the soldiers, supplied with lists of people to be seized and shot, set out to occupy key points in the capital, success appeared well within the brothers' grasp. However, when dawn broke, the profile of a small US naval force could be seen on the horizon. Two frigates and a destroyer were steaming three miles off shore. And another unexpected complication faced the Trujillo family. Lt. Col. Edwin Simmons, the military attaché in the US consulate general,[2] had uncovered the plot. The consulate informed Washington, and Simmons opened clandestine negotiations with the general commanding the country's only functional attack aircraft, two squadrons of Second World War P-51 Mustangs. One squadron was based near the capital and the other at Santiago de los Cabelleros in the north. The previous night the general had deployed the squadron near the capital to join the Mustangs in Santiago.

At first light he launched both squadrons in a bombing raid on army bases in the capital. The aircraft were unconventionally armed: without any brackets for bombs and with inoperative machine guns, each pilot was given a sack of hand grenades. Meanwhile, on the ground, the anti-aircraft defences were not so much unconventional as impractical. Alerted to the attack by the roar of propeller engines and the crunch of hand grenades bursting harmlessly around the perimeter, soldiers at the army headquarters in the city raced to the roof. Headquarters was the Fortaleza Ozama, a crenellated fortress of the *Beau Geste* style much favoured by the late dictator. On the roof were Krupp water-cooled machine guns, purchased some years before by the generalissimo's Puerto Rican financial advisor, Hector Benitez Rexach. What Rexach may or may not have known, and the soldiers belatedly discovered, was that the machine guns had been manufactured about 1905. These pre-Wright brothers weapons were capable of only minimum elevation. As a result, a sort of Three Stooges historical tableau unfolded, with troops wrestling hopelessly with their ancient weapons, while overhead, pilots in antique aircraft lobbed grenades with uniform inaccuracy.

More serious developments were visible out at sea. From the embassy roof I could see that the three warships had been joined by four more, including the aircraft carrier *Boxer*. My secretary and I completed the arcane chore of converting my report for External Affairs to book cipher. I delivered the telegram to the All America Cable and Wireless Office and went home for lunch. As I turned onto Avenida George Washington, a broad thoroughfare that runs along the edge of the Caribbean, I saw a group of American officers from the consulate standing by the sea wall, looking out to sea. I recognized them all: a vice consul, the information officer, a CIA officer, and Colonel Simmons. I stopped the car, walked over, and was making a facetious remark about gunboat diplomacy when the colonel looked at his watch and said, "Damn! They're late!" At this moment a thunderous roar rose from the west and three squadrons of Sabre jets from the Guantánamo naval base in Cuba swept low across the waterfront. They passed six times over the full length of the city. By the time they had returned to Guantánamo the coup was over and, incredibly, no blood had been shed.

This account was interrupted several times, but Rangel persevered in her attention to my story, and at the end she called her secretary on the intercom.

"Raiza, get me Elsa on the phone." Elsa Boccachiampe, the Venezuelan ambassador in Port-au-Prince, came on the line.

"Elsa," said Rangel, "are you still in touch with President Aristide at the palace?" Elsa confirmed that she was.

"Good. Call him immediately and ask him this. Would he authorize the overflight of Port-au-Prince by a squadron of Venezuelan F-16 aircraft?"

She put the phone down and I left.

At home the phone rang at about 1:30 the next morning. I groped for it. "John, can you meet me at the palace in an hour?" It was Beatrice.

"In an hour's time? What's up?" And then a few cobwebs parted. I asked "It's Aristide?"

"Yes. General Cédras has taken charge of the coup d'état. President Perez spoke to him a few hours ago and persuaded him to release Aristide to exile in Venezuela. He is sending his personal aircraft to Port-au-Prince. It should be back here about four o'clock this morning." She promised to tell me more on the way to the airport.

Rangel and I reached the airport shortly before 4:00 A.M. Apart from the blue runway lights and a yellow glow from the main terminal, it was still black. In the VIP waiting room of the military terminal were Michael

Skol, the US ambassador, Libourel, the French ambassador, Beatrice Rangel, and myself. Skol took me aside.

"John, you wouldn't believe what happened yesterday afternoon."

"What was that?" I said disingenuously.

"President Perez ordered his F-16s to scramble and buzz Port-au-Prince." Skol paused. "That would have put the wind up. At that speed, rocketing over the city, everyone on the ground, especially the army, would have thought they were American. But, too bad…it didn't happen. The palace surrendered and Aristide was taken before they could get airborne."

Aristide landed at about 5:00 A.M., accompanied by two secretaries, the chief of police of Port-au-Prince, and five members of his bodyguard. In a report to Ottawa I wrote that he "looked terrible, torn between gratitude that his life had been spared and a feeling that martyrdom with his people might have been preferable." When he emerged from the aircraft the worst of the ordeal was over. But there was one surprise still waiting for him and most of the small reception party. Within minutes of his landing, the French ambassador informed Aristide that on instructions from his government, he wished to invite the president to stay at his residence, and then, when sufficiently rested, to proceed to France as a guest of the French government. Libourel then withdrew to his residence to prepare for his guest. Aristide, the US ambassador, Rangel and I followed in a separate vehicle. Rangel was furious that the French government had the effrontery to pluck Aristide out of Venezuelan hands. I think she referred to the French manoeuvre as "diplomatic kidnapping." En route we suggested to Aristide that the image of following Jean-Claude Duvalier (Baby Doc) to France might not be popular with his supporters. Rangel also indicated delicately that it would be appropriate for him to move to the presidential suite at the Hilton that had been prepared for him.

In the course of the drive, and over coffee and defrosted canapés provided by Libourel's dyspeptic major-domo, Aristide gave us his account. It was heavily punctuated with the emotion of the previous three days. We sat in the main-floor gallery of the ambassador's large Italianate residence. The windows looked out on the fairway of the sixth hole of the Valle Arriba Golf and Country Club, from which I had once hooked a ball onto the ambassador's roof tiles. Aristide looked crumpled, a condition magnified by his short, frail stature. His face, which tended to telegraph his feelings, showed misery and flashes of anger. The extraordinary charm that I was later to enjoy was not visible.

Aristide told us that he had first learned of the plot the previous Saturday, but that after being reassured by General Cédras and other officers, he had dismissed the rumours. It was only on Sunday that he recognized the seriousness of the situation, and realized that the leader of the coup was the same Raoul Cédras, the man he had picked to be chief of his army.

On the basis of his account, Aristide was fortunate to be alive. He repeatedly emphasized that Dufour, the French ambassador in Port-au-Prince, had saved his life. Alerted that Aristide was in danger, Dufour drove to the president's home and found that it was surrounded by rebel soldiers. Weapons were fired sporadically, and one of Aristide's bodyguards was killed. The ambassador managed to get Aristide into his car, and set off for the presidential palace, where he deposited him. Bodyguards still protected him, but the situation deteriorated as the morning wore on. Soldiers isolated the palace and opened fire on its defenders.

However, as we later learned, the phone link had not been cut, and Aristide and his staff were able to appeal to some Haitians, Americans, and Venezuelans for help. By late afternoon, with no sign of the presence of loyal soldiers, Aristide walked out of the palace and surrendered. The soldiers seized him and argued about who should shoot him. Aristide's hands were tied with his own necktie, and he was led off to the Dessalines army barracks, which adjoined the palace. In the barracks he was forced to lie face-down on the floor. Again he thought that he was about to be shot. Soldiers mocked him, shouting, "To hell with democracy! Thank God the army is in charge!"

At this point, two things happened: Cédras appeared and announced that he was in charge, and Ambassador Dufour reached the Dessalines barracks by telephone. According to Aristide, this call lowered the temperature, and negotiations soon began for Aristide's exile. Late that evening Aristide was taken to the airport. President Perez's aircraft was en route from Caracas when it was found that the Haitian air traffic controllers had fled. A dozen military trucks were requisitioned to illuminate the runway with their headlights. Aristide told us that the control tower was operated by the American air force attaché.

Several times Aristide brought the conversation back to Cédras. Deeply offended by Cédras's treachery, he referred to the list of people to be shot that was being compiled by the army. Many, perhaps twelve hundred, had already been killed. Most had been murdered during the night of September 30 and the following morning. Aristide accused Cédras of greed and power-madness. He told us that he did not know what was happening to members of his family, his friends, and his cabinet. Fatigued, disoriented, and depressed, he broke into tears.

I quickly discovered how quickly Aristide could bounce back. When I saw him off at the airport bound for an OAS meeting on the Haitian crisis twenty-eight hours later, the change from a dejected, scruffy, and emotionally drained figure into a composed leader was astonishing. International endorsement, some rest, and President Perez's well-organized and high-profile treatment had produced a transformation. The new wardrobe organized by Rangel certainly helped, and so, no doubt, did the move to the Hilton Hotel the evening before.

With Aristide out of the way for a few days, Skol, Rangel, and I tried to piece together what we thought had ignited the coup. A multitude of versions circulated in Haiti. On one point everyone agreed. It was a coup waiting to happen. The long-standing antagonism of the elite had been reinforced by Aristide's charismatic populism. More incendiary was Aristide's provocation of the army. Mutual distrust had grown since the election, and had been inflamed by Aristide's decision to establish a militia group that was independent of the army and loyal to the president. Aristide had taken this step for reasons of self-preservation. To the army it resembled a remodelled Tonton Macoute. It did not take a long memory in the Haitian army to recall that François Duvalier (Papa Doc) had outmanoeuvred the regular forces by forming his own brutal secret police force, the original Tonton Macoute, and emasculated the army. The Tontons had been *déchouké* (torn apart) – in many cases literally – after the flight of Baby Doc, and the army had been attempting to reassert its position as the nation's principal political arbiter.

Through the night of September 29 and the morning of the following day the senior officers and most of the army waited to see what response there would be to Aristide's appeal for support. When it was clear that no significant response was forthcoming, that the American embassy was doing nothing to discourage the coup, Cédras and the others moved off the fence and joined it. In Cédras's case, the rebels had appealed to him to join, presumably to give greater depth and "legitimacy" to their cause.

Cédras had betrayed his president, and Aristide loathed him with a scorching intensity. Over the next three years, as de facto leader of an increasingly brutal, corrupt, and chaotic government, Cédras was demonized by much of the international community and by the international press. Evil is not a label to be lightly fastened on all the conspirators in this dolorous episode. Cédras was probably not evil, but he was unable or perhaps unwilling to curb the appetites of those around him who were.

Within days of the coup, mutual intransigence and many institutional interests slammed the doors on Aristide's return. Important elements of the two main currents of Haitian religious life opposed Aristide. One was a group of powerful Vodou priests and the other was Ligonde, the Duvalieriste Archbishop of Port-au-Prince, whose anti-Aristide views were shared by the Vatican. Aristide's rising prominence as a liberation-theology priest had made relations with Rome uncomfortable, and they deteriorated further when Aristide entered politics.[3] The Vatican emphasized its distinctive view of the Haitian political scene by becoming the only sovereign entity to formally recognize the Cédras regime.

Moderate Haitians considered that any viable solution would require Cédras's presence. On this issue more than any other, Aristide was inflexible. Messages from many of his supporters reinforced his stubbornness.

As it had been for almost two centuries, the US role in Haitian affairs had been much more harmful than helpful. Neither Cédras nor Aristide had warm feelings about the United States. Cédras was a graduate of the Fort Benning Army School of the Americas in Georgia, at that time notorious as a "staff college" for future military dictators. His disenchantment with the United States appears to date from the international isolation of Haiti following the coup. Aristide's antipathy ran deeper and for a much longer period. In varying degrees, Haitians had not forgiven the United States for the painful and humiliating occupation by American Marines from 1915 to 1934. In Aristide's case, the list of grievances was long. The Reagan administration had supported a succession of corrupt and brutal governments. Paramilitary agents had frequently tried to assassinate him for stirring up the poor with his courageous and increasingly popular liberation theology. It was no secret that several American ambassadors regarded Aristide as a "destabilizing" presence. Later, as a presidential candidate and president in exile, he was the subject of apparently fabricated and leaked CIA allegations that he was mentally unstable. Aristide was further grieved by the ambiguous role of US embassy staff during the critical period when Cédras and other senior officers were deciding which way the wind was blowing.

Aristide's strong feelings about the United States surfaced from time to time in our conversations, but never so sharply as during our meeting on Boxing Day 1991. Aristide was preoccupied with his chances of survival when returned from exile. He spoke of enemies and "other interests, …other forces," which, in his view, controlled many politicians and army officers.

"Other interests…the bourgeoisie?" I asked.

"*Non, plus haut que ça.*" More specifically, he remarked that the United States was in control of these "forces," and would determine his life and more probably his death soon after his return. I tried to soften this image, reminding him of the support he had received from President Bush, and Bush's own condemnation of the coup. The conversation was interrupted by the telephone. Madame Mitterand was calling to convey encouragement and Christmas greetings. The discussion resumed and fell quickly back into the old grooves. On the role of the Organization of American States, he was skeptical. He felt that time was running out for him, and that both OAS solidarity and the embargo against trade with Haiti were showing wear and tear. Apart from the United States, most OAS members meant well, but if their sanctions weren't backed up by the UN, what could they do? He had confidence in only a few members of the Haitian legislature. He referred to one senior member as an "ex-Macoute," who attended meetings of the chamber with a revolver in one pocket and a grenade in the other. Two threads kept reappearing: his feeling that he had no control over events, and fatalism about "the forces" opposing him. He repeated his foreboding that upon return to Haiti, "I will not last long before I am assassinated." For someone who spent long periods in hiding, who lay flat on the floor of the jeep when changing hiding places, and who had escaped an assassin's bullet or the blade of a machete at least half a dozen times, this was a reasonable anxiety.

The setting of this conversation and the absence of family at Christmas time probably contributed to his gloom. For better security and privacy, President Perez had moved him from the Hilton Hotel to a presidential mansion within the "Círculo Miltar" on the outer edge of Caracas. Well inside the perimeter of Venezuela's largest military base, Aristide had both security and privacy – for his taste, too much of the latter. He had few friends in Caracas, and in any event was not encouraged to leave the protection of the Venezuelan army. The house was vast, modern, and impressive from the outside. Inside, it was sparsely furnished, cold, and impersonal. Aristide's loneliness in this house no doubt contributed to the warm welcome he gave to me and a few of my colleagues and to the alacrity with which he took up the opportunity to move. Over the course of his stay in Venezuela, roughly five months, I visited Aristide fairly often. Haiti had become a special focus of Canadian foreign policy, and a particular interest of Prime Minister Mulroney's.

A strong relationship between Mulroney and Perez had developed over the issue. Perez paid his first visit to Canada at the prime minister's invitation just eight days before the coup. I had flown in Perez's plane, and attended the lunch at Sussex Drive, where Perez and Mulroney agreed that it would be useful to form a Haiti support group comprised of France, the United States, Venezuela, and Canada. Despite differences, particularly with France, this support group sprang into active engagement immediately after the coup. An assessment of the group in order of enthusiastic and constructive involvement would put Perez well ahead of the pack, followed by Mulroney. Bush soon became lukewarm. Madame Mitterand was much more personally committed to Haiti than her husband. Aristide would later add Prime Minister Michael Manley of Jamaica to this small group of international supporters.

Conversations with Aristide invariably focused on two issues. The first was the search for a suitable candidate for prime minister of Haiti who could serve as a bridge between the de facto Cédras government and Aristide. The second was the means by which both sides could be persuaded to accept or accommodate each other. While a number of candidates were nominated, including the former head of the Haitian Communist Party, neither the sanctions nor the leverage of this powerful group of leaders were able to achieve a negotiated solution. In the end it was the threat of force and the actual visibility of an American invasion fleet that brought down the military regime and opened the way for Aristide's return.

It can be argued in retrospect – as Aristide undoubtedly would agree – that his situation would have been politically untenable and physically

dangerous if he had worked in harness with Cédras and a largely un-
cleansed army. However, Haiti paid a heavy price for three years of truculence on both sides. Early compromise was blocked and the sanctions
failed to achieve their political purpose, while the remnants of the Haitian
economy were dismantled. Ian Martin, who had been deputy head of
the OAS/UN monitoring team in Haiti, described the turmoil of hap-
hazard and inadequately targeted application of sanctions as "mangled
multilateralism."

It is difficult to exaggerate the impact on almost every segment of
Haitian society of the three years of sanctions imposed by both the UN
and the OAS. In October 1994, when President Aristide returned in tri-
umph, the normally formidable task of governing had become many times
more difficult because of economic, social, political, and agricultural devastation. Several thousand had been killed or "disappeared," and roughly
fifty thousand had fled by sea, many of them drowning when their flimsy,
overcrowded fishing boats sank. Many more thousands were displaced
from their homes. So appalling were the economic consequences and the
rising toll of human rights abuses that by early 1994 many observers, including persons in the human rights community, had concluded that the
only "humanitarian" option was military intervention.

Through the spring and summer of that year the debacles in Somalia
cast a debilitating shadow and kept the Clinton government tied to the
sanctions policy. However, by midsummer President Clinton concluded
that there was no alternative to invasion. On July 31 the United Nations
Security Council authorized the United States to take military action on
behalf of the UN. Clinton urged Prime Minister Chrétien to join him and
commit elements of the Canadian forces to the invasion. The Canadian
government was expected to agree, given the narrowing of options, reinforced by the special responsibility that Canada had assumed for Haiti.
However, Ottawa turned Clinton down, saying that it would support the
post-invasion phase – the policing of Haiti.

Just as the "international" but almost entirely American invasion
force, which had been named "Uphold Democracy," was preparing to
land, Jimmy Carter, Colin Powell, and Senator Sam Nunn negotiated with
Cédras and found a man driven not so much by greed or power but by
a swollen vision of himself as a patriot. He saw himself in the tradition
of the founders of the first black republic – Dessalines, Christophe, and

Pétion – prepared to fight to the end to defend his country from foreign invasion and domination. The Carter team found in this noble fantasy an opening through which they could appeal to his patriotism and offer comfortable exile and immunity from persecution. The exile of Cédras and his family and that of his principal confederates was agreed, and the following morning US forces came ashore unopposed and without loss of life.

My last conversation with Aristide took place in April 1995, in the presidential palace in Port-au-Prince. I had by then left the Department of External Affairs and was at the time running an NGO program in Haiti in support of the elections that would choose a successor to Aristide. The occasion was the investiture of Brian Mulroney with Haiti's most exalted decoration. After our many sessions in Caracas and one in Washington, it was extraordinary to see Aristide presiding over his government in his own country. He radiated self-assurance and the joy of long-denied power. In our short discussion he repeated that his best and staunchest friends in the international community were Brian Mulroney and Carlos Andres Perez. Outside, on the edge of the Champs de Mars, demonstrators chanted in Creole, "*Tidid, Prezidan pou vie!*" (Aristide, President for Life!). This was emotional stuff, but I could not forget the appeal that Aristide had made just days before the coup d'état that his enemies should be treated to "*le supplice du collier.*"

POSTSCRIPT
Aristide was re-elected and returned to the presidency in 2001. Two years later he was forced to resign and unwillingly left the country for the Central African Republic in a US aircraft. He returned to Port-au-Prince in 2011 following the election to the presidency of the singer and entertainer Michel Martelly.

Between Brazil and Venezuela: *Caipirinhas*, Trestle Bridges, and Formula One Bus Drivers

During my tour as ambassador in Venezuela (1988–1992), I attended a meeting of regional heads of mission that was held in Brasilia. This is an account of my return by road and air to Caracas.

From Manaus we chugged down the Rio Negro to where it joins the Amazon. For the first half hour it was like furrowing Coca-Cola™. The Amazon is swifter, denser with silt, and colder than the Rio Negro, so that the black and the brown run separately with a clear dividing line for about eight kilometres before the Rio Negro dissolves into the larger river. The Rio Negro is remarkable for its pink dolphins – which I did not see. At its source in Venezuela it is linked by the Casiquiare River to the Orinoco (which perplexed Alexander von Humboldt, who discovered that it manages to run both south to the Amazon and north to the Orinoco[4]). Friar Gaspar de Carvajal's account of the first sighting by Europeans of the confluence of the two great rivers in 1542 is skimpy.[5] Exhausted by repeated skirmishes with indigenous tribes, he gives only a few lines to the event, including the notation that "the line between black and brown extended for more than twenty leagues" (about one hundred kilometres). It is possible that the Friar's rainy season was much heavier than mine.

It was pleasant to be on the water with a good breeze. The rain had stopped, there were no mosquitoes, and I had a cold beer in hand. The Manaus riverboats have a distinctive design with just a hint of the scalloped shape of a Chinese junk. Most of these boats have two tiers. Those with three look as if they will capsize. They are almost all constructed of wood and decked against the heat. The doors to the toilets have elegantly varnished wood on the outside. Inside, water sloshes over the floorboards.

The next morning I set off by bus for Boa Vista, the capital of Brazil's remote Territorio Roraima and another stopping point on my journey from Brasilia to Caracas. But getting to the bus station was touch and go. There was confusion at the desk. The hotel clerk had forgotten to organize transport and, probably with reason, blamed me and my less than fluent Portuguese. At length a call was made and a taxi found. The taxi driver, the usual would-be Brazilian Formula One racing nut, screeched to a stop in front of the terminal.

The bus was air conditioned, the windows were curtained and I snoozed, unaware that we were moving along the infamous BR-174 highway cut through the rain forest under Brazil's military dictatorship and through the heartland of the Waimari-Atroari tribe, who fought bloody and ultimately losing battles with construction workers, miners, and government soldiers. Our run to Boa Vista was uneventful.[6]

Not so the following day... But first I settled down in a monastically-furnished hotel. The bed was a cot, but at least the mattress, unlike the one in Manaus, was clean. The best parts were the view over the Rio Branco, a tributary of the Rio Negro, and the bar, where I ordered two *caipirinhas*. Since my first exposure to this ambrosia on a Brazilian gunboat on the Suriname River ten years earlier it had been one of my hot weather cocktails of choice.

The Rio Branco looked even better with the morning light glazing its surface. Beyond the river and just beginning to bake in the equatorial sun were the Pakaraima Mountains of neighbouring Guyana. I was booked on the wonderfully euphonious Uniao de Cascabel bus line. Inexplicably, another company had a departure to Santa Elena de Uairen in Venezuela scheduled at roughly the same time. The advantage of this for me was that neither bus was crowded. One disadvantage became apparent when after about four kilometres the asphalt surface came to an end – leaving 160 kilometres of dirt, sand, potholes, and hazardous trestle bridges to the Venezuelan border.[7] The related disadvantage, which was considerable, was that if you trailed another bus in a non-air conditioned and therefore windows-open bus, you were engulfed in dust. If you closed the windows, you would roast. In either case, the dust obscured the driver's view of the potholes. For these reasons, but much more because his machismo was engaged, our driver was determined to overtake the other bus. My notes say, "This bloody bus needs seat belts." At every flat stretch our driver floored it, and to the hoots, roars, and upright middle fingers of most of the passengers, we would pass the other bus, leaving it with its open windows behind us. But not for long. Competition had fired up both drivers. The two buses hurtled past one another until something went snap on our pothole-pummelled undercarriage. We stopped. The driver investigated and repaired whatever it was. We started up again, now mercifully well behind the other bus. The road had narrowed, the potholes grown, and our driver (a.k.a. Nelson Piquet) slowed to a less terrifying pace.

There were cowboys on the road, which was increasingly better suited to horses than buses. The bus overtook a small herd. The horses raced alongside to loud yips from the passengers. But then, again the bus stopped. This time we were faced with the challenge of a wooden trestle bridge in fragile condition. We exited the bus and walked gingerly over the blackwater creek far below. On the other side we watched nervously as the driver's assistant, walking in front, guided the driver past the broken bits of planking. He inched forward with great care, but then one front wheel slipped off a board. The passengers gasped, but Nelson backed up and extricated his bus. This process, minus the incident with the front wheel, was repeated ten kilometres further on. The passengers shared bread, nuts, fruit, and stories of fatal accidents. I contributed my bottle of *cachaza* – the cane sugar alcohol base for *caipirinhas*.

Occasionally a passenger, invariably an Indian, alighted from the bus carrying a sack or parcel of goods acquired in Boa Vista. But there were no dwellings of any kind in sight, only rough scrub, cactus, huge termite cones, and a sense of desolation. We pressed on, dodging those bits of road that had washed away. The bus wheezed up a long hill, and we were in wild and quite beautiful country. Now there were a few houses, thatched with mud and wattle walls. When the sun appeared, the mud dried to yellow and burnt orange. An Indian woman carried a huge stalk of bananas on her back. Hilltops were crenellated with dark broken rock. Some of the longer slabs showed light-coloured slashes caused by lightning bolts. The landscape changed again, this time to a desolate plateau under grey skies, and then back again to forest.

A few more bumpy kilometres brought us to the scruffy village of Pakaraima and the frontier with Venezuela. The border officials looked at us solemnly, and treated us as potential desperados and/or drug smugglers. Smuggling is a way of life in this area, and perhaps all the officials weren't in on the game. But the delay was absurdly long. Our bus and the one that overtook us – and with whom we had again caught up – comprised the only business that day, and hence the only diversion in that awful place. I exchanged accounts of the madness of the previous six hours with two young Canadian backpackers from the other bus.

It was raining in Santa Elena de Uairen when we arrived in the early evening. I asked for the "best" hotel. The backpackers opted for something cheaper – but theirs wasn't much cheaper than mine, on top of which it turned out to be a fleabag. The three of us dined together at my invitation. *Restaurant de la Gran Sabana* was chosen from their guide book as the best. It was terrible, but perhaps the others were worse. Breakfast the next morning was equally bad, and served by a surly woman. She asked how I liked my peanut sandwich. I lied, saying it was fine. Some shiny pickups and a few new houses were the external face of local gold- and diamond-mining prosperity, but Santa Elena was no prize. At our table – there was only one – we were joined by a man who explained that he was 50 percent Indian and 50 percent Black, and proceeded to tell us in detail that the *ojos azules* (Europeans) had screwed everything up when they came to the New World. None of us at the table, including the *ojos azules*, disagreed, but it was not what we wanted to hear at 7:00 A.M.

My flight from Santa Elena was on a local puddle-jumper airline, but once again, getting to the flight was a challenge. The manager of the hotel – the same crone who the previous night "forgot" to fetch the towel from the linen closet that I needed after splooshing off the grime and dust of yesterday's odyssey – said that there were no taxis in town and suggested a private arrangement with the hotel owner, who was not available. In the store down the street from the hotel a more amiable character informed me that there was a taxi, and promised to deliver it to the hotel. It arrived on time, and climbing into this vehicle in full view of the hotel manager provided a small, welcome jolt of *schadenfreude* at derailing her plans. But this was short-lived. Jesus, the driver, was cranky, and his car equipped with a live cockroach and an open bottle of rum. It was 9:00 A.M., and raining again. In the course of the drive to the airfield Jesus mellowed and offered me a swig of his rum. I poured a few ounces into a small paper cup which he thoughtfully provided. He helped himself, and we toasted the awful weather. The rum was terrible, but seemed just right for the occasion.

At the airstrip we drew up alongside a lean-to with a corrugated roof. Jesus smiled and informed me that this was the terminal building of the Santa Elena International Airport. Inside, sheltering from the rain, there appeared to be more passengers than the Canadian Twin Otter could accommodate. In fact, there were twenty-one passengers for twenty seats,

ATLANTIC OCEAN

CARACAS

ORINOCO R.

VENEZUELA

ANGEL FALLS

GUYANA

SANTA ELENA
DE UAIRÉN

PAKARAIMA MTNS

BRAZIL

BOA VISTA

LETHEM

RIO BRANCO

RIO

NEGRO

BRAZILIA

MANAUS

AMAZON R.

MANAUS TO SANTA ELENA DE UAIRÉN 870 km

---- BUS

>>>> AIR

ⲙⲙ MESA SHAPED MOUNTAINS

Wreath laying for Simon Bolivar deep in the Orinoco, author and Judy Graham

but somehow everyone was squeezed on board. The stall warning emitted a few bleeps as we climbed.

I was reminded of the flight with Judy and our daughter Fiona five months previously. We had travelled from Puerto Ayacucho in a Venezuelan navy launch to San Fernando de Atabapo deep in the Upper Orinoco, and were returning in an Arava, an Israeli-built STOL aircraft, belonging to the National Guard. The purpose of the flight was to carry a seriously ill Yanomami Indian girl to hospital. The navy suggested we accept the flight as long as we didn't mind sitting in the webbing that was strung like hammocks along the fuselage. The rear door swung down. The girl, with slivers of wood through her nose and cheeks and an insert that expanded her lower lip, was carried on board, accompanied by her petrified mother. We followed, whereupon the pilot said to the crowd of villagers, "Anyone want a free ride to Ayacucho?" Half the crowd, about twenty-five people, swarmed up the ramp. Except for the Indian girl it was mostly standing room inside. The ramp closed, and we lumbered very slowly into the air. The Arava was designed to carry sixteen fully equipped paratroopers. On the ground at Puerto Ayacucho, a crew member told us that the pilot was hoping to establish a record for passengers carried in an Arava.

Back on the Twin Otter, we had La Gran Sabana below us – huge *tepuis* (mesas), flat-topped mountains cascading water down thousand-metre rock walls. Unfortunately this spectacular landscape was shrouded in cloud and only partially visible.

We were en route to Ciudad Bolivar, and the aircraft landed at four small grass strips to exchange cargo and passengers. At Kurumatu I spoke with two Spanish nuns who had driven from their mission to collect medical supplies for the serious health problems suffered at the mission, with malaria, gastroenteritis, flu, and a local intestinal irritation caused by "spicy garlic." We took off from Kurumatu with twenty-two passengers, and this time levelled off without agitating the stall warning system. The Venezuelan pilots were stress-testing Canadian engineering. There was no door for the cockpit, so nervous passengers like me could watch and over-hear what was going on up front. On the ground at Icabaru the pilot was smoking, and engaged in an altercation with the co-pilot that apparently related to some adjustment of the controls. Who won? We didn't know, and most of the passengers didn't seem to care. Few of them bothered with seat belts. Sitting beside me was a large woman whose left buttock occupied part of my seat. This was a far cry from the image of ambassadorial luxury travel held by many taxpayers.

The good news was that I had a window seat and the cloud had by now cleared. We skimmed the ridge of a *tepui*. Water cascaded down the verti-cal sides. The pilot swept in an arc around Angel Falls. It was magnificent. We were within three hundred metres of the longest vertical drop of any waterfall on the planet.[8]

∾ ∾ ∾

Beauty and the Official Beast:
The Miss Venezuela Contest

We had four years in Venezuela (1988–1992), enough time to explore the stunning diversity of its terrain, its idiosyncrasies (good and bad), and the vitality of its plastic arts and other forms of cultural expression. These in-cluded the annual Miss Venezuela contest. To the vexation of some of my diplomatic colleagues, I was asked to be a judge three years running, and participated twice. This is the story of my first experience in this classic Venezuelan ritual.

"You're going out of town?" I asked Judy.

"That's right! If you think I'm going to hang around while you make a fool of yourself ogling naked women in front of the entire country, you're crazy." Judy was not angry, but firm.

"They're not naked…or not entirely…and besides, it's an honour," I said unwisely.

I had been invited to be one of the judges in the Miss Venezuela contest, and explained to my wife that this was a major national honour – the Venezuelan equivalent of being made an honorary referee at the Stanley Cup. More than half the country, minus the thousands crammed into the convention centre for the real thing, would be glued to television sets for the full four hours of this extravaganza. I tried to explain that in this country, ambitious entrepreneurs and ambassadors would give their right arm for this sort of image opportunity. The cameras would swivel from the girls to the expressions on the faces of the judges. All ten of us would be identified, resplendent in our dinner jackets and newly decorated with specially cast Miss Venezuela medals.

"Mm," said my wife, as she rewarded my rationale with a frosty look. "What will Ottawa say?" Good question. There was no written guidance, but only the recently lobotomized would imagine that it was politically correct in the early nineties for a Canadian ambassador to officiate at a beauty contest. My arguments would cut no ice at home, where the Miss Canada contest was the latest victim of social progress – although it has since been reinstated.

I consulted "unofficially" with a friend in Ottawa, who said, "unofficially," "Go for it." Unless an over-zealous apparatchik happened to catch a rebroadcast on a late night cable channel, I was probably safe.

The Miss Venezuela contest was (and still is) a phenomenon. It had grown into a major national enterprise with fat commercial benefits for the cosmetics, fashion, and plastic surgery industries. However, the most lucrative rewards were in television and cable rights. The winner would move on to be Venezuela's contestant at the Miss Universe or Miss World contest. No other country has placed as many of its young women as winners or first or second runners-up in these competitions. As a result, the national show, the chrysalis from which these diaphanous heroines would emerge, had an audience of over one hundred million, ranging through Latin America, the Caribbean, Spain, and parts of the United States. I was told that the contest was also very popular in several Asian countries.

The Cisneros Group and its television company, Venevision, had developed the contest, and owned the rights. The owner, Gustavo Cisneros, one of the wealthiest men in Latin America, had generously invited me. One of his executives was assigned to explain what was involved. Naively, I enquired whether the event would feature the usual sexist focus on breasts and bottoms. I was assured that this competition would be different. "It will be in step with the times," he said.

"Does this mean that measurements will not be given?" I asked.

"No measurements," he said, emphasizing that the judges would be examining the whole woman: her personality, her talents, her intelligence, and her sensitivity about the human condition – in addition to other features. To this end, he explained, the judges would have an opportunity to interview the girls the day prior to the competition. I reported this conversation to Judy, saying, ingenuously, that a serious effort was being made to reduce traditional blatant sexism. She remained unimpressed.

As judges we were a mixed lot: a well-known Latin crooner who wore a toreador hat festooned with sequins; the incumbent foreign minister; the governor of a nearby state; a fashion designer; a former Miss Universe (subsequently to become mayor of Caracas and a presidential candidate); an aging journalist whose face had a permanent vulpine cast; a plastic surgeon; and two women described by the master of ceremonies as belonging to the "jet set." The Italian ambassador and I rounded off the judicial panel.

The interviews took place in Venevision's headquarters building in downtown Caracas. The contestants appeared one by one, for this occasion demurely wrapped in opaque fabric. My fellow judges and I were allowed a total of three minutes to draw from each contestant the vital information upon which we would mark them for character, skills, awareness of current events, and humanitarian impulse. The ten of us took turns extracting this intelligence. We also had the doubtful benefit of access to brief resumés, obviously crafted by Venevision's marketing boffos. My colleagues asked questions about local pop singers, Venezuelan geography, and fashion. My questions were, "Do you think women are adequately represented in the cabinet?" "What social policy is most likely to improve family life?" and others along these lines. This approach irritated some of my colleagues, for whom I was becoming the group nerd. They also surprised and discomfited most of the girls. Although I had been misled by Gustavo's executive about the new non-macho approach, I deserved the silent rebuke of my fellow judges for pushing alien ideas into a culture that, with few exceptions, wasn't ready for them.

Nevertheless, I gave high marks to the three who gave thoughtful answers to my questions. The organizers told us that the markings assigned at this session were to be reflected in the final score given at the event itself. I gave the highest marks to the young woman from the Delta Amacuro, a remote, impoverished state that encompassed the basin of the Orinoco River and that was home more to alligators than to people. Miss Delta Amacuro was shapely, even statuesque, and unlike the other predominantly White contestants, her skin was mahogany. Her most striking feature was her coal-black hair, which had been cut and coiffed so that it resembled the deck of an aircraft carrier with a take-off ramp over her forehead. Later, when he had an opportunity to inspect her in a bathing suit, my new friend the plastic surgeon told me that she was one of probably only two contestants who appeared without the benefit of plastic surgery or cosmetic dentistry. She was very bright, and provided articulate, socially sensitive responses.

The next afternoon, while Judy was flying east with two house guests to spend several days scrambling through gorges in the Gran Sabana, I set off for the Poliedro, the huge convention centre where the contest was to take place. The judges were seated in the equivalent of the orchestra pit, a location that offered a close-up view of the cantilevered flesh parading in front of us. A warm-up speech by the oily-smooth master of ceremonies included the presentation of the judges. Each contestant was then introduced by name, by the Venezuelan state or district she was representing, of which there were twenty-six, and, of course, by her measurements. As the sixth consecutive contestant came forward with the identical 90-60-90-centimetre configuration, I whispered to the ladies on either side of me that something fishy was going on. I suggested that we go on stage and verify the measurements. They giggled and the show went on. The plastic surgeon obviously knew what he was talking about, and I began to have anti-sexist thoughts. However, I was quickly rescued from this incorrectness by the libidinous undulations of the entire cast performing the lambada.

Most of the time I sat and ogled and enjoyed the spectacle. Designed as a mega-entertainment, the competition was divided into segments, many of which were song and dance. For judging purposes the girls appeared in short dresses, bathing suits, and evening gowns. The bathing suit was, of course, the big favourite. Many states had their own cheering section, especially Vargas, Miranda, Zulia, and the National Capital. Booster teams came with placards, drums, and trumpets, all enlivening a boisterous carnival atmosphere.

Our score cards were collected following the last presentation by all of the contestants and given into the hands of the executives of an allegedly reputable international accounting firm. The results were announced and the contestants reduced to five. There were more score cards, and eventually, with great fanfare and cacophonous crowd noise, Miss Venezuela was crowned.

I should not have been surprised, but Miss Delta Amacuro had not placed – had not even won Miss Congeniality. Nor had the other two women to whom I had given high marks at the interview. However, the other judges (or perhaps the organizers, given that it was thought by some that the judging was fixed) knew what they were doing. That year Miss Venezuela went on to become Miss World.

Postscript

Many years later I told this story to a small reunion of former naval officer cadets.[9] I think they were amused, but I was totally trumped when one of my friends, a distinguished professor emeritus of medicine, explained in lively detail his experience as the official physician at the Miss Nude World contest.

BOOK TWO

History is little more than the register of crimes,
the follies, and the misfortunes of mankind.

—Edward Gibbon,
The History of the Decline and Fall of the Roman Empire

In late 1992 I left the Canadian Foreign Service and began a second career with international organizations.

DOMINICAN REPUBLIC

Stepping Back from the Precipice

This story is about a deeply troubling election – the most troubling that the Organization of American States had encountered up to that point. In April 1994 the secretary general of the OAS appointed me to lead the OAS observation mission in the Dominican Republic. I was at that time the head of the Unit for the Promotion of Democracy in the OAS. This was a Canadian-inspired and Canadian-funded innovation, and I was its first incumbent.[1]

Because I had been ambassador to Venezuela and non-resident ambassador to the Dominican Republic from 1988 to 1992, I knew many of the players and was expected to have some knowledge of the intricacies of Dominican politics. It says something about how little I knew that, before leaving our home in Washington, I told Judy that I would be back in three weeks. That was the first of May. It was almost four months later that I returned to Washington.

I don't think it was naïveté, although I have certainly been guilty of that, but there wasn't one among us – neither an observer, nor a senior Dominican politician, nor a member of the press – who forecast that summer's extraordinary sequence of events.

This was not for lack of warning signals. The previous presidential elections, in 1990, had concluded in acrimony after incidents of violence, confusion, bad organization, and accusations of fraud. Dr. Joaquín Balaguer was eventually declared the winner. Following pressure from the opposition parties, Jimmy Carter, who had come as a mediator, and others in the international community made recommendations for a major over-haul of the election process. These were accepted by the government and by the Dominican Electoral Commission (JCE). Advice was forthcoming, some paid for by Canada, but, as my team soon discovered, very little of this advice was implemented. Efforts to bring problems to the attention of the JCE were met by accusations of "intrusion." International advisors were criticized for their "aggressiveness." Meanwhile, the JCE informed the public that the preparations for the 1994 elections were "progressing well."

At this stage neither I nor my team scented fraud. Political interfer-ence, yes, because a majority of the magistrates on the JCE belonged to the government party, the Reformistas. The first person to speculate that fraud might be in the cards was the Spaniard Vicente Martin, an interna-tional consultant whose job was to advise the JCE's computer centre. The more he learned the more he was alarmed, and his knowledge was alarm-ing the Reformista magistrates. Martin was getting too close to the heart of things. He was excluded from most of the computer centre's activities. Martin was withdrawn from the country when he began to receive anon-ymous death threats, and he was soon followed by two other consultants who were concerned about their safety. Vicente Martin was replaced by a Puerto Rican, Jorge Tirado, an army veteran who always dined in Santo Domingo with his back to the wall to allow him a clear view of who was entering the restaurant – a habit he had acquired in Vietnam.

It was into this incendiary environment that the International Election Observation teams came in the first week of May. The OAS team had twenty-seven members; the International Foundation for Electoral Systems (IFES), led by Charles Manatt, a former chairman of the US Democratic Party, twenty; and the National Democratic Institute (NDI), led by Stephen Solarz, a former New York congressman, twenty-six.

Within days of our arrival the political temperature rose. The Partido Revolucionario Dominicano (PRD), the principal opposition party, ex-pected that it would go into the elections with a significant lead. However, national opinion polls indicated that the results would be very close, and this had the effect of cranking up doubts about the competence of the JCE, allegations of predetermined fraud, incidents of violence, and corrosively bitter negative campaigning. The PRD leader, Peña Gomez, a Black man of Haitian ancestry, was accused of being unstable and a participant in Satanic cults. But it was President Balaguer who played the Haitian card most effectively. His bizarre concoction was that foreign governments, allegedly the United States and Canada, were plotting to force the union of Haiti and the Dominican Republic as a means of resolving the endemically chaotic Haitian problem. Peña Gomez's Haitian blood became a regular Reformista theme, and he was accused of being the agent of this plot and the person who would implement it if elected president. Grotesque caricatures of Peña circulated. As tensions rose, so did concern about the possible breakout of widespread violence.

Increasingly important as time went on was my connection with Monsignor Nuñez Collado, Rector of Madre y Maestra, the Catholic University. Monsignor Nuñez had been the moving force in Dominican efforts to reform the electoral process. Another important ally was Danny McDonald, commissioner of the US Federal Elections Commission, who had been inserted into the OAS team by the US ambassador to the OAS, in part to keep an eye on me. The clandestine side of this scheme rapidly collapsed when McDonald and I discovered shared interests in cigars, rum sours, and humour – and became friends.

Election day was clear and warm. It began deceptively well. The passion generated by this contest pushed the numbers even beyond the usually high Dominican turnout. In fact, the turnout was extraordinary, later calculated to be 87.4 percent, by far the highest turnout in Dominican history. These numbers are absolutely unheard of in the more jaded democracies of the North. In any event, the early morning produced few problems and no violence. Cheered by the reports to this effect, I set off to visit a few polling stations in the capital.

At mid-morning I was in a slum quarter with Danny McDonald when the cell phone began ringing with calls from several observers. One of the dark scenarios projected by Vicente Martin was materializing. Large numbers of citizens were being turned away because their names were not on the voters list that had been delivered by the JCE the previous day and that had replaced the voter's list in which their names appeared. NDI and IFES were soon reporting the same phenomenon.

A meeting of the three headquarters teams was hastily assembled and an urgent appointment with the JCE was requested. This was finally granted at 2:40 P.M., by which time a clear pattern of disenfranchisement had been established. On behalf of the three observation teams, I explained our findings and asked the JCE to extend the polling hours beyond the six o'clock closing and to authorize voting by those whose names were on the earlier list. The monsignor, the US embassy, and others were making the same démarche. By the time the JCE reluctantly agreed to extend the vote, it was 6:13 P.M. and the polls had already closed. Some polls reopened, but the damage was done. The predetermined fraud had succeeded by a whisker. The JCE reported that Balaguer had won by a margin of 22,281 votes over Peña Gomez. It was later found that over twice that number had been disenfranchised.

Temperatures rose, crowds gathered, and violence was expected. In this situation the verdict of the International Election Observation teams became increasingly important. The leading members of the three teams met regularly over the following days. A key issue among us was not whether to point to problems and irregularities – we all agreed that this must be done. The debate was about whether we should openly indicate the possibility of fraud in our communiqués. NDI wanted to move in that direction. My position and that of IFES was that while fraud was almost certain, we could not at that stage prove it, and in a highly polarized and incendiary environment we should be careful not to allow our statements to raise passions to the point where we would contribute to social combustion.

Post-Election: Dangers and Dilemmas

The press in Latin America and the United States picked up on the discordant sounds. Editorials in the *Washington Post* and the *New York Times* expressed dismay, and urged the Dominican electoral authorities to conduct a thorough and transparent investigation. Writing for UPS from Santo Domingo, the American journalist Georgie Ann Geyer opened her piece saying, "It may not be the dirtiest election in Dominican history [but] it is also possible that my cat, if put in an aviary, will embrace the birds."

From election day, and onward for the next three months, all of us who were engaged faced the challenge of seeking redress, and the means of such redress for an election that appeared almost certainly stolen by fraud. That was one challenge. The other challenge was to do so – or more precisely to persuade the Dominicans to do so – without shattering the increasingly tenuous stability of the country. The two challenges were inherently in conflict. My goal, shared by Monsignor Nuñez and by US Ambassador Robert Pastorino and his successor Donna Hrinak, was to find and tread the narrow path that might lead away from the abyss.

An immediate issue was the reaction of the PRD. By the end of election day, the party was convinced that the election had been stolen by Balaguer and the Reformistas. The risk of civil convulsion was rising, and the conclusion of many that the army's loyalties were divided was unsettling. Concerned that the safety of their team was at risk, the head office of NDI in Washington ordered all of its observers out of the country forty-eight hours after the election.

Peña and Balaguer

I had met Peña before the election, but it was our first meeting after the election that was the most memorable. Phones rang, senior advisors rushed in and out of his offices. Emotions were inflamed. Some members of the PRD were advising Peña to allow the party to take to the streets and show its real strength. Parts of the city were to be torched. Fuelled by his own anger and frustration and wounded by a vicious campaign, Peña was torn between giving in to the pressures for direct action and inevitable violence on the one hand, and holding the reins of his party tight to avoid the destructive fracturing of society on the other. I made the case for country above party, and, of course, was not alone. Monsignor Nuñez was a more powerful advocate for this course. We were joined by Ambassador Pastorino and others. Part of our collective leverage was our commitment to press for a real investigation of election skulduggery. None of us were prepared to accept the results of manipulation.

Peña's choice of pacific tools over violent ones did not come easily. His spirit had been fired and his reputation first established by his role as spokesman and speech writer for Colonel Caamaño in the Constitutionalista cause in the civil war of 1964, which pitted Caamaño's troops against US

Dr. Peña Gomez and President Balaguer.

Marines. On this occasion, to his great credit, Peña eventually stood his ground, and instructed his people to engage only in peaceful protest.

With the crisis still in full spate, my role evolved from that of head of the election observation mission to that of international mediator. The OAS announced that its mission in the Dominican Republic would be extended. More and more, as events unfolded, my principal Dominican counterpart became Monsignor Nuñez. I was most fortunate to have such a wise and agreeable partner, and someone for whom almost no doors, no matter how thick, were closed.

During my time as Canadian ambassador I had met a number of times with President Balaguer. There were more meetings during the crisis. Despite the hostility of many of his supporters, which, of course, was linked to the perceived threat that I posed to the success of the electoral manipulation, our conversations were always cordial. One Dominican friend who had known the president for almost sixty years, and knew him as well as anyone outside the family, told me that a close personal relationship with Balaguer was impossible. My own impression was that notwithstanding his infirmities and great age – he was then eighty-seven – he remained a masterful political manipulator. Cunning, and with a richly developed capacity to harness human weakness to his advantage, he possessed a wonderful memory, intellectual curiosity, and, when switched on, great charm.

That I was often the beneficiary of that charm may be surprising. I put it down to chance – the chance that I had met him when he was still Generalissimo Trujillo's president and I was a young diplomat posted to Ciudad Trujillo. When I returned as ambassador, Balaguer relished conversations about this chapter of his past, his recollections of the dictators of that time and region, his role in rescuing clerics from the vengeance of the Trujillo family. I sometimes recounted political jokes that I had picked up in the capital. These conversations broke the ice and inevitably facilitated discussions on hard issues.

His response to one such joke illuminates our relationship and something of his self-deprecating humour. I embarked on it with trepidation. The story concerns a driver who has joined a long line at a well-known gas station to fill up his car with gas at a time of serious gasoline and other shortages. After a long wait, the man, who is no closer to the pumps, pulls out his pistol and starts to back out of the line.

. "*Que paso?*" demands one of the other drivers.

"I'm going to the palace to shoot the president," responds the man, and drives off to a scattering of applause. Half an hour later the same man reappears with his car at the end of an even longer queue.

"What happened at the palace?" ask several in the line who saw him leave.

"The line to kill the president is longer than the line for gas."

The president rocked gently with laughter.

This relationship may or may not explain the outcome of an incident in early June. The changing OAS role in Santo Domingo was attracting increased attention in Washington, and Christopher Thomas, the acting secretary general thought that an internationally recognized figure should be performing the role of mediator. The Brazilian, Baena Soares, had left at the expiry of his term as secretary general, and his interim successor, Thomas, instructed me to ask Balaguer if he would prefer to have the former secretary general leading the OAS mission. The response was immediate: "No, *Señor Embajador*, I would like you to stay." And so I remained, but in retrospect I suspect his answer had less to do with friendly feelings

Graham scrummed by Dominican media.

than with the hope that I would be less troublesome than the former secretary general.

Foreign Intervention?

The OAS was accused by Reformistas and others of being "interventionists" who were working to advance the ambitions of Peña Gomez. The firebrands tried to incite a frenzy of jingoism. It was not prudent to drive past one of their demonstrations without showing the national flag. The charge of intervention was a potent one in a country that had endured a long US occupation (1916–1924), CIA involvement in the assassination of Trujillo, and, more recently, the landing by a force of US Marines (1964). There can be no doubt that our activities and statements stirred an already turbulent pot. My mission had done something unprecedented in the history of the OAS. Even though the wording had been deliberately non-provocative, we had blown the whistle on a flawed election. The OAS had refused to endorse the proclaimed winner. Most Dominicans did not realize that the OAS and the other missions could only be present in the country on the express invitation of the JCE – in effect, of the Dominican government. When speaking to the media I reminded them that I was there only by invitation and repeated my increasingly tedious but fundamental mantra that "the OAS was seeking to support a Dominican solution to the crisis."

The Verification Commission: A Road to Nowhere

In order to achieve this "Dominican solution," the monsignor, I, and others urgently pressed the JCE to launch a thorough investigation. However, it was not until June 6, after many delays and arguments about the composition of the Verification Commission, that it was finally constituted. The commission was to be led by the director general of the JCE and included several competent and respected individuals. The commission reported to the JCE on July 12. On the basis of a random selection of polling sites, the commission concluded that a minimum of 45,000 voters had been disenfranchised as a result of substitution – the real voters' names had been replaced with fictitious names – and that "irregularities" had occurred in at least 1,900 polling stations. The commission noted that the anomalies did not seem to be attributable to technical malfunctioning of the computer equipment. By this point the possibility of innocent malfunction was reduced virtually to a mathematical and procedural impossibility. Nevertheless, the chair of the JCE told the press that the commission "had discarded any notion of fraud." The JCE magistrates sat on this report for three weeks.

Attempts to persuade Balaguer to discuss possible exit strategies were running into a wall. On July 28 the afternoon papers quoted Balaguer as saying that he would not sit down to discuss a negotiated solution until he was formally proclaimed victor of the elections.

That evening I sat rocking on the monsignor's patio, drinking his rum and, as usual, dissecting the crisis. In our view the president was playing with fire, but calculating that a formal declaration by the JCE would increase his leverage if he were to be cornered into negotiations.

The following morning there was a damage control session. It was agreed that we must speak urgently with Peña. In my notes at the time I wrote, "The situation is increasingly volatile and we fear that Peña, in his indignation, may push the situation toward the edge. Agripino [the monsignor] and I will seek separate appointments with Balaguer and with Peña. I called Ambassador Hrinak to suggest that she also call on Peña."

The next day, July 30, I met with Peña. He wanted President Clinton to telephone personally to Balaguer to apply pressure. I responded that Clinton was unlikely to agree, but the notion of an urgent high-level call from Washington made sense.

August 1 began badly. At a morning meeting with the director general of the JCE, I found him very discouraged. He forecast that the official proclamation of Balaguer's victory would be given within days, and would be issued without any reference to the Verification Commission. This prediction proved correct. On August 2 the JCE formally announced the election of President Balaguer for the period 1994–1998, with no reference at all to the report of the Verification Commission.

Of course, all hell broke loose. The roller-coaster crisis plunged again, with the spectre of a general strike and civil disorder. The armed forces and police issued a statement expressing support for the JCE's ruling. Fortunately, the question in many minds about how many military commanders would support the government in the event of an uprising went unanswered.

The US Role: Pressures and Suspicions

Up to this point I have said little about the role of the United States and of its ambassadors. Yet it was critically important. In terms of real leverage, it was crucial.

The US government had assigned two top professionals to the embassy in Santo Domingo. Robert Pastorino completed his assignment soon after the elections and was replaced by Donna Hrinak. I have lost count of the number of meetings I had with these excellent people. I was lucky. Our relationship was that of colleagues who had reached the same diagnosis of the problems and were looking to each other for support. But at the outset of the crisis the application of strong and consistent pressure by the US government could not be taken for granted. Haiti, on the western part of the island, was a bigger and more public headache for the Clinton administration. Washington was attempting – along with the OAS and the UN – to isolate and extinguish the illegal regime of General Cédras. A key component of the effort was to seal the Dominican–Haitian border – which the Balaguer government was not enthusiastic about. While careful not to say so openly, Balaguer had been quite content to see Aristide overthrown by Cédras.

In these circumstances, it might have been expected that the US government would have decided to pay the price of Balaguer's co-operation on the frontier by casting a blind eye on his cooked election. This did not happen. Notwithstanding the risks to effective collaboration on the border, the ambassadors and the State Department applied pressure on the Balaguer government both to block undesirable border crossings and to rectify its errors in the conduct of the election.

Many years later former US ambassador Michael Skol explained how it was that the US government did not allow the much more public pressures of the Haitian crisis to trump concerns about democracy in the Dominican Republic. Skol, who was at that time the deputy assistant secretary for Latin America, was given the lead on the crisis in the State Department, and eventually the lead role for the US government. At this time I was unaware of the strategic battle taking place in Washington that pitted Skol against Strobe Talbot, the deputy secretary, and number two in the State Department. Talbot had taken an intense personal interest in the Haitian file. He was accustomed to getting his way, and was attracted by Balaguer's ploy to trade Dominican support in plugging the porous border with Haiti, thus further isolating the Cédras military regime in Port-au-Prince, and Dominican co-operation elsewhere, for tacit American acceptance of Balaguer's consolidation of his victory in the tainted election. Skol took a different view. If he had lost the battle with Talbot, the final outcome in Santo Domingo would have been very different.

After this success Skol visited Balaguer in Santo Domingo and told him bluntly that the US government wanted a solution to the crisis that reflected democratic principles. In his comments to me long after, Skol admitted that his tactics might have appeared "harsh, even imperial," but he believed that they were necessary to convince Balaguer that the US government was not bluffing. At about the same time, the US ambassador to the OAS raised the possibility of OAS economic and diplomatic sanctions against the Dominican Republic.

Countervailing pressures were again at work. It was very soon after the elections that my innocence about the privacy of telephone conversations was shattered. I discovered what most others had known – that a sophisticated eavesdropping industry was blossoming in Santo Domingo, and that tapes of my cellular phone discussions had become a popular item in some quarters. In a clumsy attempt to persuade me to be more "understanding" of the government's position, the president of Balaguer's party invited me to listen to a pirated tape of one of my conversations with Peña Gomez. He implied – quite wrongly, I thought – that my objectivity was tainted. I was more annoyed than embarrassed about this tape. A senior associate of Peña Gomez tried a similar tactic. He was also threatening to expose my presumed "bias." The meeting was held under the flame trees in the garden of the old OAS building. Like many others, it was held outside in order to avoid electronic eavesdropping. The concern by both sides about where I stood was understandable. There was a great deal at stake.

Pressure was also being applied at OAS headquarters in Washington. One or two OAS ambassadors, unhappy with the OAS's pursuit of democracy in Santo Domingo, complained to Christopher Thomas that my activities as mediator in Santo Domingo exceeded my mandate. Thomas, who was getting cold feet as the election crisis heated up, called to say that he intended to recall me to Washington. I mentioned this to Donna Hrinak. She was horrified, and suggested that I speak to Michael Skol on a secure line. Skol and I had been friends and colleagues when we were our respective countries' ambassadors in Caracas. I spoke to him on a confidential line, and by the next day Thomas had backed off.

By this time I was increasingly a target of press attention. My own nerves were fraying and I wasn't getting much sleep. I decided to call Dr. Jordi Brossa, who had been my physician thirty years before, when he had been one of those involved in the plot against Trujillo. Jordi received me warmly and prescribed potent pills.

Deadlock and Extrication: Ten Days in August

Having conferred the next presidency on Balaguer, the JCE had written itself out of the picture. As this would not have happened without Balaguer's personal blessing, he had either concluded that he could ride out the storm or had calculated that confirmation as president-elect would strengthen his hand for the days ahead. For the monsignor and myself it became clear that the only remaining path out of the worsening crisis lay in direct negotiations between Peña and Balaguer. Our energies were bent in that direction and our shuttle diplomacy accelerated. However, it was not immediately successful. Balaguer was elusive, and Peña was exasperated and losing patience. On August 1 we learned that Balaguer had passed four hours in the cemetery meditating by his mother's tomb. Eventually persistence prevailed. We met separately with Peña and Balaguer.

Graham and President Balaguer in the palace.

As it happened, Balaguer was more responsive to the idea of a direct meeting with his opponent than was Peña, whose advisors were opposed to any one-on-one meeting of their leader with Balaguer. They were convinced that the slippery octogenarian would trick Peña into a bad deal. They were also concerned that directly consorting with the president would lower their moral ground. With the solid weight of many friends and senior colleagues against it, Peña resisted the proposal. It was not until the end of the first week in August that he succumbed to the argument that a continuing stalemate would harm both him and the country.

Peña attached the condition that the meeting must not be in the palace, but on neutral ground. I reported this to Balaguer, who immediately set wheels in motion for the meeting to be held in a library near the palace. It had been agreed between Balaguer and Peña that only four people would be present: the two principals, with Monsignor Nuñez and myself as witnesses.

Pie in the Library

At seven o'clock in the evening, August 9, the monsignor and I arrived at the library to find a surprisingly familiar setting. The furniture, consisting of table, settee, lamps, and chairs, had been moved from the president's reception chamber at the palace and set up there. The president, looking very composed, had already taken his place. Peña appeared within a few minutes, looking less composed. Balaguer invited me to open the proceedings. I made a brief statement about the purpose of the meeting and expressed our pleasure that the principals had agreed to attend. The president indicated his willingness to discuss any proposals that Peña might wish to make. At this point, to our surprise and dismay, Peña interjected to say that his colleague, Hatuey de Camps, was outside and would read a statement articulating the PRD position. Balaguer, without betraying any hint of displeasure, consented. De Camps entered the room and read a statement that essentially reiterated the PRD position that in view of the magnitude of the fraud, the government must agree to fresh elections as soon as possible, and that no other course could be considered. The intention of de Camps' intervention was clearly to freeze the dialogue and intimidate Peña.

The monsignor and I had been told that afternoon that Peña, under tremendous pressure from his senior colleagues, had given them the assurance that he would only meet with Balaguer, that he would negotiate nothing. However, still uncertain about how their leader would stand up to Balaguer, they had extracted Peña's assent to have a senior colleague set out the party's position in inflexible terms. Having apparently accomplished this purpose, de Camps left the room.

For his part, Peña repeated the party's "all or nothing" stance, insisting that the May 16 elections lacked legitimacy. The meeting continued for some time along this sterile path, and both the monsignor and I began to despair of any positive outcome. Attempting to dispel the chill that had fallen over the room, Balaguer showed no impatience with Peña's stonewalling, always addressing Peña as "Doctor." He admitted no wrongdoing, but began to peel away Peña's truculence with words of understanding for his frustration, and appreciation of his opponent's patience, given the strong support he had received across the country. The atmosphere was palpably lightening, and from the softer tone of Peña's interjections it was evident that Balaguer could sense the change. Speaking very slowly, in his normal, slightly quavering, voice, he reminded his opponent that the elections had ended in a virtual tie, and then suggested, "Why don't we share the pie?" Peña responded, "What does this mean?" The president paused, and said, "Me, two years, and you, two years." As he said this, he bent forward and extended his hand toward Peña. Peña rose and, without any haste, grasped Balaguer's hand. The meeting broke up with Balaguer inviting Peña to his house the next day at 11:00 A.M. to work out the details. Monsignor Nuñez and I were invited to attend this meeting.

Eluding the press, the monsignor and I drove back to his residence, where he poured Cuba Libres with a generous hand. Our shocked reactions were identical. Peña, as his people had feared, had been seduced by the wily Balaguer. There would be no recourse to fresh elections, and the two men and their parties would share equal time at the public trough over the next four years. Having inserted the thin edge of an astute political wedge, Balaguer presumably anticipated that the damage done by this Faustian deal to Peña might mean that he, Balaguer, would occupy the palace not just for the agreed two years but for the full four. Over the next few hours several people dropped by. The last to come was Peña, and at his invitation the monsignor and I offered our opinions about the agreement reached in the library. Upon leaving us Peña passed the night in heavy consultation with senior members of his party.

Neither the monsignor nor I were present for these discussions, but we understood that the "pie" was received with deeply divided reactions by senior party members. Clearly, in the minds of its leaders the PRD had won the election. For a major party that had been out of power for eight years, half of the pie was more attractive than the uncertainties of another election. Not surprisingly, then, many of those present favoured accepting the Balaguer proposal. The arguments were long and intense. It was only in the early hours of the morning that those who argued that neither the party nor the leader would ever be forgiven by the traumatized party base finally convinced Peña to decline the offer.

At ten o'clock that morning, Monsignor Nuñez and I called on President Balaguer at his private residence to inform him that we would not support the arrangement agreed to on the previous evening. The president accepted our position. He offered no counter-argument and expressed his hope that the OAS would continue to support the mediation process. Shortly after our departure, Peña arrived to deliver his message that the deal was off. Balaguer responded equably, and the two, with a few associates, set about to work on the formula that we had hoped would emerge from the meeting in the library. The central points of their agreement, which became enshrined in *el Pacto de la Democracia*, were the non-re-election of an incumbent president and the holding of new elections within eighteen months. Advisors from both sides were assigned to develop a draft.

"Hallelujah!" we said to ourselves when told of this development. We were now six days from the inauguration, and events were moving swiftly, but they were still on a characteristically switchback course. Confusion and disagreement arose over other important issues, including the scheduling for the embedding of these changes in the constitution by the Constituent Assembly, the timing of the new elections, and problems relating the percentage of votes required by a presidential candidate to avoid a second round of voting. In Peña's presence President Balaguer presided at a press conference that afternoon at which he outlined the terms of the agreement and announced that the Democratic Pact, incorporating this agreement, would be signed at the palace that same night by the three principal parties. To our surprise, Balaguer also publicly acknowledged the role of the monsignor (and the Church) and myself (and the OAS).

The signing of the pact was a catharsis after four months of almost constant civil peril. The media was present in full force, and so too were most of the leading citizens, the party chieftains, the diplomatic corps, and congressional figures. The setting was the opulent Salon of the Caryatids in the presidential palace, where I had first met Trujillo and Balaguer at a New Year's levee. The forty or so nymphs that encircled the entire chamber had lost none of the buxom charm that I recalled from my first exposure to them. The principal change was that Balaguer had recently upgraded them from plaster to marble. Little else had changed in the palace, the tawny-coloured domed Italianate building that was the only architectural success of Trujillo's long dictatorship.

I was seated at the president's left. At his right sat Cardinal Nicolás Jesús López Rodriguez, who early on in the crisis had pronounced anathema on all "foreign intervention," including that of the OAS. However, the ceremony could not begin, because Peña, whose presence was key to the event, was not there. Peña, sleepless now for a day and a half, had spent the afternoon and evening in a crossfire of advice from his political colleagues about whether he should share centre stage with Balaguer. Monsignor Nuñez, who had been tipped off about Peña's predicament and his reluctance to participate, personally appealed to him. It was this intervention that persuaded Peña to attend, rescued the pact from becoming a humiliating fiasco and the country from suffering more trauma.

The half-hour delay caused by the Peña problem was, for me, spent in very agreeable conversation with the president. I had learned from the time when I was ambassador that Balaguer was happier talking about the past than the present. Almost all of our meetings were prefaced by stories about Trujillo. On this occasion I enquired about how Trujillo got on with the other dictators of that period – some of whom were his temporary guests, in flight from their own countries. "Batista, no," Balaguer replied. "He didn't particularly care for Batista, nor for Somoza." He remarked that Trujillo liked Juan Peron and the Venezuelan, Pérez Jiménez. "What about Franco?" I asked. The answer came readily. Trujillo admired Franco. "Despite many differences and contrasting styles, they got along." On the subject of Franco, it occurred to me to ask Balaguer if he could confirm a story I had heard the previous week from Monsignor Arnaiz. The monsignor, a Spanish prelate, was taking leave of Franco before setting off for Santo Domingo – this was just after Balaguer's first authentic electoral victory, in 1966, when Generalissimo Franco asked the monsignor to convey cautionary advice as well as congratulations to his friend. The advice came in three parts: beware of expectations – with power you must expect to lose friends and gain enemies; don't make promises; and don't invite to the palace those who want invitations, invite to the palace those who don't want invitations. Balaguer emitted a wheezy chuckle and said, "Yes, that was Franco's message."

Peña, of course, fell squarely into the last category. At last he arrived, and the solemn reading and signing of the pact began. Peña's delay and the refusal of some of the designated witnesses to sign cast a light shadow over the event. However, all was neatly, if ephemerally, papered over in the president's speech later on. It was not the soaring oratory of his middle age, but not bad for a frail, blind man of eighty-seven. More importantly, the pact signalled to the country that the worst was over.

On August 15, the day before the inauguration, Donna Hrinak and I held our last meeting. The issue was whether or not she should attend the inauguration. Almost her entire senior staff were opposed, arguing that Balaguer had made a mockery of the democratic process and should be deprived of any public approval by the US ambassador. The most vehement advocate of this line was the director of USAID. The State Department had left the decision to the ambassador's discretion. My position was that the compromise embodied in the pact would not have been realized without her tireless work, that of her predecessor, and the support of her government. I said that her non-attendance would, in effect, signal a repudiation by the US government of a solution that had avoided civil conflict, and one that we had all laboured so hard to obtain. I added that foreign investors and the business community would interpret this as a vote of non-confidence in an economy already battered by months of uncertainty. She said that there would be another meeting with her staff.

That night I was having a late supper when my cell phone rang. It was Donna. She had decided to attend the inauguration. All of the senior staff tried to dissuade her, with one surprising exception, her military attaché.

The next morning, August 16, we threaded our way separately through a boisterous crowd outside the legislative building. I had mixed feelings about being recognized and about a few placards that read, "Graham and the OAS: Get out." But by far the greater number of derogatory signs were directed at the American ambassador.

Following his swearing in, the president, smart in a dark morning dress and with his black silk top hat on the table beside him, rose to speak. His address was appropriate to the occasion. There was no triumphalism. Instead, there were a few gracious references to Peña Gomez, reflecting the spirit of the pact. In deference to Peña's wishes, Balaguer announced that he would ask the Constituent Assembly to reduce from 50 percent to 40 percent the degree of support for the leading presidential candidate required to avoid a second round of voting. With that, the curtain finally came down on four months of tension, uncertainty, and high drama.

Epilogue

Since May 16, we had confronted the challenge of persuading the government and the JCE to engage in a transparent investigation of a major fraud. Our second task was to continue to protest the fraud until a route out of the electoral crisis could be found without exacerbating the existing tensions on both sides to the point where the stability of the state was seriously endangered. On the first, we were thwarted. A full investigation of the fraud was never completed. The second was more successful. From the beginning, the mediation effort was an attempt to create space within which Dominicans could devise and apply a solution. In the end that is what happened.

The personality, the cerebral strength, the tenacity, and the guile of Joaquín Balaguer permeate this entire episode. He ruled as an omniscient constitutional despot. In the manner of his mentor, Trujillo, his grasp of detail extended beyond the capital into towns and villages throughout the country. He used the weaknesses as much as the strengths of his associates to his benefit. He may not have known the minutiae, but I believe it must be assumed that he approved the fraud in advance. Inside that tight, highly personalized system, reinforced by sanctions of fear and economic penalty, it is unthinkable that such a major decision could have been taken without his consent.

So, why did a wily old bird like Balaguer give his consent? Why did he not anticipate some of the problems involved in inviting experienced international observer teams? My speculative answer is that when he had rigged elections before, he had been slapped on the wrist (by Jimmy Carter and others), but had gotten away with it. Presumably he believed that however clumsy some of the manipulation, the JCE would rationalize and defend the results, and that in the end the international observers would grumble but accept a *fait accompli*. He had little reason to think otherwise. Up to that point the OAS had never so unequivocally cast into question the legitimacy of national election results. When we blew the whistle, we took the government and the JCE by surprise.

It is tempting to judge Balaguer by the standards of a more distant, putative mentor, Niccolo Machiavelli. The author of *The Prince* would have assigned him high marks for his ruthlessness, his masterful command of human psychology and political dynamics, and his commitment to the dictum "It is much safer to be feared than loved." But guile was not the only test of success for Machiavelli. He respected the positive results of political action that bound a people more closely to their leader. Balaguer's conspicuous failures in education and electrification would drop him several points. Machiavelli also recommended that statesmen facing policy crossroads "should opt for the lesser of two evils." In 1994 the "lesser of the two evils" for the president was a compromise with Peña Gomez, the sometimes flawed and finally tragic leader, who had much earlier placed country over party.[2]

HAITI

"The Pencil of God Has No Eraser" (Haitian Proverb)

I

The events described in this and the following chapter took place in the spring of 1995, when I was running a technical support operation on behalf of the International Foundation for Electoral Systems (IFES), in preparation for what was to be the second free election in Haitian history. My team was working under contract for the UN.

Garbage collection arrangements in Port-au-Prince are probably unique in the western hemisphere. Each block, or sometimes each grouping of blocks, has its own designated garbage zone. There are no dumpsters. Garbage is taken by bucket, wheelbarrow, or handcart and piled in a rising fetid heap at the side of the street. It's ripe, but downtown, when the wind blows moist and noxious off the bay, the heady effluvium of sewage overpowers the smell of garbage.

The dumping ground near my office served as a constantly replenished smorgasbord for the neighbourhood fauna: rats, the size of small rabbits, chubby pigs, and street dogs. There were no cats; in this part of town few survive the pot. Once every couple of weeks, with surprising regularity, a truck backs up to the pile. Gaunt men appear with spades

Note the citation on the cart for a verse from Exodus.

and the heap disappears into the bed of the truck, leaving a wet, garnished splotch on the road.

For the residents of this quarter, reaching a consensus on the location of the dump site had been easy. It was to be in front of that rotting oxymoron *La Ronde Pointe* (whose sign says "*Rond ointe*"), an ex-nightclub owned by former president Jean-Claude Duvalier. The club had been sacked, or, in Creole, *déchouké*, the day after he left the country with his dollars and his felonious wife. That was eight years before this visit, and apart from the patina of decay, and the squatters behind the rags that sheathed the empty window frames, it was the same ruin I had seen on a visit shortly after the dynasty had fallen.

I remember that corner, its garbage, and its stink vividly. The graffiti changed after former President Carter's visit in February 1995. One wall read in Creole, "Jimmy Carter, false democrat." Alongside, the same hand had written in English, "Jimmy Carter dickhead." Carter had negotiated the exile to Panama of Cédras, the general who had overthrown Aristide and who had ordered his troops to oppose an American invasion. Carter's crime was to save lives, many Haitian and perhaps a few American. The mob had wanted the general's blood at any price.

The roadway is not busy, but the traffic is diverse. Armoured Humvees pass, carrying American or Nepalese troops; men and boys, their shirtless backs slippery with toil, push and drag two-wheeled carts with towering loads of flour, charcoal, motor oil, or ice; once I saw the entire carcass of a car being trundled down the road by two men. By some Malthusian calculation, human labour is cheaper than that of mules.

I never understood how the children in the neighbourhood were still capable of showing even in short flashes the spontaneity and joy of being children. The remains of *La Ronde Pointe* is at the intersection of Rue Harry Truman and Rue Marie Jeanne. My office was six doors down from the ex-nightclub on Marie Jeanne. Some of the kids shined our shoes or washed our cars during the day. At dusk there was always a group of three waiting for us to leave. They were between eight and eleven and they waited for a handout, usually a few gourdes apiece (a gourde was worth about eight cents) and some good-natured teasing. Someone had told me that Haitians also appreciate gifts of soap, so I remembered to bring some tablets of hotel soap. I flicked these into the air for the children to catch, and was amazed by their wide grins when they recognized the soap. Hygiene in Haiti, especially in that putrefying neighbourhood, is enormously important. Families would disrobe, females partially and males completely, to scrub themselves by a fractured water main across the street.

Two weeks into my contract, the corner was the scene of a human *déchoukage*. It took place around eleven o'clock in the morning. I was in the office talking to a civilian member of the United Nations about the election when shouting in the street drew us to the window. A young man was attempting to outrun a mob that was chasing him down Marie Jeanne, but his hands were tied behind his back and his closest pursuers were striking him with sticks. I didn't know it then, but there were two victims. They were alleged to have been seen stealing. The value of the theft was probably under five dollars. In this culture, if a thief is caught, retribution is swift. Probably because it scarcely exists, justice is telescoped into self-appointed judges, juries, and executioners. Accusations are shouted and a mass of people forms.

I called the UN military on my radio. They arrived with their Humvees thirty-five minutes later. In the meantime, not really understanding what was happening, I went outside. One youngster lay dead, beaten to death. The other was sprawled by the garbage heap, alive but perhaps fatally injured, with a long gash on the back of his head. I called again, this time for an ambulance. It came after the Humvees. I walked back to the office numb with horror. Justice, I told myself, had been a pretext. For me this was the Haitian version of fox hunting – killing for entertainment. My

Haitian colleagues neither shared nor comprehended my reaction. What had happened was, in their context, an expression of natural law. After a time I accepted that my view was too simple, but I still didn't understand. If I was going to go on working with Haitians, there were some steep cultural walls that I would have to climb.

Four days after the killing I was in my ancient, gorgeous, termite-ridden hotel, the Grand Hotel Olafson – gingerbread, architectural whimsy, big saucy rats, and dry rot – made famous by Graham Greene, who used it for the setting of his novel *The Comedians*. Early in its life, for nine years after about 1917, during the US Marine occupation, it had been used as a hospital. It was Sunday morning, and a local church service was being shown on the hotel's one TV set perched above the bar. A woman was conducting the choir, her hips swinging to the music. In the apse, a band – piano, guitar, and goatskin drums – played the accompaniment. The singing was in Creole and the melody was somewhere between a Gregorian hymn and a traditional soft Haitian folk song, at times with louder Vodou syncopations. Behind the counter was a splendid papier mâché bust of Desalines, the first emperor of Haiti, and a large lady bartender. She asked me if I had been to church.

"No, not today."

"Why not? Why don't you go to church?"

"I'm lazy."

"Hmmph. You know…Haitians pray a lot. Haitians pray more than they do in other countries."

The majority practise Vodou, and most blend their Vodou with Catholicism on Sundays. I considered a tart reply, but held back. Surprisingly rich, wonderful choral music filled the room.

∾ ∾ ∾

"The Pencil of God Has No Eraser"

II

Haiti, with its stygian complexity, its bewitchery, and its insoluble challenges, became a thread that ran through my diplomatic

*and international careers. My first visit was in 1960, to a country
controlled by Papa Doc Duvalier and his Tonton Macoutes. The
last was in 2010, shortly after the earthquake, when I led a small
team on behalf of Jimmy Carter's Friends of the Inter-American
Democratic Charter. This story, like the last one, is from 1995.*

I used to know some yuppie settings where the inhabitants renovated and
adorned their bathrooms to the point where they became the centrepiece
of the apartment: burnt orange and chocolate ceramic tiles, deep pile
around the toilet, an adjoining box room made over into a sauna, thick
six-foot towels in solid colours, and, for the minimally deranged, perhaps
a toilet seat that plays Handel when activated.

The one bathroom in our small, hot, crowded office in downtown
Port-au-Prince was not quite like this, but it did nevertheless hold a natural position as a centre of attraction for us, even more so during the regular power outages that cut out the water pump.

One morning toward the end of April it was discovered that the security guard had somehow broken the stout lock on the bathroom door
during the night. Left to itself, the bathroom door would not close. This
was disconcerting, particularly for the eleven women in our twenty-
seven-person office.

Michel, the office cleaner and general handyman, addressed the problem with a Rube Goldberg solution. The door opened outward, and he
attached the end of an eight-foot length of sisal rope to the inside door
handle. Snuggled between the barrel of diesel fuel for the generator and
the cardboard box containing flashlights so that the generator could be
found, the toilet occupant, sitting or standing, could close the door by
pulling on the rope. Privacy required constant pressure on the rope.

Michel's experiment was not well received. However, it took two days
of rising abuse before he devised an alternative method. Because of the
configuration of the door frame and the wall, it was not possible to at-
tach a simple hook latch or deadbolt on the inside of the door. Undaunted,
Michel nailed a deadbolt to the outside. This solution involved delegated
privacy control. Once in the bathroom, the user required a confederate
on the outside to push home the bolt, remain discreetly nearby until the
occupant shouted or knocked to be released, and then withdraw the bolt.

In abusive Creole the women made it known that they did not wish to have Michel performing this role.

As the bathroom drama entered its fourth day, there were other developments. The first was that negotiations with the landlord to fit a functional lock on the door that could be operated from the inside were stalled by the landlord's reasonable insistence that the nocturnal blundering of our security guard was not his responsibility. Secondly, there was a rising incidence of constipation. Notable exceptions were those struck down by "Danse Macoute," the Haitian version of the "Aztec Two-Step."

The third development was not related to the bathroom, but to what the UN military command perceived as the vulnerability of our office. Our job was to organize and enter on computers the information required to place the names of some twelve thousand candidates on ballots for the next elections in a country with only one previous experience of free elections. It was accepted that if our machines and data base were destroyed, a highly sensitive election timetable would be derailed. During the previous election campaign a mob had burned down the offices of the Election Commission. The UN had promised twice-daily patrols by armoured Humvees. However, it was seven days before they found our location.

On this, the fourth day of the toilet crisis, we received a visit from a military team comprised of a Bahamian naval lieutenant-commander, a captain of cavalry from Djibouti (the camel corps), a Pakistani police lieutenant, and two trucks from the United States Corps of Engineers. Because it was an unsavoury part of town, the few windows in our grungy, two-storeyed, low-ceilinged office were already grilled. The engineers were there to fasten thick iron mesh over the grill work.

I walked outside to see the work in progress. The street was better than most in this part of town, but the harbour with its memorable fragrance was only four hundred yards away.

"What purpose will the iron mesh serve?" I asked the engineer sergeant.

"It'll keep out hand grenades, rocks, and most of a Molotov cocktail."

The next day a new functional bathroom lock was installed, and the neighbours complained that our fortifications had lowered the tone of the street. Everything considered, they had a point.

BOSNIA

Black Past, Grey Future?

For seven months in 1996 and again for seven months in 1997 I was sent to Bosnia by Elections Canada to work with the Organization for Security and Co-operation in Europe (OSCE). I was there as senior elections officer for a large area in northwest Bosnia. The title of this chapter is adapted from that of Rebecca West's masterly volume on pre–Second World War Yugoslavia, Black Lamb, Grey Falcon.

Before I left for Bosnia, in early March 1996, I found an old Serbo-Croat phrase book in my basement. In large print on the cover it declared, inaccurately, "With this book you need never be at a loss when conversing with Serbo-Croat-speaking people." However, there were some useful phrases inside, such as "Where can I buy a rifle?" and "How many men-of-war are lying in your harbour?"

Thus equipped, I stepped onto the shell-scarred apron of Sarajevo Airport with four companions: a former (and, I thought, still active) Russian intelligence officer, an airsick Dane, a Swede, and another Canadian. The Russian impressed me as a hardened international: his luggage included a tennis racquet. We were all taking up long-term assignments with the OSCE, the instrument chosen by the Dayton Peace Accords for delivering legitimate elections, human rights, and democratization. It was a raw afternoon with snow on the ground and the feel of more to come. We piled our luggage into the back of a van and set off for the centre of Sarajevo. Exploratory conversations that had begun that morning in Vienna shut down as we drove through a corridor of devastation.

The shock was just beginning. A few days later I took the long drive to my post in Bihac, in northwestern Bosnia. Neither my briefings nor CNN had prepared me for the human desolation. The peace was only five months old, and most of the day's journey was through ruins. Towns and villages were gutted, some by armed conflict, but most burned or blown up by one or other of the opposing ethnic forces. Bosansko Grahovo was a grim example. It had been a town of about 3,000 people, with small lumber mills and a furniture factory. On this first visit, there was not a living thing except for one mournful dog standing in the snow by a row of dilapidated terrace houses. I travelled with a kind of hollow pain somewhere between chest and stomach.

I also learned that to move about Bosnia you needed not just a road map but an ethnic map as well. Take the town of Drvar, a Tito stronghold during the Second World War. It was important to know that it was 99 percent Croat, but it was essential to know that before the Bosnian war it had been 97 percent Serb. Prijedor had been 44 percent Muslim, 42 percent Serb, and 6 percent Croat. In 1996 it was about 98 percent Serb – and so on, with similar dramatic inversions across the country.

After places like Bosansko Grahavo and Drvar, Bihac wasn't so bad. The centre of what became known as the Bihac pocket during the Bosnian war, the town was my base for seven months in 1996 and another seven months in 1997. The climate is not unlike that of Ottawa. The winter is as long but not as cold, which is just as well, as there was almost no central heating. The food is *haut cholesterol* – fried beef, mutton, veal, and fat-laden french fries. Because of the demented driving, the roads are more dangerous than the minefields. But the setting is splendid. Bihac lies in a wide valley, astride a turquoise river. It was predominantly Muslim before the war, and is now even more predominantly Muslim. The electronically magnified voice of the muezzin heralds the day at 4:55 A.M.

Bihac had not been physically overrun. It had withstood a siege for almost as long as Sarajevo, and with that city, Srebrenica, and a few others, shared the much-caricatured distinction of having been designated a "safe area" by the United Nations. Unlike Srebrenica, it survived. The United Nations and its military arm in Bosnia, UNPROFOR (United Nations

Protection Force), can take no credit for this. Survival was largely the result of astute and ferocious local military leadership and the resilience of the community. Almost encircled by the Serbs, Bihac had one open corridor running north to the Croatian frontier. It was sealed when a rebel Muslim group led by Fikret Abdic established a *modus vivendi* with the Serbs. The fighting among Muslims in this "pocket" was the most vicious and costly of the war. It was a conflict that coloured everything – more than the three-year battle with the Serbs. From the highest level of local government and from the deputy commander of the Bosnian army we received threats that if we, the OSCE, persisted in allowing Abdic's party to run in the elections, they would be "unable to protect us from the consequences." (Under the terms of the Dayton agreement, all parties, including that of Abdic, had a right to run.)

A secondary but still disconcerting inter-Muslim consequence of the war was the widening of divisions based on degrees of religious orthodoxy. A moderately secular pre-war population split into zealous and non-zealous communities, a change brought about by pressure from those Muslim countries that provided material support during the war. At one end of this spectrum, Muslims consumed huge quantities of local spirits and supported the Miss Bihac contest. At the other end, a group of zealots blew up a nude statue because it offended their mores. Blowing up statues in Bihac was not difficult, as there was almost unlimited access to explosives and statues.

By any standard this was a catastrophic, brutal set of overlapping wars. Over 150,000 were killed (the majority of them non-combatants), and horrific numbers executed, recalling and certainly exacerbated by memories of past conflict. During the Second World War far more Yugoslavs were killed by internecine conflict than by the Germans, Italians, and Bulgarians combined. Atrocities committed by Ante Pavelic's Ustashi (Croation Fascists) against the Serbs appalled even the German commanding general in Zagreb.

Approximately three million people, well over half of the population, were displaced from their homes. The Hague Tribunal identified some 20,000 cases of rape. Few of the guilty parties were arrested. When I was living in Bihac, the sense of unrequited justice was deep. General Ratko Mladic and Radovan Karadzic, the Bosnian Serb military and political leaders respectively, still ran free, and in towns and villages where mass graves were being uncovered there was corrosive anger about the lower-level villains who had not been named by The Hague. There were many people who could identify perpetrators of executions, rape, and other atrocities. They could not comprehend how the international community could allow these persons to remain free.

A judge I came to know quite well in the small town of Sanski Most spent about half of his time searching for and documenting bodies, many of them those of people he knew. Although not a cheerful man, he was remarkably pleasant. I could only marvel at how he could smile and talk normally about normal things.

The cumulative impact of these horrors did little to incline the people to trust international institutions. In Bosnian Muslim areas UNPROFOR was particularly vilified. Some UNPROFOR units were regarded as almost useless, such as, for example, the Bangladeshis, who were caught inside the Bihac pocket unprepared for a Bosnian winter. In this case it was the UN logistics unit, not the Bangladeshis, who were the culprits. The French were distrusted because they appeared to favour the Serbs. Many of the forces in the Bihac area, both UN and belligerents, were active in the lucrative black market. For 5,000 Deutschmarks you could pay a UN soldier – or a unit of soldiers – to hide you in an armoured personnel carrier and take you to Zagreb, out of the war zone. In most cases the fault cannot be assigned to identifiable units. Some did excellent work. In the Medak pocket near Bihac in September 1993, the Princess Patricia Light Infantry fought a major engagement, news of which was suppressed by the Department of National Defence in the aftermath of Somalia. In the Medak incident the Canadians were interposed between Croat and Serb forces when the Croats attacked. The Croats fell back with serious losses, while the Princess Pats suffered only light injuries. The fact that the United Nations forces operated under a hopelessly restricted mandate, determined by New York, was not understood – and, in the circumstances, understandably not understood. Bosnian public offices called attention to the failure of United Nations to prevent horrific tragedies such as Srebrenica by placing placards on their windows and walls castigating the UN.

Most of us were regarded as guilty, if not by deed, then by association. Subject to some individual variations, the international community, including the OSCE, were seen as one grey, pusillanimous, pro-Serb amalgam.

As the senior elections officer for Una Sana Canton (Muslim) and Canton Ten (Croat), an area that covers about one quarter of the Bosniac/Croat Federation, my job was to work with a team of internationals based in Bihac and four satellite offices to help set up and run the election process in the region. We tried to work closely with canton presidents, local mayors, party and election officials, and police chiefs. It was frustrating, frequently irritating, often entertaining, and always challenging.

Sometimes we met with the head of the secret police, a trim, well-dressed man who used his steely grey eyes to engage in "Who will blink first?" contests. We guessed that he had learned this technique in secret police school. In our experience he always won. The secret police in Bihac, and presumably throughout Bosnia, were the best paid, best equipped, and smartest of all Bosnian public servants. They read all of our faxed confidential reports and listened to our car radio communications. Their intercept staff spoke English, Russian, German, and probably French. A few of us used Spanish on the car radio – in large part for security reasons, but sometimes just to annoy the secret policemen. This practice soon led to a competition in offensive invective. José Maria, a Spanish friend, swept the board with "*Eres un mao poreiro!*" "*Eres*" means "you are," and *mao poreiro*, as José Maria recounted, was the working title assigned in the Middle Ages to the farm hand whose task, in the event of fumbled navigation, was to facilitate the fertilization of the sow by the boar.

The team in Bihac was as eccentric as it was eclectic. It included a Danish judge who produced aquavit and raw herring for the summer solstice; a Finn who maintained the only freshly ironed beret in the Balkans; a Polish colonel whose forte was protocol; an officer of the Polish foreign ministry allegedly sent to spy on the colonel; another Pole, whose preparation for his job as elections officer was a four-year assignment in North Korea; a Russian (the one with the tennis racquet) who, as supply officer, hoarded the supplies; two German Swiss, a French Swiss, and an Italian Swiss (*les Fromages Suisses*); an American who drove a Harley-Davidson and who was regularly and jocularly accused of being with the CIA; our well-organized admin officer; the media officer, another American, who had once worked in Dan Quayle's press office and who published a delightfully satirical underground newspaper. Eventually most people earned nicknames, most of which were affectionately offensive. A young German diplomat was the "Neurotic Teutonic," and a craggy Czech colonel was "Testosterone." Less charitable names were assigned to those who came into our orbit only periodically: a bombastic Italian general became "Il Duce," and a high-ranking Canadian military officer was known as "Half-track." For reasons still unclear, a senior American at headquarters was "Foreskin." One story in the underground newspaper about happenings at headquarters ran with the title "Roll Back Foreskin." The operations centre in Sarajevo, for reasons that I will leave obscure, was called "The Jock Strap"; a Canadian working there was "Cactus Plant." In what began as a playful initiative, but was to prove foolhardy, I gave nicknames in Serbo/Croat to a few of my locally engaged friends. I was soon rewarded with my own tag, "*Veliki Magaratz*" (Big Donkey). Although our group in Bihac sometimes resembled the cast of a Monty Python film, most of the team proved to be very good, and some were quite extraordinary. The internal chemistry was rumbustious.

I ought not to have been surprised, but I learned that in work settings like Bosnia and in other international assignments you are much more exposed to the colour and texture of national idiosyncrasies than you are in the more cocooned platform of an embassy – and, of course, the local population is more exposed to yours.

The elections of 1996 and 1997 have been described as the most complicated ever supervised by an international organization, in large part because of the massive displacement of citizens. The process was girdled with safeguards against fraud, but our design proved excessively complex. In the end, parts of it were almost incomprehensible, especially for those Hungarian, Lithuanian, Kyrgyz, Romanian, and Bulgarian polling station supervisors whose English (the OSCE official language) was mediocre.

A major challenge for Bosnia was the determination of priorities, and thus of the expenditure of energies and money. And a key issue was the skewing of these priorities. Our OSCE mandate encompassed human rights, structural democratization, and media development as well as elections. The local people had other requirements: economic rehabilitation, jobs, water, sewage, rebuilding schools, and repairing hospitals. But elections were the centrepiece, and were driven by a different agenda. They were a fundamental part of Dayton, but they had also become the exit strategy for the United States.

The elections in 1996 and again in 1997 were compressed into unrealistic time frames by Washington's concern for American political realities. The United States had originally committed itself to withdrawing its military forces in December 1996, but President Clinton's advisors insisted that they be withdrawn before the US elections in November. As the US military presence was essential in order to provide a secure environment for the Bosnian elections, this election date had to be scheduled well prior to US withdrawal. Many of us considered this timing counterintuitive. There was only the thinnest of scabs over the war wounds, and real anxiety that premature elections would reopen them. The 1996 elections were intended to legitimize the constitutions of the two entities set up under Dayton (Bosnia and the Serb Republic), facilitate the reintegration of peoples, and democratize. They did legitimize constitutions, but in both entities they also consolidated the power of ruling parties that were not only inclined to authoritarianism, but also gang-infested. Reintegration did not occur, ethnic cleansing continued, albeit in less violent form, and, faced with these realities, American military withdrawal was delayed.

There were other reasons for anxiety about the time frame. We were dealing with governments that were not only concerned with different priorities and had no real interest in accommodating a multi-party system, or such other basic conditions of a democratic society as freedom of the press, freedom of assembly, and freedom of movement. These were governments with no tradition of democracy and little interest in democratic norms except in so far as elections served to reinforce their authority. In every case the ruling parties saw themselves as representing a special trust to defend territory, religion, culture, and the memories of those who had given their lives in the same sacred cause. The guns had been silent for only a few months, and the bitterness of conflict was still fresh, so this was a powerful point of view. When they said, "Anyone who is not with us is against us," we did not accept their point of view, but we could understand it.

Astonishingly, the 1996 elections passed peacefully. No one was killed. No polling stations were burned down. There was fraud, some of it in our area, but not much. And all this less than a year after the cessation of hostilities. "Why?" we asked ourselves. One reason was that the local election officers had worked more conscientiously than we had expected. A second was that our preparations had been effective. And third, we had excellent logistics support from the Canadian forces based in our area. But

Graham and ex–Soviet T-55 tank.

as we began to fill our glasses we realized that a key reason had nothing to do with our work. The election would not have been successful without the willing and highly motivated co-operation of the ruling parties. In the end, they ensured that electoral workers were able to do their job. They obtained their objective of legitimizing and consolidating their ethnically based political systems. In other words, this was a success for the process, but not for democracy.

On the eve of the elections I was interviewed in Bihac on what I was assured was a background-only basis by a *Globe and Mail* reporter. The following morning my remark that "the elections in Bosnia were like the game *Snakes and Ladders*, but with more snakes than ladders" was the "Quote of the Day," a feature of the *Globe* at that time. My colleagues in Bihac were pleased. Sarajevo was not.

By the end of September 1997 many of us were feeling jaded and troubled about the disproportionate priority accorded elections at the expense of more basic institution-building activities. Parliamentary elections for the Serb Republic were announced. A repeat round of the 1996 elections for Bosnia and Herzegovina was being planned for 1998. In a dark mood I included the following paragraph as part of my weekly fax to headquarters in Sarajevo: "We move from one election to another. There is a feeling that we are caught on an unstoppable railway – a diabolical machine with no fixed destination that crashes through an ever-thickening jungle of political and technical challenges with a diminishing and exhausted crew. And there is a question about whether the passage of this juggernaut is improving or complicating the political landscape through which it runs." There was no reply.

In the relatively few cases in which the outcome was in doubt, one ethnic group was attempting to retrieve political control of the municipality from which it had been expelled by force. In these electoral contests, "free and fair" had little meaning. Such was the case in Drvar, which was part of my area. The new Croat inhabitants had been displaced from about forty different municipalities, to which in most cases they could not return.

Both the OSCE high command in Sarajevo and the international press concluded that Drvar would be the most combustible part of the country for the two days of elections. Helicopters descended on Drvar. One contained Robert Gelbart, the United States Assistant Secretary of State, who appeared to have been badly briefed. On arrival he strode into the polling station dedicated to Serb voters and harangued the Croat staff for "deliberately delaying" the Serb voting. (A subsequent investigation determined that there had been no significant or orchestrated delay.) He was joined by a gaggle of VIPs and a British major general, whose bodyguards clattered into the polling station carrying their automatic weapons and tried to set up a satellite telephone between two ballot boxes. Gelbart's personal bodyguard, dressed in civilian clothes and carrying a submachine gun, stood watch in front of the door to the polling station. The young Hungarian election supervisor protested that guns were specifically prohibited from polling stations, but was rebuked by the general. The Serb voters, many of whom had fraudulent papers, were confused and irritated by the uproar. The Croat-staffed polling station committee was threatening: "You push us, then you run the polling stations. We will go home." A crisis was building.

Meanwhile, about three hundred yards away, Colonel Grant, the commander of the Canadian Battle Group, and I were trying to land in a helicopter, but couldn't set down because the landing area was already crowded with helicopters. We hovered, the downdraft from our machine

VELIKA KLADUSA — ZAGREB ↑ — BELGRADE →

CROATIA

CROATIA

CAZIN

BIHAC

REPUBLIKA SRPSKA (R.S.)

· KULAN VAKUF

BANJA LUKA

BOSNIA HERZEGOVINA

BRUTANAC
SREBRENICA

R.S.

LI VIVO

SARAJEVO

FEDERACIA BOSNA
I HERCEGOVINA

SPLIT

ADRIATIC SEA

R.S.

SERBIA

MONTENEGRO

200 Km

DUBROVNIK

⫽ BOSNIAN FEDERATION
☰ REPUBLICA SRPSKA R.S.

stripping plums off the orchard below, until one helicopter was moved. The rest of the day and a good part of the night were devoted to damage control and the negotiation of another polling station for the Serbs. This was tough, because the Croats knew that an extra polling station made it that much more likely that they would lose the municipality.

Elsewhere in the town, the Canadian military were containing a volatile situation, setting up extra polling stations, feeding and comforting ten busloads of Serbs who were spending the night in a parking area above the town, and, not least, calming the British general.

On the second day my team and I woke up in Canadian army tents to heavy rain. It was unusually – and blessedly – heavy, and lasted all day. The rain reduced interethnic collision in Drvar. It also stopped the return of the helicopters and their passengers. In the end there were no fatalities, and the Serbs had the opportunity to vote, or to try to vote (some were seen by my staff forging documents). But enough had voted, and the

Croats lost Drvar to the Serbs. Across the country the OSCE-imposed elections led to some "returns," but by and large Bosnia remained a frozen ethnic checkerboard.

It goes without saying that a vital ingredient for international effectiveness in war-torn societies is good co-ordination among the international players under sound leadership. In 1996 and 1997 this ingredient was not in place in Bosnia. Instead, the international presence was often characterized by turf battles, personality conflicts, and lop-sided competition between Bosnian needs and the political agendas of Russia, France, and the United States. Abrasions at the centre were frequently reproduced in the field, with the inevitable result that they diminished the already tarnished credibility and leverage of the international community.

There were many areas of controversy. One was the United States Train and Equip program. Mutual deterrence was part of the Dayton strategy. This involved efforts to build up Croat, and particularly Muslim, weaponry, skills, and military organization so that the previously superior Serb army, with its competent former Yugoslav officers, no longer threatened. In conversation with a Train and Equip officer just before I left Bihac, I enquired about his current task.

"Well," he replied, "we're teaching the Bosnian army how to shoot straight."

"Why would you want to do that?"

"For Christ's sake," he retorted, "haven't you seen the walls of the buildings around here? They look like Swiss cheese. Ninety-nine percent of the shooting is off-target."

"Yes," I said. "We should keep it that way."

ॐ ॐ ॐ

Sex, Sports, and Diplomacy

Working in immediate post-war Bosnia was gruelling, but we also frequently found it eccentrically comical, because so much of the learning experience involved cultural collision – and the need for more humility than most of us possessed.

Halid Lipovac, the mayor of Cazin, a Muslim town in northwest Bosnia, and Fikret Dragonovic, his deputy, looked uneasily at their dinner guests: a Polish colonel, a Swiss human rights officer, an American advisor, two interpreters, and myself. Cazin was frowzy and war-torn, its appearance only partially relieved by an old Ottoman fortress built on an escarpment at the edge of town.

A round of *losa*, a semi-lethal local beverage that resembles slivovitz, had not softened the brittle atmosphere as both sides groped for common ground. I don't suppose that the decor of the municipally-owned hotel – dark wood, poor lighting, and cherry-velvet upholstery – was much help. Most of the broken glass had been replaced, but some window frames were still sheathed in plastic. The war had stopped only five months before, and there hadn't been time to cover up all the ravages of Serb mortar and rocket fire. This was a duty occasion for both sides, and none of us was looking forward to a collision of cultures.

Another round of *losa* appeared. Dragonovic reached for his glass, stood, lifted his beaky nose, and intoned the Bosnian toast: "*Zvilili.*"

"Gentlemen," he said, ignoring the interpreters, "I propose tonight that there should be two topics of conversation: sex and sports." He was trying to break the ice.

Throwing non-sexism to the winds and attempting to bring to a close the lengthening silence that followed the translation of this initiative, I said, "*Gospodin* [Mister] Dragonovic, you said that there should be two topics, but you have mentioned only one." When this was translated, the Bosnian side actually beamed. Our side was not expecting this agenda in a rustic Muslim corner of Bosnia, but now that the conversation had been propelled downward, it gathered momentum.

The diners were wrapped in smog. I had brought cigars, good hand-made Dominican coronas. The Bosnians only knew thin black cheroots. The mayor was enchanted, and intended to cut his cigar into pieces to share with his friends, but Dragonovic insisted on smoking his. There was no cigar cutter, so I demonstrated that the tip could be cut by using one's teeth. Dragonovic chomped deeply, removing almost an inch of cigar, and the rest started to unravel in his mouth.

Spewing shards of tobacco leaf and puffing deeply, Dragonovic told dirty jokes. Invariably they featured the respective taboos of Bosnian mullahs and Croatian bishops: pigs and girls.[1] Unfortunately, etiquette called for reciprocity, and it was soon clear that on our side I was the only one with a supply of moderately obscene stories. I responded with a story about crazed parrots and prostitutes. Dimly recalling a historical Bosnian animosity toward Rumanians, for my second story I substituted Ceauşescu for Fidel Castro.

This demented cultural interchange was beginning to work. The *losa* was also playing its intended role. But the key to success was more the quality of the translations than the quality of shaggy parrot stories. Zena, one of our two interpreters, was in shock, so translation in both directions fell on my assistant, Maryanne Rukavina. Maryanne, Croatian-born but raised in Chicago, gave an eighties punk rock dimension to the evening. She was twenty-three and attractive, with short, black hair. Because the hotel had no heating, she had zipped up her black leather jacket, so not one of the estimated five tattoos on her body was visible. However, her rings were. She had six in her left ear lobe and two in her right, and a turquoise stone was set in one nostril. Black leather boots completed the ensemble. However, she managed to look slightly less raffish than Dragonovic, who was wearing a baggy double-breasted suit in garbage-bag green. Maryanne was splendid. She carried all of the indelicacies with seamless aplomb.

Maryanne had come to Bosnia during the war, and worked for eighteen months in a clinic for women who had been raped when armies swept over towns and villages. At the war's end she applied for a job with the Canadian Army near Bihac, but because her appearance was too exuberantly nonconformist for the Canadian Army, she was hired instead by the OSCE in Bihac.

Midmorning, two days later, Maryanne and I were sipping bad Turkish coffee with her friend Adita in Bozanki Petrovac, another small town. The rough tablecloth was speckled with mould, and the mould fit with the devastation of the town, and with the tank tracks imprinted in the asphalt beside us. The April sun, dappling through the chestnuts overhead, was just warm enough to allow us to sit outside. As usual, the customers were nearly all men. They were drinking coffee or beer and they were all smoking, mostly the foul and cheap local *Drina* cigarettes. Beer is two German marks; coffee, one. Where did they get the money, in a town where unemployment is at least 80 percent?[2]

The three of us had just had a disagreeable meeting with the mayor. We had failed to obtain his agreement to establish a non-partisan local election commission. I was berated for representing an organization that was ignorant of his community's history, insensitive to its needs, and too close to its enemies.

As we stirred the thick coffee, Adita, who lives in Bosanski Petrovac, said to me, "You should not be upset. Poric (the mayor) is a fool, but there is reason for his anger."

"You mean that he blames us for not stopping the Serbs?" (Unlike Cazin, Bosanski Petrovac was overrun by the Serbs.)

"Yes, but that's only part of it. You and the OSCE come here to tell him that he must spend time and money on electoral organization. What would you do in his shoes? There are no jobs, half the roof is missing from the school, the factories are in ruins – and you've seen the shambles at the hospital. If we're lucky there's electricity three hours a day, and water is not much better. Only half the remaining houses in this town have been repaired enough for people to live in them. What would your priorities be? And besides, what does he want elections for? Do you really think he believes in democracy, or the rights of an opposition he despises? Another mass grave was found on the road to Sanski Most just last week – and there will be more. The Muslims in this town – and now there are only Muslims – don't want to hear about reconciliation."

Adita was bright and she spoke her mind. Some of the premises I had brought with me from Ottawa were lying smashed at my feet. Adita was doing a good job. Before the war her town had been 40 percent Serb, and during the Serb occupation it had been almost 100 percent Serb. Now, with the exception of a few elderly people, there were no Serbs at all.

"Adita, what happened when the Serb militia came to put you in trucks? Weren't there some friends and neighbours or Serb leaders in the community who tried to prevent it? It's hard to believe that the hundreds of people you've lived in peace with would all turn against you."

"No, they weren't all like that. But there were some horrible surprises. People you trusted, people whose children you'd looked after. But you're right. There were some who didn't like what was happening."

"What did they do?"

"They did nothing."

"Couldn't they have said something?"

"No. It's very simple. Their own people would have killed them."

This is what they believed. It is not necessarily what would have happened.

The Psychologist, the General, and the Beauty Contest

This is another story about cultural collision that descends, as most of them do, into black humour.

"You are a strange person." The remark was addressed to me by Drojic, the gaunt, sour, grey-faced chief of protocol, who was filling in during the unexplained absence of the mayor of Sanski Most. Jasmin, the interpreter for our Sanski Most Field Office, was embarrassed. His hands and eyes appealed to Drojic to offer alternative language, but Drojic was already looking forward to telling the mayor and his chums how he had told the foreign intruders to stuff it. He would have been dismayed to learn that Jasmin, as he told us later, had blunted the sharpest barbs.

"Why are you in this office? Why is your organization in this country?" Drojic snapped. "We, the Bosnians, drove the Serbs out of this town six months ago. Not only did you not help us, you stopped us from recapturing the towns in the north – Priejedor, Banja Luka – and that's where Muslim families have lived for centuries." There were elements of both truth and fiction in this statement – mostly truth. It was a swamp to stay away from, and soft soap wasn't going to get us anywhere.

"*Gospodin* Drojic, I am here because your president, Alija Izetbegovic, signed an agreement in Dayton. He and the other presidents [of Serbia and Croatia] agreed that IFOR [the Implementation Force] troops would come and enforce the peace, and that the OSCE, my organization, would be responsible for human rights, elections, and political stabilization. That means that when you and your mayor threaten to evict the leader of the opposition party, one of the very few people in this community prepared to oppose your party, you are violating the rules that your president agreed to. We are not here because talking to you is fun."

"Hah, you are mistaken." Drojic glared at us across the drab, unheated meeting room, then continued, "The reasons have nothing to do with politics." He paused.

"And the reasons are?"

Drojic stiffened. "In this municipality, 4,613 houses and apartment buildings were destroyed. Another 10,000 were badly damaged. Returning residents and refugees were assigned houses according to family size. Bobic [the evicted opposition leader] was given an apartment with two rooms. This was a mistake. He was not entitled to two rooms."

"That was three months ago. Why wasn't he told immediately that a mistake had been made and assigned another apartment?"

"It was the hospital where he works. They own the apartment. He's a psychologist. Maybe they didn't tell him."

"But now that he is working for the opposition, you're telling him?"

Only slightly nettled, Drojic replied, "Muslim families are coming from a refugee camp in Croatia. Where do we put them? Is the OSCE helping? As usual, not at all. Besides, Bobic is an inappropriate person."

"Inappropriate?"

"Yes. The neighbours complain about drinking parties, too much noise, unorthodox clothes – and girls."

"Girls?"

"The place was a brothel."

If even some of these accusations were true, Bobic was beginning to sound like the best thing that had happened to grim, depressing Sanski Most since the liberation. At this moment the door opened and General Alegic, the mayor, appeared. Puffy-lipped, baggy-eyed, with a six-day beard, Alegic was a seedier, slightly beefier Yasser Arafat look-alike. We were invited into his office. It had heat and a military decor: a mounted Kalashnikov and a shelf lined with mortar shells. He distributed plasticized bilingual business cards that describe him not as mayor, but as "Chief" of Sanski Most. The former commander of an army corps, and still a warlord, he wore his power, his avarice, and his dirty deals with a rough effervescence.

This was not my first meeting with Alegic. His conversation, like that of his assistant Drojic, was spiked with accusations about the incompetence or indolence of the OSCE. However, unlike the sparring with Drojic, the exchange of insults that had begun between Alegic and me was for reciprocal entertainment.

Drojic and I gave short summaries of our respective positions. I informed the general that the blatant, politically motivated eviction of the only significant opposition leader in the municipality would bring him grief. He would be subject to sanctions by the OSCE electoral tribunal that could cost him money or some of his authority or both. Finally, I reminded him that Sanski Most needed money from the international community.

The general pushed out his bottom lip. "Once again you have come to make my people nervous. Look what you have done to Drojic."

"General," I replied, "if we didn't come, citizens of this town would not dare to vote against you."

Alegic favoured me with a toothy smile. "Vote against me? The people like me. They like the party."

The meeting concluded with the general saying that he would consider the eviction decision. A week later we learned that the notice had been withdrawn – a small victory, probably a temporary one, and a loss of face for Drojic.

An Improbable Celebration

My colleague Luke and I celebrate by attending the cantonal beauty contest. We can't believe that in tired, battered, conservative, Muslim Bihac they are actually holding a beauty contest. Luke is the former intern in Dan Quayle's press office, mentioned earlier, the editor-in-chief of our satirical and highly libellous underground newspaper, and the OSCE's Bihac press officer.

It is pouring with rain, but we are overcome with curiosity, and with my Venezuelan beauty contest credentials I regard myself as an authority in this area. We join about four thousand people jammed into the town arena. The shell holes in the roof have recently been repaired, so most of the rain is kept out. Almost everyone appears to be under the age of twenty-three. Roughly 3,750 are smoking. There is a wall of smoke through which violet shafts of light are gyrating. The whole place throbs with acoustically defective, hyper-amplified heavy metal. The audience claps and screams. We have never seen such enthusiasm in six months in Bosnia. Maybe, although this seems very unlikely, the contestants are performing a Balkan version of *Carmina Burana*. From the back of the arena who can tell? Smoke has made the stage invisible. We climb to a narrow catwalk that hugs the wall near the ceiling and extends over one side of the stage, which is now more or less visible. We can see the contestants dancing. They are wearing identical tubular pant suits cunningly designed to eliminate any pectoral outline. In Venezuela, the crowd would howl with rage. This crowd is berserk with joyful abandon. There has been nothing like this evening for three long, bloody years of siege. The war is over. This is catharsis.

~ ~ ~

More Generals and the Ice Cream Men

Bosnia at this time was characterized by mismatched encounters between occasionally earnest, usually cynical, sometimes corrupt internationals and frequently depressed, equally cynical, often corrupt locals. There was a generous sprinkling of decency on both sides, but, like Haiti, it was a place more imprisoned than enriched by its history.

I wake to the sound of Kalashnikovs. The deeper crumps are hand grenades being thrown in the river. The reason for the explosions – or part of the reason; nearly everyone in Bihac has a gun and likes to shoot—is the Muslim festival of *Bajram. Bajram* also explains the freshly skinned sheep hanging in the fork of my neighbour's tree. Traditionally, the sheep are roasted on a spit over a wood fire. This is just as well, as there is no electricity. Snow in the mountains has knocked out the power line from Croatia. No electricity also means no water, because the pumps have stopped. Breakfast is all right. I cook it on a gas stove and heat up some of our emergency water for a bird bath.

Outside, the rain is falling on last night's snow. I have been a month in this remote corner of Bosnia and each day brings a fresh variation on the theme of pathological intolerance. This day is no different. Haris, the driver, Maryanne, the interpreter, and I head southeast for a meeting in Drvar with the "Ice Cream Men." The Ice Cream Men were the monitors of the war, and now of the peace. They are mostly retired military officers and were appointed by the European Union Commission. They have a longer title, but everyone calls them the Ice Cream Men because they are dressed in white from head to toe. This is to identify them as visibly neutral, making them less likely to be shot at.

We are going to a different corner of Bosnia, but there is the same mix of grandeur and horror in the landscape as I saw on the first drive in from Sarajevo. This time there are towering cliffs, crags, long open valleys, and an abundance of rock. One of the first phrases I learned was *"mnogo kamen"* – "lots of rock." From a distance, the villages of grey fieldstone clustered on the lower slopes fit perfectly into this wintry splendour. Closer, it's clear that everything has been disfigured by war. Mile after mile of destroyed and abandoned villages and farmhouses. Broken roofing tile provides a few filaments of colour. Most of the houses were deliberately burned or dynamited by one or other of the retreating armies – or else by the owners themselves, determined to leave nothing to the enemy. In this sector it was the Serbs who were the most thorough practitioners of scorched earth. Most of what remained was looted. The looters left pathetic piles of rubble: sinks, bed springs, a man's jacket, a child's bicycle, and, curiously, a pair of yellow plastic ski boots. I approach for a closer look. "Stop!" Haris shouts. Until recently he was a Bosnian soldier. "Don't go near them. Serbs leave booby traps – and you never know where they have planted their mines."

It's easy to tell when you are entering a front line area. The forest, when there is one, is shattered: trunks and branches have been hacked away by shell and rocket fire. This battlefield is signposted with old ammunition boxes, shallow trenches, and a burnt-out tank. We climb into a heavily wooded area and then climb down in looping switchbacks until we reach Drvar, once Tito's headquarters. In 1942 and 1943 it was a partisan base and a popular Wehrmacht target. Rebuilt partly as a shrine, it was knocked about again last year. But the setting is unchanged. Flooded fields around the town perimeter reflect the snow-covered Dinara Alps. The sun flashes briefly from behind the clouds.

Dieter and Trevor, the Ice Cream Men, take us to meet Father Topic, the Catholic priest. Topic is a Croat, a refugee from Serb expulsion. He serves a community that is almost entirely Croat and that occupies the patched-up homes and apartments that still legally belonged to the Serbs until they were driven out five months before.

Topic is depressed by his parishioners. "Most of them don't want to work. A man summed it up yesterday. He said to me, 'Why should I work in the fields? When the crop is ready the Serbs will come back and take it.'"

"They don't believe that reconciliation is possible?" I ask.

Topic's exasperation is masked by fatigue. "No. Any talk of reconciliation frightens them. You must understand, everyone in Drvar is a refugee. Most lost their homes four years ago. They move to another town, it's attacked, and they move on again – or they're ordered to leave by their own army. Drvar is a Serb town, it's not home to the Croats. But they're tired."

"What about the UN and the humanitarian organizations? Do they motivate the people to work?"

"No," says Topic. "They hand out food and some money – and that's part of the problem. Of course, at the beginning we couldn't survive without them, but now the incentive is gone. Most of them won't work if they don't have to."

The next day is bright, but colder, and despite layers of sweaters, pyjamas, and socks, I am still chilled in my unheated bedroom. The ceramic stove downstairs radiates heat in a two-metre arc. Its best feature, probably its only redeeming feature, is ornamental. The electricity and the water are still off, and I am adjusting to last night's adventures at the wildly misnamed Tropicana Restaurant, where I was kissed by an unknown war veteran. My colleagues at the table, who were not kissed, laughed hysterically. He was a friendly drunk showing his affection in the traditional way. Unfortunately, this is the second such occurrence in two weeks. The first involved a fiddle player for the Tamborski Orkestra, also drunk and also unshaven. Heidi, a blonde, red-cheeked Austrian, smiles at the unshaven part. "Now you know what it's like." She is genial and a determined feminist, allegedly on her second volume of recorded sexist remarks by the male international staff.

A week later the Polish colonel, Aryana, the colonel's interpreter, a Swedish major, and I set off at eight o'clock in the comfort of a warm Volkswagen. A snow-covered mountain road takes us to Kolin Vakuf, a battered but still attractive village overlooked by a huge Turkish fortress. Two semi-hostile armies, one Croat, the other Bosnian Muslim, face each other across the swollen Una River. Disagreement about which army should control the village is festering dangerously. A meeting has been called to find a solution. Four generals and the OSCE have been invited. The Muslim general is Atif Dudakovic, a local war hero. He wears a permanent pit-bull expression and has an ego the size of the mountain behind us. The Croat is Mirko Glasnovic – more subdued, but also with an impressive war record. A Canadian citizen, Glasnovic is a former sergeant in the French Foreign Legion and before that a sergeant in the Princess Patricia Light Infantry. The others are Major General Kearley, the British divisional commander, and Brigadier General Jeffreys, the Canadian brigade commander. Kearley is backed up by five tanks and infantry, Jeffreys by three armoured personnel carriers.

The Polish colonel, the Swedish major, and I are witnesses to the negotiations, not participants. We stand shuffling in the cold, waiting for things to start. Sentries are warming themselves by a wood-fired iron brazier. The scene is beginning to look staged, like a set from a film about the Russian front in 1943. A British officer invites us into his command post for tea. The tea is English "char" – hot, sweet, premixed in a large aluminum canister, and welcome. The command post is an ancient stone farmhouse. On an inside wall is posted a glossary of useful expressions with their Serbo/Croatian phonetic equivalents. The first is "Ne postazi. Ya sam kiri Britanski" – "Don't shoot. I am a British soldier."

The meeting starts. Krasnovic agrees not to do anything provocative provided Dudakovic does nothing provocative. Dudakovic agrees not to do anything provocative provided that… The tension has dropped, so the meeting is not a total failure.

Back to Bihac through the same wild terrain and bleak desolation. The first time I passed through this ravaged landscape, the horror drove so deep inside that I thought it would never leave. After a month the dull, sick feeling was still there, but less intense, as if some sort of neurological insulation had lacquered my antennae.

Back in Bihac that evening there was an invitation to meet with an international group of Bosnia watchers at the Pink Flamingo Disco. Jean-Pierre, another Ice Cream Man, offered to drive, but didn't know the location of the club. Our administrator, Christian, one of the Swiss fromages, supplied what proved to be hopeless directions. Bihac is not that large, but we drove all over town, stopping periodically so that I could get out of the huge white armoured Mercedes to ask directions in my almost non-existent Bosnian. The drive gave us a chance to talk. I told Jean-Pierre I was puzzled by what seemed to be a frosty relationship between Trevor and Dieter, who were supposed to be working as a team. "Well," said Jean-Pierre, "that's because they are still fighting the Second World War. Both are too young to be veterans, but Trevor was a lieutenant colonel in the

British Army and Dieter a major in the German Air Force. They get prickly about history."

Finally we found the Pink Flamingo. The place was jammed with young people, mostly men, some on crutches, and most of them recently demobilized soldiers. They sat or stood with their beers and cigarettes, glancing morosely at the dancers through the thick smoke. In most cases these were women dancing with other women.

Aladin, one of our local staff, was nearby. Over the din I shouted to him, "Why are the men more interested in beer than girls?"

Aladin paused. "It's hard to say. But people don't have jobs. Things are tough. Sometimes they commit suicide, occasionally with hand grenades, in places like this."

"Is that why there's usually a curfew?"

"Maybe. Two nights ago the bouncer here shot a customer, a soldier who'd tried to pull a gun on him. Lots of blood. The soldier was OK."

Three months later the Polish colonel, Maryanne, and I entertained General Dudakovic for lunch at Gurman's, Bihac's least bad restaurant. It was a warm day and the owner had set the table on the terrace at the edge of the Una River. Dudakovic arrived accompanied by a brigadier and a colonel. His bodyguard patrolled nearby and his chauffeur sat in a new Mercedes 300. At our suggestion the general ordered the food, a ventricle-clogging succession of local dishes: soup with bits of mutton, *Bosanski lomax* (a heavy local stew consisting of steak, mutton, turnip, and other root vegetables, and garnished with pickled cabbage), and fruitcake compote. This was served with local beer and Dalmatian wine.

After several months I was getting to know the general, in part by direct contact and otherwise through second-hand accounts. Trevor had told me one fragment of the story. He and others were trading war stories with the general when someone spoke of the famous meeting in no man's land in 1915 when soldiers from both sides stopped shooting and exchanged Christmas greetings. Dudavokic then recounted what he described as a similar experience. It was the last month of the recent war, and the general's army was advancing across Serb lines. Dudakovic was at a forward command post when he was greeted by a bewildered soldier. The general recognized the Serb uniform, but the Serb, assuming he was addressing a compatriot, asked what route he should take to get back to his unit.

"What happened?" asked Trevor.

"I shot him," replied the general.

Dudakovic was in his usual ebullient and pugnacious good humour – and we had to take him seriously. At this time he was one of the most influential and potentially dangerous players in northwest Bosnia. He was also the most successful, most enterprising, and without doubt most courageous general in the Bosnian army. The survival of Bihac against vastly superior Serb, Croat, and rebel Muslim forces was largely due to his leadership. Between mouthfuls he told war stories. The one I recall most clearly concerned his attempted entrapment of an opposing army by pretending that Bihac had been captured by units of the rebel Muslim army. He organized the townspeople to celebrate their "liberation" by shouting in the streets.

"We fooled some of them, but before we could suck them all into the trap they smelled a rat. And do you know where I got this idea?" he asked.

None of us ventured a guess.

"From the English film *The Eagle Has Landed.*"

Conversation was moving easily when I made the mistake of shifting it to economic subjects. The general's eyes glazed over, and the brigadier intervened to provide useless information about a recycled five-year plan. The subject was dropped, glasses were refilled, and Dudakovic put down his knife and fork.

"I am going to tell you something that I have told no one else in the international community," he said, moving his eyes slowly around the table. We were accustomed to his theatrics, but he had our attention. "The Muslim rebels, under their leader Fikret Abdic, are planning an operation in the area of their former headquarters in Velika Kladusa. This is extremely serious, and I must take pre-emptive action to prevent a disaster."

"But…," the Polish colonel interjected.

"I know, I know. Any armed operation on my part would be in direct violation of the Dayton Agreement. But what else should I do? What would you do in my position – if you had to decide between respect for an agreement made in Ohio or the defence of your own șoil, for which thousands of your comrades have given their blood?"

"General," I said, "you wouldn't be telling us this if you didn't want us to do something. If we are to do anything, we will have to know more

about this crisis. Until now, we have heard nothing about a potential attack by the rebels. What evidence do you have?"

"Of course, we have evidence – but you will understand that the sources are very confidential."

"General, unless you can persuade us that the threat is real, we are going to be skeptical. You must know that because you have given us this information we must speak to General Couture or General Kearley. They are going to be suspicious." General Couture was the Canadian brigadier general in Coralici, which was nearby, and General Kearley was the British major general in Banja Luka.

"Yes," said Dudakovic. He was not pleased when the conversation took this turn, but neither was he surprised. "I can tell you that my people have detected large-scale smuggling of arms into the Velika Kladusa/Cazin axis over the past week. Of course, the arms come from across the Croatian border. Tudjman knows about this." Tudjman was the president of Croatia and one of the sinister players in the Bosnian war.

"Can you identify the location of the arms caches? This is an IFOR job." IFOR was the NATO-led multinational peacekeeping force.

"Look, I can take you to my camp at Cazin. Last night a military bus was ambushed on the road toward Buzim. There are twenty-two bullet holes in the bus, which is now at the camp."

That evening we sat down to another meal of supercharged cholesterol, this time with Christian Couture, the Canadian brigadier. He was unaware of the crisis, had no information about accelerated smuggling, wondered about whose bullets had made holes in the bus, and shared our skepticism. He also deployed armoured personnel carriers on the access roads to the camp where Dudakovic's army was quartered. The Bosnian forces far outnumbered the Canadian, but Dudakovic knew better than to spring Couture's tripwire.

∾ ∾ ∾

The Road to Srebrenica

In early September 1998 I returned to Bosnia to supervise another set of elections for the OSCE. Although I did not learn about my assignment until I reached Sarajevo, my final destination was Srebrenica, and it may be inappropriate that the first stages of a roundabout journey to that dark place should be tales of whimsy. However, they loosely fit the pattern of this book.

I had not expected to reach Bosnia via Rome. The usual route from Canada in 1998 was through Frankfurt to Zagreb and then into Bosnia by car or bus. But that was with Air Canada, and Air Canada was on strike. There were about a thousand people, or so it seemed, lined up at the gate in Pearson Airport waiting to board a 747 that was wearing a giant wristwatch whose strap was buckled over the forward hump of the aircraft. It should have been an advertisement for Brunswick Sardines, not Bulgari timepieces. However, the Alitalia schedule offered an eight-hour stopover in Rome before my evening flight to Split on the Dalmatian coast, time enough, I thought, to renew an old acquaintance with a beautiful city. I was on my way to take part in what proved to be another counterproductive election organized by the OSCE. An excursion in Rome struck me as therapeutic preparation for post-war Bosnia.

But what to do in the few hours available? I settled on three objectives: a city tour, lunch in a Roman restaurant, and an Italian haircut. Each goal was accomplished, but not as planned. From Leonardo da Vinci Airport an express train whisked me into the central railway terminal, where I had been told I would find tour buses. After a half-hour search I found that one tour bus had moved its starting point to a new and unadvertised location. I was guided to a different tour company, but its bus had engine trouble. I boarded an imitation trolley belonging to a third company, only to be told to get off, because it wasn't taking passengers.

Time was passing and it was very hot. "To hell with a tour," I muttered. I would get a haircut. It was Monday, and I soon discovered that Italian barbers don't work on Mondays. The only possibility might be the railway station. I walked back and found a sign featuring scissors and a comb. The arrow pointed down. At the bottom of the staircase was a long, dimly lit tunnel that ran under the tracks. Beyond another arrow was a small shop with "*Pelecuria*" on the door. Inside it contained the absolute minimum of furnishings and a small, ancient Roman with a white smock and a mournful moustache. He looked 105 and embalmed.

"*Buon giorno*," I said cheerily. No reply. He motioned me to sit. Pointing at my head, I said, in what I thought might be Italian, "*Normale*." Through a long session in which he said not a word, I began to worry less about my hair and more about what a straight razor would do in his trembling hands. I survived, but not much hair did. I emerged in the sweltering heat looking like an elderly marine recruit.

Still no buses. Fed up, I took a taxi to the Trevi Fountain. It sounded cool, and the sculpture is magnificent. However, the fountain and the sculpture were almost completely screened by a thick ring of tourists. Perspiring and tired, I was beginning to think that the Visigoths who had sacked the city in the fifth century had been misrepresented by revisionist historians.

I lunched in a trattoria. The pasta was a skimpy *puttanesca* and ridiculously expensive. Muttering darkly to myself and walking away from the trattoria, I spotted a sign that read, in English, "Scooters for Rent." Inside the shop I was cheerfully received. They would certainly rent me a scooter.

"What about a licence?" I asked.

"Licence, *signore*? Forget it – no licence required."

"And a helmet?"

"Don't worry. Yes, there is helmet law, but is not enforced."

"OK, but would you rent a scooter in this town to someone who has never driven one before?"

"*Non c'è problema.*"

I wasn't sure, so I took a test run on the cobbled lane outside the shop. The machine was amazingly basic: accelerator, brake, turning signals, and horn; no gears. Very slowly I set out into the afternoon traffic, nervous and awkward, like someone doing a practice run for the film *Roman Holiday*. Herds of scooters whizzed past. From the narrow Via del Lucchesi I turned left onto Via del Corso – the Pantheon on my right, through the Piazza Venezia, the blinding white monument to King Victor Emmanuel on my left and the Forum behind it. I swung right, by the Theatre of Marcus Claudius Marcellus, onto the west bank of the Tiber. Past the tomb of Tiberius and the mausoleum of Marcellus's uncle, Augustus. Sightseeing at twenty kilometres per hour and watching out for the gyrations of Roman drivers was nerve-racking, but I was beginning to enjoy it. The wind in my face was cool and no one had sworn at me.

Back at the shop the manager was renting a scooter to an American couple as I came up. "How did it go?" he asked.

"Great. I hit one Fiat, one Ferrari, and one Cardinal." I was treated to a tired smile.

It was early evening when I arrived at the hotel in Split – and there were complications. To save money the OSCE had assigned two persons to each room. This would have been all right if there had been two keys, but my unknown companion had the only key, and he was asleep in the room. His routing, from Vancouver via Frankfurt, had delivered him to the hotel that afternoon. Bushed with jet lag, he had gone straight to bed. Repeated loud knocking eventually produced the sound of muffled cursing, and a dazed and dyspeptic gentleman, even older than me, opened the door. Still grumbling, he went back to bed while I unpacked. I removed my breakables, starting with a duty-free bottle of gin. "Hmph," said Phil Shirer, a distinguished labour lawyer from Vancouver. "I have one of those." Next came an airline-size bottle of dry vermouth. "Hmm," he mumbled, evincing more interest. Finally, I drew from my luggage a small jar of picked onions. "My God!" said Phil, getting out of bed and shaking my hand. Martinis were prepared and the old curmudgeon and I bonded.

The next day Phil and I were in the much shot-up Holiday Inn in Sarajevo serving martinis to a small group of friends, most of them from my previous incarnation in Bosnia. These reunions invariably generated a stream of anecdotes. The most curious story that evening was told by Luke, a good friend and colleague from Bihac – and the recipient of my Mickey Mouse watch when he was transferred to OSCE headquarters in Sarajevo: I thought that in times of need it would help him with perspective, as it had for me. The story was set in Bihac during the Bosnian war. Luke had only recently heard it from a Bosnian friend who had been trapped in that town throughout the siege. He began, "You fellows know about the Bangladeshi battalion in Bihac during the war?"

"Sure," said Soren, a Danish judge and my apartment mate for several months in Bihac. "It was late fall and they were rotated into the so-called UN Safe Zone still wearing tropical uniforms. They were hustled into Bihac because the French had withdrawn ahead of schedule. Their supply ship hadn't arrived and the UN logistics people in Zagreb had neglected to get them warm clothes. They would have frozen if the citizens of Bihac hadn't taken pity and loaned them overcoats and sweaters."

Goran, a Croatian friend, added, "Many of them had to share crummy East German Army sleeping bags."

"That's right," said Luke, "and it does involve the same idiots in Logistics. But that's not the story. Sometime in February they sent in five thousand field rations of freeze-dried pork stew. As good Muslims, the Bangladeshi soldiers wouldn't touch the stuff. As you know, Bihac is largely Muslim, but most of them were less strict, and all of them were very hungry. So what happens? Inevitably, the people in Bihac learned about the shemozzle. It didn't look as if the Bangladeshis were going to give away the rations. What was there in bloody, besieged Bihac that a Bangladeshi soldier could possibly want in exchange for a pork stew? And by this time the UN had finally sent in warm clothes. You can imagine all the late-night brainstorming. Cash, of course, was a possibility, but for some reason that wasn't working. The commandant's orders or a code of conduct? Who knows? Finally somebody had a brilliant idea. There were porno films in Bihac. Yeah, a lot of porno films in normally quiet, conservative Bihac.

Next day there were two converging lines of citizens and soldiers – a good outcome for both sides."

"A great story," said Carolyn, an American and another former colleague from Bihac, "but is it true?"

"I can't be certain," replied Luke. "I'm telling it as it was told to me – and knowing Bihac, you have to admit that it's plausible."

"It's true," I said, "at least I think so. And there's more to the story." Luke's account had stirred a memory of a convivial evening the year before in Cazin, a small town near Bihac. The hosts were Matthew, a former British army officer, and Laura, an Italian. Both were working with the OSCE. One of the guests was Indira, a tough, smart, whisky-throated Bosnian who had been the interpreter for Colonel Meunier, a Canadian who commanded the Bangladeshi regiment in Bihac.

"You remember Indira, Colonel Meunier's interpreter? She was there, and she told me that a key player in this saga was a West Indian named Oscar, a civilian working for the UN and, according to Indira, a very cool guy. Oscar buys a TV set and VCR in Zagreb and sets this stuff up with a few chairs in an empty UN container in Bihac. He made a fortune charging the Bangladeshis five Deutschmarks each to watch twenty minutes of their own porn."

Once started there were more Indira stories. Apparently Colonel Meunier had the annoying habit of walking around the perimeter of his base every day with his interpreter, and about one third of this route was visible to Serb snipers in the hills surrounding Bihac. Indira made a point of keeping Meunier between her and the snipers."

Indira had dark-side stories too, and I had made a note of one of them. In February 1995 Jimmy Carter was concluding negotiations with President Karadzic of the Republika Srpska. For once it looked as if there would be a positive outcome. The Serbs had agreed to halt attacks on safe havens such as Bihac, Sarajevo, and Srebrenica. On the day following the day when Carter had understood an agreement would come into effect, a Serb bombardment was launched at Bihac, including cluster bombs in the town centre. These are fragmentation bombs designed not to destroy strategic installations but to penetrate flesh. Colonel Meunier immediately dispatched a message to the office of Akashi, the top UN officer for Bosnia, reporting this violation. Within a few hours a reply was received from the UN headquarters in Zagreb that read, "What is the nationality of the officer reporting this incident?" Inured, or so he thought, to UN casuistry, Meunier was incredulous. The bombardment continued.

When the party was breaking up, Finn, a Norwegian judge, told me that he had arranged to have me observe the elections in Srebrenica, the darkest of all the dark places in Bosnia. Like Bihac and Sarajevo, Srebrenica had been declared a safe zone by the UN early in the war, which meant that its integrity and the safety of non-combatant citizens would be assured by the UN.

The UN's performance at the time of the Bangladeshi farce in the winter of 1994/1995 foreshadowed the much darker tragedy of Srebrenica only a few months later. In Bihac the cumulative impact of dithering by the UN in New York, the pathetic condition of the Bangladeshi troops, and ultimately a UN refusal to allow air strikes against the encroaching Bosnian Serb and rebel Muslim forces brought this city to within a hair's breadth of a bloody collapse. Although NATO urged air strikes, the UN command held back, fearing that aircraft would be lost to Serb surface-to-air missiles (SAMs) allegedly deployed to the region on orders from Belgrade. For the same reason, they suspended airdrops of food and medicine. In the end, although greatly outnumbered, Bihac survived three years of siege. Robust Bosnian Muslim (or Bosniak) military leadership under General Dudakovic held the perimeter until August 1995, when Croatian President Franjo Tudjman finally ordered his army to attack the Serb forces. Tudjman was not responding to UN appeals. He acted because he recognized that Serb control of Bihac would threaten the security of Croatia. By then, almost five thousand lives, mostly non-combatant, had been lost in the Bihac pocket.

The script is chillingly similar, but unlike Bihac and Sarajevo, Srebrenica did not survive. Menaced by encircling Bosnian Serb forces, the commander of the Dutch UN contingent based in Srebrenica appealed for air strikes. Once again NATO officers supported the request, but apart from some minor sorties that were "too little and too late," the request was opposed by senior UN military and civilian officials. They feared that a show of UN strength would provoke attacks on other UN contingents. While it is conceivable that this calculation may have been correct, the result led to the retreat of the Dutch and the massacre of approximately eight thousand unarmed Bosnian men and boys – the worst atrocity in Europe since the Second World War.

Sitting in the war-mottled Holiday Inn sipping martinis, our conversation occasionally slipped away from jocular anecdotes to the dark side. Someone asked, "Is the common perception of UN decency and rational purpose a delusion?" It was a fair question, because our work with the OSCE was profoundly affected by UN decisions. The martini party consensus went something like this: if we set aside failure to act as a consequence of the veto system in the Security Council, the UN is still left with responsibility for colossal preventable tragedies. The worst was the Rwanda genocide, and in the next tier was Srebrenica. With an effort, we widened the context and concluded that, even with ghastly lapses, on balance the UN record is not so bad. But as Carolyn observed, "Cold comfort for the Bosnians."

The next day there was a briefing at OSCE headquarters and I met Belem, a very pleasant young Spanish woman assigned as my partner for the Srebrenica elections. In the afternoon we climbed into our crumbling Opal (the odometer read 369,925 kilometres) and drove from Sarajevo out of the Bosnian entity, now "cleansed" and separated into Bosniak and Catholic Croat enclaves, to the Republika Srpska, equally "cleansed," from all but the Orthodox Serb. Both entities were part of the dysfunctional Federation of Bosnia and Herzegovina. From the border we headed northeast through wooded hill country – not the dramatic landscape of the Bihac and Drvar areas, but disfigured in the same way, with smashed villages and blown-up farms.

The long siege had taken a heavy physical toll on Srebrenica. Artillery and mortar fire had destroyed or damaged 60 percent of the homes and buildings. The city's one hotel was missing windows and most of its plumbing, so most of the international community assigned to Srebrenica was lodged in nearby and less damaged Bratunac. This was convenient, as we were able to commune with the people on arrival. Our quarters were in the Hotel Fontana.

Surprisingly, the most accessible and sociable of the internationals were the IPTF, the International Police Task Force – surprisingly, because the IPTF in many regions of Bosnia had a reputation for insularity and mediocre competence. The officers in Bratunac were French Gendarmes and, almost as surprisingly, their immediate boss was a superintendent from Scotland Yard. Once, after only a few days of acquaintance and with perhaps excessive jocularity, I greeted them with, "*Bonjour, les flics.*"

There was a short silence, and then one replied, "*Non, non, monsieur, nous ne sommes pas les flics. Nous sommes les poulets.*" I was unaware of the Gendarme nickname.

Asked about their professional challenges, they said they were tough. The town was grey, sullen, and depressed. No surprise. Srebrenica had 70 percent unemployment, and agriculture was hazardous, as the fields had been heavily mined. 75 percent of the residents were refugees from their own homes and dependent on foreign handouts. Asked about crime and violence, the superintendent responded that there was a great deal of violence, wife-beating particularly. A Gendarme remarked that it was so common that the men in this region seemed to regard battering their wives as a form of foreplay.

"Can you do anything about it?" I asked.

"No. No woman ever reports it. And it is not just fear. The brutality is accepted. It's part of the culture."

Bratunac lies on the left bank of the Drina, one of the great rivers of the Balkans, which forms the frontier between the Republika Srpska and Serbia. One evening I walked along the road that leads to the bridge linking the two countries. Mist on the river had turned Serbia into a long smudge, and the far end of the bridge was dissolving. I was fishing my camera out of its case to take a picture when I looked up and saw a local policeman rapidly approaching. He pointed sternly at my camera, making it clear that no photographs of strategic installations were permitted. A ridiculous prohibition. The bridge and its predecessor had probably been there for 150 years. There was no column of tanks, in fact no traffic at all. The policeman's action was part of the lingering paranoia that gripped this godforsaken region.

Srebrenica and Brutanac had been thoroughly "cleansed." The two communities had been Muslim by a wide majority before the war. The people living in Srebrenica at the time of our visit were 100 percent Serb, and were not pleased with the OSCE system, which encouraged voting by the original inhabitants. In Srebrenica this ensured that the Serbs would have only minority representation on the municipal council. The elections in 1997 (Bosnia was awash with elections) had produced these political inversions across the country, with Bosniak, Serb, or Croat mayors governing residents the majority of whom were of an ethnicity not their own. The idea was not just the application of a democratic principle, it was to facilitate the reintegration of former residents. Under enormous pressure from the international community, all municipalities reluctantly complied. The one exception was Srebrenica. In February the new mayor and the Bosniak councillors attempted to enter Srebrenica. They were blocked by angry Serbs, and the accompanying OSCE car was stoned. Total obstruction led the OSCE to impose an international, a former American army officer, as mayor, with wide discretionary powers. He was not well received. Nor were we.

Like the previous postwar elections, the voting in 1998 had brought almost no positive change to the Bosnian political landscape. In most cases the corrupt, militant, single-ethnicity parties remained frozen in place. The respected International Crisis Group described these elections as "a giant process of ethnically motivated social engineering." Their judgment on the elections that Belem and I were observing was that they "had not even dented" the power of the entrenched parties.

Under the OSCE rules, the surviving former Bosniak residents of Srebrenica had the right not only to vote for a Srebrenica slate that included Bosniak parties, but to vote in person in Srebrenica. However, the OSCE were not taking any chances. Two busloads of Muslims, all women, came from Tuzla, about two hours drive from the other side of the ethnic boundary, and voted in the two polling stations that were allotted them. Because these stations were located on the rural outskirts of the municipality and away from most of the Serbs, the elections in Srebrenica passed without serious incident.

By the time balloting was over, clouds shrouded the steep hills encircling Srebrenica and it began to rain heavily. An ugly place in sunlight, it looked much worse in the rain. We were there only a few days, but Belem and I could not will ourselves to ignore the ghosts of Srebrenica, real or imagined. Back in Brutanac, we talked about it. What had happened was a grotesque, totally unforgiveable crime, but we agreed that the crime had deep roots. The poison with which Milosevic had infected Yugoslavia was insecurity – the spread of corrosive distrust of once respected neighbours because they belonged to another religious/ethnic group. At the outset, insecurity about the intentions of others was artificially created by means of lies and innuendo. Like anti-Semitism after 1945, it did not come to an end. In the mid-nineties, little more than a generation had passed since the horrors of the Second World War. Serbs recalled the atrocities of Ante

Pavelic, the leader of the Croatian Fascist government set up by Hitler, and the founder of the notorious "Black Legion." Armed by the Germans, this regiment was composed of fanatical Croat Ustashi and Bosniak Muslims. While the Black Legion proved impotent when faced with Tito's partisans, it was the instrument both of Nazi genocide against Balkan Jews and gypsies and Pavelic's own policy of genocide against the Serbs.

Bosnian Serbs were still nursing these, as well as other more recent, wounds. In 2006 Naser Oric, a Bosniak military commander in the Srebrenica area, was sentenced to two years in prison by the International Human Rights Tribunal in the Hague. Journalists estimated that hundreds of Bosnian Serbs, mostly unarmed, had been killed by Oric's soldiers between 1992 and early 1995. In *The Broken Road*, the final volume of his brilliant trilogy describing an odyssey on foot from Northern Europe to Istanbul between 1933 and 1935, the travel writer Patrick Leigh Fermor grumbles about the Balkan pathology of a thousand years of oppression and conflict: "The frontiers have changed again and again…and each step in these struggles has been marked by horror: ambush, assassination, burnt villages, uprooting and massacres leaving behind them the curses of fear, hatred and irredentism and thirst for revenge."

In Srebrenica the Serbs we met in town were voters, or those involved in the mechanics of the election process. They and Slobo, our driver, and Sanja, our interpreter, were uniformly taciturn. We steered away from the massacre, but it was evident that they were in denial about what had taken place three years before. They took their cue from the wartime president of the Republika Srpska, Radovan Karadzic, who declared that "nothing had happened in Srebrenica." Karadzic, who was also a psychiatrist, a poet, and a former snake oil salesman, remains in prison in The Hague awaiting sentence for genocide and crimes against humanity – crimes committed over two decades ago. He is there with his colleague, General Ratko Mladic, the Bosnian Serb military commander responsible for the siege of Sarajevo and the liquidation of Srebrenica. The Bosniaks, unable to decide which of the two was the bigger beast, have bestowed on both the sobriquet "Butcher of Bosnia."

PARAGUAY

El Supremo

In July 1998, the Washington-based International Foundation for Electoral Systems (IFES) sent me to Asuncion with a small technical support team in advance of the presidential elections. I was in Paraguay for just under a month.

Paraguay was not a wholesome democracy when I was there in 1998. In fact, it never was. The country's closest approach to democratic normality up to that point had occurred in 1993, when Juan Carlos Wasmosy, who represented the Colorado, the ruling party of the preceding dictatorship, was elected president. Despite the fraud and horseplay of that election, the opposition made a good showing. In 1996, Wasmosy's anointed successor, General Oviedo, the head of the army, wishing to accelerate matters, attempted to overthrow his president. After much shuffling back and forth, Oviedo was imprisoned and Raul Alberto Cubas became the governing party candidate with the unusual platform, "Me in the Presidency, Oviedo in power." This entire cast was to experience unhappy trajectories, but more on that later. The country faced other problems. Paraguay was close to the top of Transparency International's ranking of corrupt states. Confronted by the press with evidence of massive embezzlement, a government senator responded, "Why not? These are the perks of office." It was in this setting that the recently established Paraguayan Election Commission invited IFES[1] to send a technical support team.

I was the leader of the IFES team, and my first call on the magistrates in the Commission was unwisely scheduled for two hours after the arrival of my connecting flight from Brasilia – which was just before my luggage arrived in Santiago, Chile. My wrinkled and generally scruffy appearance was a shock to the soberly attired commissioners. A bad start, I thought. However, the next morning a beautifully gift-wrapped silk tie was delivered to my hotel from the commissioners.

The commissioners quarrelled among themselves, which complicated our technical support mission, but, unlike many of the politicians, they were looking for results that more or less resembled the will of the voters. And, like most Paraguayans, they were delightful as individuals. The chief commissioner, Dr. Carlos Mojoli, was very genial, but eccentric even by Paraguayan standards. He had three hobbies: fishing, shooting, and motorcycling and managed to practise at least two of these pursuits simultaneously. Several months previously, Richard Soudriette, the head of IFES, was invited to join Dr. Majoli on his fishing boat. Casting near the shore, Richard snagged his lure on the branch of an overhanging tree. Richard was about to cut his line when Mojoli produced a submachine gun from his cabin, which he fired until the offending branch fell into the water. I will return to Dr. Mojoli.

Paraguay was frustrating, entertaining, and often enchanting. The city of Asuncion gave the impression that time had stopped about 1926. That was the feel of the architecture, the hotel lobby furnishings, the public transport system, the restaurant menus, and the courtliness of the citizens. But nothing spoke of the distant past so much as the pace of life. Leisurely movement was embedded in the culture. The siesta was sacrosanct. Almost everything stopped at noon. The tobacco men, who rolled cheap (5 cents each), foul, pretzel-shaped cigars in the market, hitched their hammocks under the public tables.

Before scattering to different destinations within the country, my team, from seven Latin American countries, met in Asuncion for a final briefing. Because the cellular network was limited, our communications would be by fax. "How should we address you?" one of the team enquired. Salutation protocol is given more emphasis in Latin America than in Canada. The previous evening I had been reading the exceptionally dolorous history of Paraguay. A long chapter is devoted to Dr. Francia, who was president from 1811 to 1840. In many ways he reminded me of Trujillo:

efficient, incredibly brutal, and a megalomaniac. Francia instructed all Paraguayans to address him as "*El Supremo.*" Such was the chemistry of our team that with a straight face I suggested that they send their faxes to "*El Supremo.*" And so they did. One of them still does.

Manuel Herrera and I remained in Asuncion. Manuel was a consultant with Mexico's Electoral Institute and a former professional soccer player. Still athletic, he persuaded me to run each morning at an ungodly hour. Each morning before breakfast we were picked up by Julio Cesar, our driver, and taken to the city park, which lies between the Paraguay River and the railway tracks. The circumference of Julio Cesar's waist was only a little less than his height. That he barely fit into our rented car and that the steering wheel dug into his belly never seemed to affect his sunny, garrulous, and earthy nature, nor his morbid interests.

On our drive to the park we were brought up to date on the scandals and criminal violence of the previous day. We were also taught amazingly offensive epithets in Guarani, the original language of Paraguay, to hurl at miscreant drivers. "Señores, say this loud and you will get respect." In our view, informing a tough, evil-tempered Asuncion driver, "Only mushrooms would grow in your swampy crotch," was more likely to get us shot. Wednesday was Julio Cesar's bumper day. As we climbed sleepily into the car he would show us with great relish a copy of a weekly tabloid that specialized in the most grisly crimes of the past week. This paper, which is no longer in circulation, was mostly comprised of excessively graphic photographs of victims, severed body parts, and distraught relatives.

In the park, Manuel and I ran along the perimeter trail and then inland toward the railway tracks. If our timing was right, about 7:45 A.M. we would hear the rumbling, clanking, and snorting of the commuter train. This was a joy to behold. The ancient wood-fired locomotive belched smoke and sparks, and a bright orange glow could be seen through the many holes in the walls of its rusty furnace. The three passenger carriages looked slightly crumpled, as if they had rolled over once or twice. All that was missing from this wonderful tableau was the thunderous pursuit of rebel horsemen shouting "*Viva Zapata!*" or perhaps "*Muere Supremo!*"

Meanwhile, the election campaign was getting testy. Especially disquieting for us was the escalating vendetta between Dr. Mojoli and the president. Rooted less in politics than in personal antipathy, the feud was rapidly becoming politicized and deteriorating into tantrums. Wasmosy accused Majoli of exceeding his mandate as election chief. Majoli fired off verbal shots warning the president off his turf. Wasmosy ordered troops to remove the stone wall that surrounded the cluster of election offices and warehouses. Furious, Majoli instructed workers to rebuild it. The election was now only two days away. At election headquarters Majoli told me he feared that the arch villain Wasmosy intended to seize the Commission's buildings, depose the commissioners, and take control of the election machinery. This seemed unlikely, but in that overheated political cauldron nothing was impossible if the governing party feared it might lose. I was in touch with Maura Harty, the US ambassador, who shared these concerns. She was in direct contact with Wasmosy.

Although aware of the diplomatic pressures on the president, Majoli wasn't taking any chances. He showed me into one of his warehouses, where he produced a small plastic case and said, "Have a look at this." Inside was a .45-calibre automatic with extra magazines. Engraved on the grip in small print were the words, "Made in Canada." I was surprised, but this was not the moment to enquire about the exact provenance of the guns. Majoli said, "There are lots more. See that pile on the shelf…and we have dynamite."

Wasmosy did not invade, the election passed relatively peacefully, and Cubas was elected president. There were gross irregularities and much intimidation, but the OAS and other observers judged that a plurality had voted for the governing party.

The postscript is messier. Wasmosy was indicted for fraud and sentenced to four years in prison. Released by President Cubas, General Oviedo fled to Brazil. Argana, the new vice-president, a jovial politician who had teased me about fomenting trouble in the largely Canadian Mennonite community, and an ardent opponent of Cubas's soft-on-Oviedo policy, was assassinated. Unproven accusations were made that Cubas and Oviedo were involved in the conspiracy. President Cubas resigned the day following Argana's assassination to avoid impeachment by the legislature.

Plus ça change.

KYRGYZSTAN

Boiling Toilets and Fermented Mare's Milk

This story encompasses two presidential elections in Kyrgyzstan, the first in 2000 and the second in 2005. On both occasions I was an observer with the Office of Human Rights and Democracy (ODHIR), which is a branch of the Organization for Security and Co-operation in Europe (OSCE). The story opens in Bishkek, the capital of Kyrgyzstan.

From the balcony of the Hotel Pinara in Bishkek I looked out on rows of yellowing poplars and bare hills. Beyond was a white wall of high mountains, hazy in the bright sun but gorgeous in the evening and in the early morning light. Breakfast was very much like that in Bosnia: fish, cheese, salami, fresh pomegranate, and wonderful yogourt. That evening I dined at a Siberian restaurant with an enterprising young Swiss colleague. He knew Canada better than I, having cycled from Vancouver to Newfoundland three years before. The daily special was borscht and "meat à la French," which my Swiss friend decided was horse.

Outside I gave paper money in the local currency to a small beggar boy. He was carrying a sign in Cyrillic that I couldn't read. The note was probably worth about five dollars, as I didn't have anything of lower value. Apparently no one had ever given him such a treasure. He looked at me with amazement, then ran off lest the foolish philanthropist change his mind.

We had just had our first briefing for the presidential elections by the leaders of the ODHIR/OSCE team. The incumbent president, Akayev, was seeking another term, although the constitution said that he couldn't. Until about four months before our arrival, Akayev's image as a reformer and political moderate stood out against a backdrop of unreconstructed Soviet hacks in the rest of central Asia. This was no longer the case. We were told to expect manipulation, voter intimidation, and harassment of opposition organizations. The election campaign had failed most of the usual tests. There was virtually no free press, and several journalists who had the temerity to criticize the government were on trial or in jail. We wondered what we were doing observing a pre-cooked election. ODHIR/OSCE hoped that its presence could be a deterrent to blatant irregularities, and of some educational value to embryonic civil society election organizations. The movement of bureaucratic wheels was also a factor. The decision to observe had been made before Akayev had turned his back on "free and fair."

The briefing discussion moved from the political to the mundane. We were told a) that the cheap local vodka was potentially lethal; b) to keep passports and wallets well hidden; c) not to expect help if we were attacked; d) that local drivers would drive at speed as close to pedestrians as possible; and e) not to make a face if you didn't like the food. The head of mission added that the Kyrgyz are very hospitable. It was not clear from what he said whether this was a warning or a compliment. I soon learned that the Kyrgyz were hospitable to a fault.

The next morning six of us set off with a driver in an ancient seatbelt-less, and almost springless Mercedes van to our destination in Karakol, the small administrative centre of the Issyk-Kulskaya *oblast* (province). Karakol is at the eastern tip of the spearhead-shaped republic; geographically, the spear is aimed at Sinkiang, the huge province in China's northwest. To the north is Kazakhstan, to the west are the ancient cities of Tashkent and Samarkand, and to the northeast, Alma Ata, cities of the Silk Road, the tales of whose splendour were carried to Europe in the Middle Ages. The squiggly and wildly indented eastern frontier resembles a fiendishly difficult Rorschach test.

The drive was spectacular. Dry, dun-coloured flatlands around Bishkek soon gave way to the foothills of several mountain ranges. Running diagonally to the northeast along the Chinese frontier is a long parapet of rock and ice. This is the Tian Shan mountain range, whose peaks rise to over 7,400 metres. Mountains are always visible in Kyrgyzstan. Only 3 percent of the land is flat and only 8 percent arable.

There were occasional villages along our route. The rustic architecture of most of the houses reminded me of all the films I had seen of the Russian/ Siberian countryside – wood frames, mostly white, with small windows and corrugated roofing. The attractive ones have a central balcony on the second floor, elaborately shaped and carved with gingerbread. Pale blue is the favourite colour for window and door frames. The villages are the descendants of the old caravan stops along the network of silk roads. In the fields were large herds of horses, bred for transport and consumption. The early onset of winter had driven the yak to lower pastures. Traffic was now mostly horse traps and Kyrgyz riding on horseback. By the roadside, fishermen peddled trout, fished from glacier-fed streams.

After about four hours of gorges, switchbacks, forest, and scree, we came to Lake Issyk-Kul, a huge crescent-shaped lake 120 kilometres long. Ivan, our driver, told us that Stalin, and later Brezhnev, once had hunting dachas nearby. The lake is salty, and so full of minerals – including some carcinogenic waste dumped accidentally by a Canadian gold mining company – that it doesn't freeze, even in the harshest of winters. We parked in a grove of beech trees and lunched on borscht in a yurt that smelled of charred fat. Outside, the turquoise lake glittered blindingly behind the trees. Beyond rose the white palisade of another mountain range.

The bedraggled town of Tyup at the eastern end of the lake was snow-covered, and as we climbed toward Karakol and the Tiam Shan mountains, the snow lay even deeper on the fields. Farmers were hacking at the semi-frozen ground in an attempt to save the potato harvest, of which, we were told, over 60 percent was lost. Even at 1,800 metres, this much snow and cold at the end of October was most unusual.

Karakol was splotched with melting snow and looked bleak and dilapidated. The key to our apartment wouldn't work, and a fight was breaking out among the interpreters who were waiting for us. They had discovered there would only be two jobs between the three of them. The two males were telling us that we couldn't hire Rosa, a young Kyrgyz woman with gold front teeth, because she was nursing a baby and therefore would not be available full-time. We hired Rosa. Eventually a working key was produced. We lugged our packs inside, including my emergency bottle of duty-free Scotch, and looked around.

"Keith, look!" I shouted. "You can boil an egg in this toilet." A plume of steam was rising from the toilet bowl and the pipes were rattling. I had discovered the only source of heat in the apartment assigned to Keith and me. Keith, a starchy ex-Sandhurst Englishman, was overdressed for Karakol and certainly for our apartment. Threadbare carpeting ran halfway up the bedroom walls. It was Keith who discovered that the tap marked in red was for cold water and that marked in blue was for hot water. Herbert (Swiss) and Louise (Belgian), the leaders of our small observer presence in the *oblast*, invited Keith and me to join them for dinner. Keith opted for an early night.

The restaurant was one of the grungiest I have ever been in. Roughly patched chairs, splintered linoleum tabletops, and vivid tropical island murals were lit by over-bright neon strip lighting. Our neighbours were young Kyrgyz who were throwing back the dollar-a-bottle vodka that we had been warned about. We checked the two rooms upstairs. The first was set up as a nightclub and the other had little cubicles with curtains. Louise and I agreed that it was a temporarily inactive brothel. Unsure about the dining options in Karakol, we went downstairs and ordered dinner. The beer was drinkable and the horse *shashlik*, cooked on a charcoal grill outside on the street, was very good. After dinner we were joined by Rosa and several of her girlfriends. Although the gold teeth took a little getting used to, the Kyrgyz women were beautiful: light bronze complexions, lovely chestnut eyes set wide apart, and stunning features. Steel teeth I could not get used to, perhaps because they reminded me of that James Bond film.

Rosa persuaded us to have another look at the nightclub, now booming with action. We danced to the awful cacophony of a Russian punk band on tape. Louise was ordering wine when an inebriated Kyrgyz army officer approached our table and insisted on buying us a bottle of champagne, which he could not remotely afford. Totally embarrassed, we resisted his offer, until one of the girls explained that the offer was being made because we were guests in his country, and that he would be grievously offended if we refused. He was also wearing his pistol. As soon as we could we made our way downstairs, and found that the young Kyrgyz in the bar/restaurant had become belligerently drunk. A sad and bewildered group – intoxication was one of their few entertainments.

Back at the apartment the cold was intense. Despite a layering of socks, sweaters, and long johns under pyjamas, we had difficulty sleeping. Next morning Keith and I complained to the landlady, who performed some magic with the central heating, redirecting the scalding water from the toilet to miniature radiators in our rooms – and to the red tap in the bathroom.

That night, after we had spent the day visiting election and party officials around the *oblast*, Herbert invited the men in his observer team to join him at the local Turkish bath. With reasonably based suspicion about what might lie in wait in a Karakol Turkish bath, the others declined. After a short drive through the forest, Herbert and I arrived at a crumbling ruin. The chamber for the Turkish bath was still mostly intact, and Herbert speculated, on the basis of the elaborate tile around the plunge pool, that it had been part of a czarist hunting lodge. The attendant tossed logs in the furnace, the ancient pipes groaned, and soon we were able to enjoy our first Kyrgyz Turkish bath and the mixed pleasures of the icy cold and poorly illuminated plunge pool.

On election day we squelched along, through deep mud, to as many polling stations as possible. Once inside we tried hard to be inquisitive and businesslike. For their part, the Kyrgyz tried, with great skill and charm, and sometimes with success, to transform the observers' visits into social events, at which we were expected to try the pickled vegetables and other local delicacies. The borscht was multi-coloured, thick, and delicious. A particularly memorable treat at one polling station consisted of fried bread spread with rancid yak butter. The food is prepared in advance by local families to fuel the workers at each polling station over the very long election day, and washed down with chai or locally distilled beverages. As in many countries, the elections were treated as a national festival. In rural areas – and our *oblast* was mostly rural – it was an occasion for gossip and socializing. The best clothes are worn. For the women this meant brightly embroidered blouses and camisoles. The men's winter togs included sheepskin coats and long, occasionally vividly coloured woollen or burlap robes cinched with large metal buckles. Many of the horsemen wore fur hats, but most Kyrgyz men in rural areas wore the traditional felt hat, the *kalpak*. These are splendid: usually bone white, they are cone-shaped, with upturned rims, and beautifully embroidered in black thread. A measure of the status of the *kalpak* is that it may be worn in the mosque. I brought

*Kyrgyz elder
wearing a kalpak.*

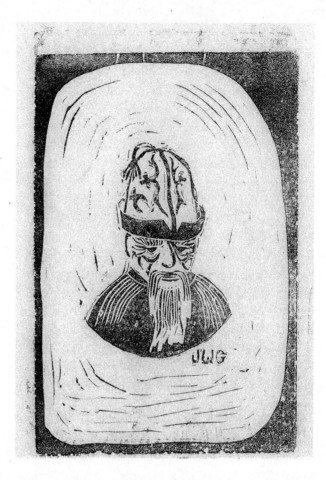

back six, plus a fur hat, for family, friends, and myself. Like the women, the men were often strikingly handsome, some with thin droopy moustaches and wispy beards.

In many villages we were a curiosity. Several people told us that we were the first non-Russian, non-central Asian foreigners they had seen. In the days before and after election day we were plied with questions about our countries. As in Bosnia, jokes were regarded both as tests of character and as icebreakers. I found that mine often left my audience puzzled – for which, of course, I would blame my interpreter. They ended up being more interested in my accounts of Canada, another country of mountains and long, harsh winters, especially relating to stories of crops destroyed by insects, floods, and early winter storms.

Back to Bishkek

Of course, Akayev won. But he would have won anyway without the massive fraud, a small part of which I saw in Karakol. He had apprenticed as a Soviet autocrat and it was not in his nature to take any chances. Akayev had no credible opponents, even counting those he had put in jail. Four and a half years later, his electors, unhappy with the corruption and incompetence of his administration, drove him out of office. The ensuing instability and risks of inter-ethnic violence troubled the neighbours, especially the Russians, Kazaks, Uzbeks, and Tajiks. The Americans were also nervous – like Canada, they are members of the OSCE. The result was pressure on ODHIR/OSCE. And so it was that five years later, in July, we were back in Kyrgyzstan to monitor a fresh election with a new slate of candidates. This time the observer team was under different, overstressed management. Although most of us were experienced observers, we were lectured like impish teenagers and potential sex maniacs. Bob Pym, from Nanaimo, compared notes with me, and we concluded that our leaders' sensitivity with respect to sex may have been related to the mission's informal, hugely successful, well lubricated, and notorious farewell bash in Bishkek in 2000, which concluded with a Russian stripper.

The small group assigned to the Fergano Valley flew from Bishkek to Osh, another ancient silk road town and the capital of the *oblast*. Kamilla, a young Uzbek woman with whom I was paired, and I were met by Sultan, our driver, and his battered Audi. We drove through blazing heat: it was 44 degrees centigrade. The Fergano Valley is Kyrgyzstan's bread basket, comprising most of the country's sparse arable land. We passed fields of cotton, watermelon, rice, and corn, and a vast network of irrigation canals fed by a girdle of glaciers. One large canal still bore the name Staliniski. This remnant of the past, like the statues of Lenin and Marx, was a reminder that nomadic Kyrgyzstan, unlike the Baltic states and Eastern Europe, had no history of democracy, and in consequence did not experience the same sense of liberation when the Soviet empire unravelled. Distance from Moscow insulated them from bureaucratic inanity and cultural bruising, but it did not free them from it. Many Kyrgyz families mourn family members killed in the Afghan war. But the country did benefit from membership in the USSR in the form of an infrastructure of roads, airports, hospitals, telecommunications, schools, and universities.

By late afternoon, Sultan had us installed in the Swiss Guest House in Jalal-Abad, our base of operations for the next four days. Apart from the mountain views, there was nothing remotely Swiss about it. There was no air conditioning, but it was comfortable, and by the standards of Karakol the Swiss Guest House was five-star.

On election day Kamilla woke me up at 5:20 A.M., well ahead of the agreed wake-up time. She was a would-be female Genghis Khan, very bright and impatient with old geezers. We had occasional sharp exchanges. Sultan was waiting, and we started our long circuit of polling stations. As it had been five years before, in Karakol, election day was festival time. The best summer clothes were worn and most of the men wore the traditional *kalpak*. Food and non-alcoholic drink were available. We were invited to partake of the Kyrgyz tradition of sharing bread – delicious round bread with a local design baked in the centre – but there was less of the abundant hospitality we had experienced in the north.

The heat was too much for the radiator, and Sultan stopped frequently to top it up. We topped up too. I can't recall a time when I took in so much liquid. Sultan stopped in a small village and returned to the car with large glass mugs of *jarma*, a local beverage made from yogourt, water, and whole wheat grains. It's like an unsweetened Indian *lassi*, only lumpier.

We climbed a gentle slope above the Fergano flatland until we came to a small and foul-smelling polling station. It was empty except for a goat and a policeman who was fast asleep. Awakened, he summoned the polling station chairlady. She was delightful, and took us to the bank of a spring-fed river where we filled up our water bottles. Sultan's car, which had conked out again, was also treated with spring water.

Election day went surprisingly well in Jalal-Abad, and generally in the rest of the country. There was intimidation and some vote stuffing, but very little violence. It was fascinating – and, of course, dehydrating.

Our visits to the police, political parties, and election authorities completed, Kamilla and I accepted Sultan's suggestion that we visit his friend the mullah, halfway up a foothill overlooking the town. We wound slowly up into the forest and stopped beside a tiny mosque set within a copse of conifers. At the bottom of the mosque there was space for no more than three people crammed together. The minaret was only about twenty feet high, and inside there was a narrow ladder to the top. A beautiful setting for prayer, but not much accommodation for the faithful. We said as

much to Sultan. "Ahh," said he, "I will ask the mullah to explain." Sultan disappeared and eventually returned with the mullah and his small son. The mullah told us that in clement weather his small group of parishioners place their prayer rugs on the grass outside the mosque. What happens in inclement weather was not made clear, but I suspect that it involved umbrellas. The mullah, who seemed pleased to see us, instructed his son to bring a "container" from a neighbouring farmer and talked to us about the tangled history of Jalal-Abad. The son returned with a pitcher of thick, off-white fluid. Sultan exclaimed that we were greatly privileged. This was *kymyz*, or fermented mare's milk. It is the "national" drink of Kyrgyzstan and its pungent taste defies the usual adjectives. My encyclopaedia describes it as "one of the most difficult [of the central Asian nectars] to get used to." We sat in the mullah's garden eating the watermelon that I had brought and sipping *kymyz* with varying degrees of real and pretended relish.

GUATEMALA

San Marcos and the Election of 2003

In 2003 I was invited by the OAS to observe the municipal, legislative and presidential elections in Guatemala. Democracy in Guatemala had been struggling with narcotics-fueled corruption and a landed elite largely unwilling to cede their privileges, prejudices, and political control. This is an account of that election, its consequences, and of my experience in San Marcos, a small province bestride a drug route in a remote corner of the country.

"... *every time the lid is lifted from four centuries of injustice, the social ferment begins to bubble over and a further wave of brutality is the only way to restore 'order'. Guatemala allows the grass roots to sprout and then mows the lawn.*"

Ronald Wright wrote this dismal epitaph in his classic study of Guatemala, Belize, and Chiapas, *Time Among the Maya*. At the time he was writing, in the mid-eighties, Vinicio Cerezo's democratically elected government had put an end to a brutal procession of military governments, notably those of Lucas and Rios Montt, but the military, in league with the old-money elite, was still keeping the grass short.

Twenty years on, and thanks in part to the energy of the international community, Guatemala had a good election – better than Cerezo's and probably the best election in sixty years. Accused of large-scale embezzlement, the previous president, Alfonso Portillo, skulked rapidly out of the country when his designated successor and prospective protector, Rios Montt lost to Oscar Berger.[1] The new president's program bore some functional resemblance to that of President Juan Jose Arevalo, who in 1945 boldly tackled health, water, education, labour law, and land tenure. But then Arevalo and his successor Jacobo Arbenz took on too much too fast for the political paranoia of the times. Arbenz was famously dislodged by the United Fruit Company (aka *el pulpo* – the octopus) and the CIA, with the blessing of the Eisenhower administration in close collaboration with the army and the elite.

Berger opened his administration with surprisingly reformist panache. He acknowledged the country's 'sinister' past, rebuked his predecessors and cited the scorching report of the United Nations Truth Commission. He made commitments to 'restructure' the army – which meant compressing the size and reforming the culture of the military establishment. It is difficult to underestimate this undertaking in a country where a privileged and intransigent military has long intimidated civil authority and slaughtered non-combatants with impunity. The Commission noted that 83 percent of the victims of the conflict were indigenous people and that acts of genocide had been committed. The military were only lightly tethered to their barracks and remained an inhibiting spectre for civilian government and civil society.

The scale of Berger's challenge and that of all subsequent presidents was huge – and his achievements, like those of his successors, have been disappointingly modest. Guatemala has one of the hemisphere's most lopsided distributions of wealth. The disequilibrium of land tenure has not changed significantly since the massive appropriations of peasant and indigenous land by dictator Justo Rufino Barrios and his successors in the last quarter of the nineteenth century. Although small parcels of land have been redistributed by succeeding administrations, 2 percent of the population continues to control about 65 percent of the land. Infant mortality is over twice the average for Latin America and the Caribbean. Murder has been escalating.

For about one quarter of adult Guatemalans, as in many other parts of Latin America, the hand that lifts them from poverty and malnutrition is that of the family member who mails or wires a remittance cheque from the United States, Mexico, Europe, or Canada (over 90 percent of these cheques are sent from the US). The other helping hand is the narcotics transshipment business, which carries many others well above the poverty line.

The catalogue of grievances gives the impression that Guatemala is still caught in a relentless cycle of racism, discrimination, and repression. There are criticisms, both domestic and international, that fundamentally nothing has changed. Not nearly enough has changed, but charges that the cultural divide and its practical consequences are as bad now as they were thirty years ago are overstated. World Bank and the United Nations Development Program (UNDP) statistics show gradual upward movement in areas such as life expectancy and literacy.[2] The physical perils of involvement in political or labour activity have declined. My discussions in 2003 with many Guatemalans, including indigenous persons, involved in development, education, and human rights indicated that forms of discrimination were beginning, ever so slightly, to moderate. They also suggested that the cultural lens through which some in the *ladino*[3] population traditionally see the indigenous people, either as an asset for exploitation or as a threat to their security, is beginning to change. The walls of discrimination, especially the indirect ones, are still indefensibly high, but they are being scaled by small numbers of enterprising individuals.

However, these changes must also be seen in the context of how the indigenous population has fared in relation to the *ladino* counterpart. While there is overall statistical improvement, the gap in the quality of life between a rural *ladino* and a rural indigenous household is actually widening.[4] In other words one effect of national economic advance has been to enlarge disparities.[5]

Ronald Wright remarked that "Latin Americans have enormous trouble with the idea that cultural diversity and national unity need not be incompatible."[6] This remains especially true in Guatemala where cultural sclerosis and exclusion have undergone very slow generational change. Up to now progress along this road has depended largely on nudging from the international community. Pressure from within is a new and still not fully matured phenomenon. While the OAS was encouraging a mobilized civil society in Guatemala, the president, Alvaro Arzu, abominated the boldness and lack of respect shown by civil society towards his government. I was present in 1999 when he admonished the General Assembly of the

OAS meeting in Antigua: while civil society in some countries might be 'civil', he explained, in Guatemala it remained 'uncivil', leaving his foreign minister, Eduardo Stein, rushing about for the next three days attempting to put the flowers back into a broken vase.

The Election

In compressed and greatly oversimplified form I have given an update on Guatemala's social and political setting and have indicated that, dark as it is now, the shadows were longer when I returned to the country in 2003. At that time, looking at Portillo's botched legacy and poor prospects of winning another term for the party if it played according to the rules, the question arose as to why the government would bother to have international observation. The answer was in part wishful thinking that the president's candidate, Rios Montt, and his FRG party[7] could win, coupled with the view that, if he did win it would be important, as in past elections, to have the international validation and legitimacy that an OAS observation can confer.[8] The government would also be aware that regimes with dodgy governance records in Latin America often needed the blessing of the OAS and other major observer organizations to secure and maintain development assistance from the Bretton Woods institutions.

The UPD (Unit for the Promotion of Democracy and my former job) had seven months' lead time to prepare for the first round in November, but not much cash. No funds were available for elections from the OAS regular budget. The organization had to solicit contributions from the donor community for each election observation. As concern grew through the summer of 2003 that a mix of sophisticated manipulation, dirty tricks and raw intimidation could unsettle the Guatemalan electoral landscape, the OAS and the European Union recognized that a major effort would be required. Election infrastructure is always huge. In Guatemala the voters list ran to over five million eligible citizens.

A comprehensive observation in a potentially unstable election requires scrutiny of all the major election functions and a presence, if possible, in all the departments – an expensive undertaking and a difficult one in an environment of hemispheric parsimony. Short on donor funding, the observer mission under a former president of Peru chose to put its primary investment in a group of long-term observers and sectoral experts.

The Canadian embassy played a significant part in this process as Canadians made up almost a quarter of the OAS short-term observation team. The ambassador, James Lambert, lobbied hard and successfully to obtain Canadian funding to help underpin the OAS mission.

By the end of September, experts had been assigned to monitor voter education, voter registry, vote counting procedures, logistics, the training of election officials, and to organize a quick count.[9]

The Portillo government's support for the candidacy of Rios Montt in the face of a constitutional provision barring former dictatorial rulers was a major vexation to election planners. The decision by the FRG-packed Supreme Court to allow Rios Montt to run escalated concerns about the environment in which campaigning would take place and the integrity of the process itself. Portillo's government supported Rios Montt's presidential ambitions with state funding. One example was the doubling of the number of former members of the para-military Civil Defense Patrols entitled to pensions. These rural patrols had been employed by the Lucas and Rios Montt regimes to secure villages and combat guerrillas. Often reinforced by press-ganged Maya, the civic patrols became part of the control apparatus that systematically violated human rights. By the end of the campaign there had been a flood of death threats and some 20 party activists had died in incidents related to the campaign.

Distressed by the prospects of increasingly turbulent elections, the OAS and European Union missions joined other international démarches, including that of Canadian Foreign Minister Bill Graham, to press the Guatemalan government to increase its security measures. The government was receptive, but there was apprehension about how increased security would be applied. The contamination of police forces by narcotics traffickers had been rising in frontier municipalities. Portillo's police force had become more corrupt and less competent. Much more competent, but greatly feared in many areas, was the army. Indigenous and opposition leaders wanted the army kept on a tight leash.

In this climate both OAS and EU missions increased the assignment of long-term observers throughout the country. Thirty-four were sent by the OAS and fourteen by the EU. OAS long-term observers spent between two months and six weeks in their departments prior to election day. The use of long-term observers is an increasingly vital tool of election missions. Complaints that election observation is too narrowly focused on election day itself was shifting from accounts of what was happening at the polling station to pre-identified weak spots in the process – such as abusive government control of the media, election transport, election financing, intimidation, lack of transparency in the computer registration of voters, and improper security of ballots.[10] Identifying the deficiencies in advance and then discreetly encouraging national electoral authorities, in this case the Supreme Electoral Tribunal (TSE), to address the problems requires skill, diplomacy and adequate lead time.

Although it was always assumed that a second round between the run-off presidential candidates would be necessary, the activities of the OAS mission (including long-term observers) and its expenditures were focused primarily on the first round of the elections where most of the serious difficulties were expected. Past elections had shown that the elections for mayor, which are decided in the first round, generate more potential for violence and irregularities than any other. Especially in rural communities, the mayor is the local 'cacique' or 'chief' dispensing patronage, controlling the municipal registry of citizens, and determining who is assigned the best (and worst) stalls in the local market. Mayors belonging to Portillo's and Rios Montt's FRG party enjoyed additional leverage; the police in an FRG municipality, e.g., did not look closely at political or other abuses committed by the municipal administration.

The job of the long-term observer was to enter these political cauldrons and find a way, in collaboration with local authorities and civil society groups, to lower tensions and increase the prospects of a reasonably fair election. The impact of well-selected and well-motivated observers who are sensitive to local culture and knowledgeable about recent history can be significant. I was not a long-term (but rather a middle-term) observer, but had had enough exposure in Guatemala and other places to assess the work of those who were – and to know that this work was mirrored in many of the departments where tensions were high and there were suspected deficiencies in the process. Combined with discreet prodding of the government and TSE by the OAS and EU headquarters missions, the work of the long-term observers in helping to defuse problems proved critical to the success and 'relative' tranquility of election day.

The Case of San Marcos

Fausto was my driver. I was not sure whether he was the worst driver I had ever had or just the second-most frightening.[11] To be fair, he was not wholly responsible for the frightening parts. The mountain roads with narrow, bending lanes frequented by local rattletrap trucks, bore their share of the responsibility. Fausto had groovy sun glasses and drove a six-cylinder pick-up with machismo relish. He complained that he did not get enough sleep. This was partly due to late nights and mostly due to his stomach, which rumbled at night – sometimes during the day, too, causing him discomfort. His diet consisted almost exclusively of deep-fried chicken and Coke™, and he disliked health food lectures. Fortunately, when fatigue was loosening his concentration, I was able to take over – but only after swearing that the OAS, who were paying him, would not be told.

On arrival in San Marcos we asked repeatedly for directions to the Hotel CRINAP. No one had heard of it, most doubted its existence and, after an hour, so did we. Finally we were able to reach one of my new colleagues by cell phone and were directed to the hotel – so new that its cement staircase was still under construction. This and the fact that each room was crammed with beds explained its cost – $7 a night. Fausto asked about the curious nomenclature of the hotel which resembled no known Guatemalan hostelry.

"Yes," they agreed. "It's strange. The proprietor used the first initial of each of her six children."

One of them, aged about thirteen, was the acting manager when I arrived. Given the modest amenities of the CRINAP, this was not demanding – with one exception. The CRINAP advertised hot showers and this was important since we were in the mountains where, by November, the nights and early mornings were frosty. Heat was supplied to the shower head by means of a canister of butane, ignited with a switch. On the second morning, instead of producing controlled heat, the canister emitted a blue flame, a loud crump and then died. Until four days later when I was able to move to another room, also crammed with beds, I took my showers short and cold.

As it was one of the four most conflictive departments in Guatemala, San Marcos illustrated many of the issues facing observers. Of its twenty-nine municipalities, the TSE identified eleven with problems rated medium to high. The most common was intimidation. In the remote highland town of San Miguel Ixtahuacan the FRG mayor, who was running for reelection, scarcely troubled to mask his machinations. A nearby hamlet which favoured the opposition was warned in writing to support the mayor or face nasty consequences. A number of persons approached the OAS alleging having had death threats made against them. In San Miguel Ixtahuacan, on the basis of flimsy pretexts, about 900 citizens (almost 10 percent of the municipal electorate) had been disenfranchised through the citizens' neighbourhood registry controlled by the mayor – the same mayor whose personal protection was a pair of ferocious and startlingly white-furred and blue-eyed huskies.

In these circumstances observers must decide what course to follow – whom to speak to – the police, the local party leaders, and/or the TSE – and in what terms. The OAS provided general guidance but no prescriptions. More often than not there is little opportunity to check with headquarters, especially when the connection is a capricious satellite telephone. While certainly not always welcome, in Guatemala the observers generally enjoyed the advantage of respect as representatives of the international community. The point was often made that we were the 'eyes of the outside world'. Fortunately this view still had resonance in 2003. Wearing vests and caps with the identifying insignia of the OAS was not only fairly safe, it had a positive impact. Visibility is a key function of all observers. It magnifies the deterrent effect that is a vital component of all election observation. The visibility factor also underscored the need for observers to project their messages to thousands more by speaking on local radio and TV. Being careful to avoid any remotely partisan comment, the three of us in San Marcos gave about a dozen local media interviews in the last week before the elections. To counter the intimidators, whose threats tend to be more effective with the illiterate, we emphasized the secrecy of the ballot. We spoke encouragingly, if not always honestly, about our confidence that the process would be fair and peaceful. The "we" were Alan Oliver (American), Domingo Mateos (Spanish) and I. They were excellent companions.

We called on party leaders, including mayors, the military commander, and the department governor. At a meeting facilitated by the governor we were able to make a presentation to a specially assembled meeting of police chiefs from all municipalities in the department.

I also made a point of calling on the local bishop, Monsignor Alvaro Ramazzini. As expected, the bishop was well informed. He was also hospitable, genial, and courageously active in defense of indigenous parishioners and others suffering at the hands of Rios Montt's henchmen. He had a passion for justice in a place where it was in very short supply. And, importantly, he was willing to share his local knowledge. His outspoken criticism from the pulpit of the barbarous behaviour of local drug lords, most of them supporters of Rios Montt, had earned him death threats. Catholic priests and nuns in Central America enjoyed no immunity from violence. Archbishop Oscar Romero of El Salvador, six Jesuit priests, including my friend Father Ignacio Ellacuria, the rector of the Universidad Centroamericana in San Salvador, many other nuns and priests, and, five years earlier, Bishop Juan Jose Gerardi of Guatemala had all been assassinated.

Inevitably, reports of this remarkable man spread beyond the mountains of San Marcos. Preparing notes for this chapter, I found that the bishop had been awarded the prestigious *Pacem in Terris* award in 2011. Previous recipients have included John F. Kennedy, Martin Luther King, Desmond Tutu, and Jean Vanier. It was Monsignor Ramazzini who told me that his nickname for the province was San *Narcos*.

Leaving the bishop's residence, I noticed a queue of people, mostly Mayan, across the street lined up to purchase tortillas at a tiny bakery set into the side of an old stone house. Unlike the usual wheat flour or yellow corn patties, they were an unappetizing grey colour. I asked about the flour.

"It is from black corn, *señor. Muy sabroso* (delicious)." And so it was. I bought several and extras for Domingo and Alan. Fausto declined his.

The bishop had advised me about civil society organizations operating in the department. Very few were prepared to put their heads above the parapet in San Marcos and traditionally there had been little dialogue between civil society and government at the municipal level. Nevertheless this set of elections marked the first major participation by Guatemalan civil society in election observation, including MIRADOR, a coalition of four human rights and humanitarian organizations which fielded many thousands of registered and sometimes haphazardly trained observers. In my case I was fortunate to share time on both election days with a member of a group of indigenous women observers – a tiny body of only forty for the entire country, but it was a beginning. Irma Raquel, resplendent in traditional costume, had no funds for transportation, so, breaking another of the OAS rules, I invited her to accompany me. The result was much improved outreach and a better grasp of the difficulties faced by indigenous women.

We broke for lunch at a rustic fish place built on stilts. Irma Raquel was hesitant about entering. It may have been the first time she had been in a restaurant, however modest. She may also have been nervous about the location – or about being seen with me. The village was Ocos on the Pacific coast, less than a kilometre from the state of Chiapas and the Mexican border. As she explained later, the beach we were perched on was a busy transit route for drugs. She didn't say, but it seemed possible that this route was the source of employment for some of the diners at neighbouring tables. Reminders of the fruits of this industry were the occasional large, invariably gaudy houses that stood out like bad plastic Christmas tree decorations from the surrounding shacks. Sometimes there was a Cadillac Escalade or similar in the driveway to complete the image.

Election day was not quiet. By the end of the day police swat squads had been deployed to five municipalities in the San Marcos department to deal with disturbances. In one town rioters broke into the voting centre and burned all the ballots. Lynchings were threatened, vehicles burned, votes were bought and four municipalities rang with accusations that names had been removed from the voters list. Crowd control was almost non-existent and a child was asphyxiated in one highland voting centre. Yet the news in San Marcos was not all bad. The majority of otherwise problem-prone municipalities had an orderly election day – a far better result than had been forecast early in the campaign. Even troubled San Miguel Ixtahuacan had a good election. Despite disenfranchisement of many, enough voters found the courage to defeat the mayor and his huskies.

Rios Montt was defeated, but because Berger did not have 50 percent of the vote, a second ballot for the presidency was necessary. This meant that Alan, Domingo, and I returned to San Marcos in December. As a veteran of the Hotel CRINAP, I made noises about upgrading. The choice in San Marcos was limited. I opted for the Hotel Esmeralda and the others reluctantly agreed. OAS observers were allocated a set amount *per diem*. If you found cheaper accommodation you could pocket the difference. We received no salary, so for many the extra money was a powerful incentive to stay in flop houses like the CRINAP at $7 a night. The Esmeralda would put us back $17. It had a dining room, central heating and each room had no more than two (or at most three) beds. The one drawback was the paintings in the public rooms. They were uniformly macabre, involving men doing inquisitorial things with whips.

The many incidents in San Marcos and three other largely indigenous departments could not spoil the sense of relief in the country that the process had survived more or less intact. With a few exceptions where reruns were necessary, the combustible local elections were over. By comparison, the second round on December 28 was a cake walk. Despite the incidents and the high level of intimidation, the elections conferred unquestioned legitimacy on the new Berger government. For the OAS, the EU, the Carter Center and other smaller missions, and for bilateral donors, including Canada, it was effort and money well spent. Unfortunately, Ronald Wright's forecast that change and a bridging of the cultural divide would be painfully slow has proven correct. The political reversal in 2014 of the court conviction of Rios Montt for genocide shows that Guatemala is still mowing the grass.

VENEZUELA

Hugo Chavez: Much Loved, Much Loathed

By 2004 Hugo Chavez had overtaken Fidel Castro as the most interesting, polarizing, and charismatic leader in the hemisphere. He was squeezing his country's free press, politicizing his judiciary, militarizing his administration, intimidating his opposition, mismanaging the economy, failing to cope with rising domestic violence and eroding constitutional checks and balances. The dark side of Chavez is very dark and stands in puzzling contrast to his successes. Frequently a clown who took adolescent pleasure in Bush baiting, he was also a genuine socialist reformer. Illiteracy all but disappeared. Education and free health care became almost universally available. Improving the quality of life for millions at the bottom levels of society was no small achievement.[1]

Additionally, Chavez kept one foot on the democratic side of the thin line that separates democracy from full-blown authoritarianism. He was proud of his 'democracy' and to his credit eventually installed what is, or was, probably the most tamper-proof voting system in the Americas. In 2004 the constitution still retained a clause which required a sitting president to submit to a recall referendum if confronted by a petition with 2.4 million signatories. In June 2004, at the culmination of a robust anti-Chavez campaign, this figure was reached and the president reluctantly acceded to the constitutional requirement. Few of the players, either national or international, emerged from the ensuing mud-slinging fracas unscathed.

Initially uncertain that he would win a free contest, Chavez took some precautionary steps by eliminating some of the basic freedoms, including full access to the voting computer centre, essential for effective electoral observation. Only when his popularity had been fortified by massive public spending and when his polling signalled that he would comfortably defeat the recall referendum did he make some concessions for international observation. When confident that he would have a majority, he decided to ice his cake with authentic international validation – the sort of certification that the OAS, Carter, or the European Community could provide. By this time only a few weeks remained before the referendum date and the European Community concluded that (a) too many restrictions remained and (b) there was too little time to assess the fairness of the pre-referendum conditions. The OAS and the Carter Center agonized over these deficiencies, examined Chavez's concessions and, knowing that their final judgments could not be based on an in-depth evaluation, decided to accept the insistent appeals of the Venezuelan opposition to be present. Having achieved the actual holding of a national referendum, the opposition were desperate to have every possible international support, including the impact of reputable international monitors.

I was invited by the OAS to participate as an observer and, using some of my vanishing leverage, persuaded the OAS to accept three others from the Canadian Foundation for the Americas (FOCAL)[2]. I was assigned to Valencia, a city of about one million persons, the third largest in Venezuela and the capital of the state of Carabobo. (A curious name because literally it means 'clown face'. Carabobo was the site of a major victory of Simón Bolivar's rebels over Spanish troops in 1821.)

On arrival we had two days before the voting to identify our polling stations and familiarize ourselves with the region's political idiosyncrasies. The latter was going to be problematic without long-term observers to furnish intelligence. I suggested a series of visits to key people to fill in part of this gap. With surprising speed we fixed up appointments on both sides of the political fence. Henrique Salas Römer was easy, as I had met him during my incarnation as ambassador to Venezuela. He is a former Governor of Carabobo and was the centre-right presidential candidate defeated by Chavez in 1998. He and others told us about potentially troublesome polling areas, gave us a grim account of the government's attempts to disenfranchise the 'disloyal', and enlarged on their scepticism about the transparency of the process. As I recall, a colleague and I were offered access to confidential intelligence on government abuses, which I declined as the arrangement would have compromised our neutrality.

One of our meetings on the government side was with the commandant of the state's military garrison. After the usual civilities I said, "General, there have been press reports that a military presence has allegedly intimidated some opposition activities in Carabobo." The general snorted: "You should not believe opposition rubbish. If there is a problem, it is you. The obvious partiality of the OAS is disturbing the calm of this region."

"Hmm," I said to myself, and thought of Bosnia. The refrain was familiar. Giving us short shrift, the general concluded the interview.

My meeting with the Archbishop of Valencia took a different course. I was offered cakes and coffee in Monsignor Jorge Liberato Urosa Savino's cathedral office and treated to a tirade about the iniquities of Chavez. The Archbishop had become a national figure for his denunciations of the government from the pulpit and in pastoral letters. He also spoke with great warmth of his time in a Canadian seminary. Looking at me with what seemed to be some diffidence, he said that he could even recall the words of the Canadian national anthem. He then sang "O Canada" in French. Two years after our meeting he was promoted Archbishop of Caracas, and not long after that, Pope John Paul appointed him Cardinal.

On referendum day we devoted most of our time to checking on procedures in polling stations, speaking to the poll officers about problems (very few), and briefly interviewing the official representatives of the government and opposition in each polling station. In 2004 Valencia was still a fairly prosperous city, and many of the polling stations on my list were in middle income to wealthy neighbourhoods. Wearing a vest and cap emblazoned 'OEA' (OEA is OAS in Spanish), my colleague (a Paraguayan lady) and I were immediately recognizable. This was a good thing because the presence of the OAS (or other well-known international observer organizations) was often a deterrent to voting shenanigans. My previous experience of elections, including several in Venezuela, had been that of a generally pleasant or at least civil reception. This was not the same. Walking along the queue to reach our first polling station, my colleague and I were greeted rapturously. We were astonished. As more voters recognized us, joyful shouts rang out, "OEA, OEA!" and "Viva la OEA!" There was a rippling of applause along the line, and the same welcome followed in several other polling stations. Not quite the reception that Allied soldiers received in Europe on entering a recently liberated town or village, but it must have been close. The big distinction, of course, was that in our case it was undeserved. One of my Canadian recruits elsewhere in Valencia told me that a very attractive lady had embraced him and invited him to her apartment for "refreshment," an invitation he had with difficulty declined.

Turnout across the country was close to 70 percent. The queues were exceptionally long, remarkably so in the scorching August sun, but people were in buoyant good spirits and somehow, at least in that part of Valencia, we were the reason. What was happening? Valencia was part of the opposition heartland. Most of its supporters believed absolutely that the recall would succeed, but only if there was an honest tabulation. Greatly exaggerating our powers, they believed that we, especially the OAS, were the guarantors of that honest tabulation and therefore of their victory.

This was not to be. Late that night it became clear that recall had been defeated. By early morning it was apparent that the "no" side had a comfortable margin of about 8 percent. The results were soon acknowledged by the OAS and the Carter Center.[3] Yesterday's euphoria turned rapidly sour. From heroes we became backstabbers. Word reached us from head office to be discreet. We packed our caps and vests, stripped our vehicles of OAS logos, and slunk out of town incognito.

UKRAIПE

Night Train to Ternopil

Ukrainian national elections in October 2004 failed to give any candidate the 50 percent or more required to gain the presidency. Run-off elections were called for November. Contaminated by massive fraud, these elections were annulled by the Ukrainian Supreme Court, which called for fresh elections to be held December 26. Discreet guidance from a few Western NGOs, but most of all, popular reaction to the fraud, especially among the young, powered the impressively successful Orange Revolution. I participated in the November run-off election as an observer for the OSCE, and in the December re-run election as an observer for an all-Canadian team. This team was created by the Canadian government to attract a domestic constituency in western Canada, despite sound warnings that a one-flag observer mission runs major credibility risks. This story draws from both experiences.

I was not an attractive sight. Dishevelled and fragrant from seventeen hours of airports and economy seats, I stood in front of the young woman responsible for hotel reservations and mission assignments. Her office was in the Hotel Rus in central Kiev. I and three hundred others formed the mission of the Organization for Security and Co-operation in Europe (OSCE) that was assembling for deployment across Ukraine for the November presidential elections. She smiled tightly and asked for my name.

"It's Graham; John Graham," I said.

"Ah, Mr. Grim," she muttered, skipping through her file to G. "We are sending you to Chernobyl."

"Chernobyl!" I gasped. Good God, they're sending me to the most radioactive location on the planet! Chernobyl was fresh in my mind. Before leaving I had read a question listed under "restaurants" that a black-humoured Berlitz author had inserted in my Ukrainian phrase book: "Is this food radioactive?"

"No, no," said the young woman, laughing. "Not Chernobyl – Ternopil." The problem was less her articulation than my defective hearing. "And you leave tonight by train. Ternopil is far; is near Polish border."

The destination was an improvement, but this was still not good news. I had just come from Atlanta via Chicago and London, my luggage was somewhere in Heathrow, and all I could think of was a bath and bed.

Fortunately there was time for a bath and a few repairs before setting off for the train station. I found a Ukrainian-speaking colleague, a veteran of the first election round in October, who took me to a labyrinth of small stores under street level, where I bought toilet articles, socks, and underwear. There was a difficulty about pyjamas. After a long search I presented my colleague with a pair of pink and decidedly feminine pyjamas.

"No!" she said.

"What do mean, 'No'? They fit. I'm tired and don't care what sex they're intended for."

"The salesperson will refuse to sell you a female garment. Believe me. I know."

Eventually I found gender-appropriate pyjamas and there was still time for borscht before leaving for the station.

Passazhirskiy Railway Station is astonishing. Floodlit, and gleaming in the rain, its giant portals of moulded aluminum suggest intergalactic rather than railway travel. Inside the huge vaulted entrance hall is a fountain set among full-size palm trees in iridescent puce plexiglass. Henri, our team leader, who had travelled this route many times, joined a line of slouching men in black leather jackets to buy tickets. "The sleeping cars," he said on return, "are just like those on the Trans-Siberian." None of his flock, a group of fourteen, jumbled in age and nationality, had experienced the Trans-Siberian. It sounded to us like prolonged discomfort.

Briefing papers warned us to expect "irregularities." The first round of elections, a month before, which reduced the presidential candidates from fifteen to two, had drawn a sharp rebuke from the OSCE. But as we boarded the train we had no notion of the scale of mischief and manipulation that was being planned by government apparatchiks across the country.

Once in the train we divided into sleeping compartments by random choice. The system was unisex, with no reserved berths. The bunkmates in my compartment were a young Ukrainian man, an elderly American man, and a middle-aged Hungarian woman. It was midnight, but the American and I tried to make conversation as the train clumped slowly out of the station. The body language of the Ukrainian said that we were not "cool" travelling companions. The Hungarian gave us a flinty look, and conversation sputtered out. The one paradoxically bright spot on this expedition was that I did not have my suitcase. My companions' bags left space only for my briefcase and shopping bag.

The sleeping car conductor came by, offered us tea from an enormous nickel-plated samovar, and lowered the vinyl-sheathed upper bunks. The arrangements were basic: a sheet, a blanket, and a pillow, but no curtains. It was already midnight. The lights were dimmed, and we prepared for bed. The Hungarian lady opted to sleep fully clothed. At this point, I realized that there was no ladder for the upper berth, and I had conceded the remaining lower to the marginally more elderly American. An upper berth was no problem for the athletic Ukrainian. Eventually I managed it by leveraging myself on the American's berth below me and the Ukrainian's upper opposite.

The train pitched and thumped through the night. Exhausted, I fell asleep, to be awakened several hours later by my aging bladder. Now, I realized, a fresh set of adventures would begin. The compartment was in total darkness. Pushing back the blanket, I stretched an arm toward the opposite bunk and probed for an edge. Propped by my arms, one foot explored the bunk below. The train was in spasmodic lurching mode, improving the chances that I would find a groin rather than vacant mattress. My toes touched something un-groinlike, then settled on mattress. The American was still asleep, and I made my way down the corridor to the washroom at the end of the carriage. There was a wash basin that didn't work and a toilet, opening onto the tracks, that did. The washroom was also inexplicably equipped with a galvanized bucket suspended from a hook over the wash basin. I returned to the compartment and managed to hoist myself onto the berth without incident.

Shortly after dawn, we drew into Ternopil station. Wet snow was falling. The temperature was dropping, and by nightfall the snow had become a blizzard. Snow continued to fall for the next seven days, with one twenty-four-hour break.

The first day was spent listening to disturbing reports from opposition politicians and election administrators about government interference and intimidation. The most credible information came from tough and intrepid women administrators. Three out of five senior government-appointed election officials in the Ternopil *oblast* had been dismissed on orders from Kiev because the government candidate, Viktor Yanukovych, had not received enough votes.

The election environment was darkening, but I was anxious to get back to the hotel. I spent a lot of time thinking about bed – my first real bed in three days. In the post-war Soviet period the Hotel Ternopil had been a spa for mid-level state, military, and party officials. Tourism was actively discouraged, because this area of the Ukraine bristled with westward-pointing ballistic missiles. This circumstance may explain why the hotel, including its window frames, was not built to international standards. Outside, the snow was driven by a howling gale, and within half an hour of my burrowing under the covers, three of my windows had blown open. I jammed them shut with bits of sock and climbed back into bed, only to watch the curtains billow at a 45-degree angle in front of the "closed" windows. I was huddled in bed wearing my fleecy, jeans and a scarf over my new Ukrainian pyjamas when the phone rang.

"Allo," said a silky voice, "my name eez Irena." I put the phone down and fell asleep.

The next day was the last before the elections. Zevile, my Lithuanian colleague, and I set off on a wide arc to the north to monitor the preparations. The blizzard was unabated, with visibility occasionally reduced to about sixty metres. Sections of the road were swept clean by the wind, while long stretches were snow-covered. In this part of Ukraine there are few ploughs and no salt. In the autumn, trucks drop small cones of sand at intervals of approximately forty metres along one side of the highway wherever there is a gradient. With the arrival of snow or freezing rain the resident peasant emerges from home with a spade and hurls sand erratically across his or her section. This system does not offer a uniformly non-slip surface. I suggested to my colleague that we should snap on our seat belts. Hers was fine, but mine was broken. When I reported this to Miroslav, the driver, he showed no concern. The safety device was the icon of the local Virgin that was clipped below the rear-view mirror. The next day another Ternopil team vehicle slid on the icy road and crashed, requiring the medical evacuation of a German observer.

Perched upon a low hill at the top of our circuit was the splendid Holy Archimandrite of Pochaev, a monastery from the fourteenth century, built, according to legend, where holy men had seen "the footprint of the Mother of God." Its parade of gold onion domes, some with swirls of blue and green, glowed against the grey sky. A gilded gazebo sat on a cushion of snow in the courtyard between one large and one very small cathedral. We had been warned by the opposition that the abbot and his monks had been invoking both divine and secular powers to persuade the villagers to vote for Yanukovych. The monastery exerts powerful influence and collaborates closely with Kiev-appointed officials who support a political alliance with Russia. "Why the political connection?" we asked Ludmila, the interpreter, by this time swathed, like Zevile, in a skirt rented at the monastery gate. "Well," she explained, "the superior of the Metropolitan, the chief of the Ukrainian Orthodox Church in Kiev, is the Patriarch of the Russian Orthodox Church in Moscow. This man, the Patriarch, was a colonel in the KGB." We were shown a flyer, apparently produced by this alliance, instructing party workers to ensure a good turnout for Yanukovych. The monks ignored us.

November 21, election day, was a blur of snow and polling stations. We were reminded early on that bars and bottle stores do not close for elections. I was hailed by a tottering voter who kept insisting "*Je parle français*," until it was clear that this was the sum total of his vocabulary. Another, with equally inflammable breath, gold teeth, and handlebar moustaches assumed that anybody could understand Ukrainian if the language was spoken at full bore. They and others belied the myth that vodka leaves no incriminating scent. In a hamlet almost literally in the shadow of the Pochaev monastery, a farmer took our interpreter aside as we trudged through the snow and failing light and explained hastily that the church and party officials had threatened the village with "reprisals" if the population did not vote heavily for Yanukovych. He then left, for fear of being spotted talking to us. Meanwhile, my toes were beginning to freeze, and I thought unhappily about my warm, waterproof hiking boots, somewhere, I hoped, in the British Airways lock-up in Kiev.

Henri passed on a report from the October election that all prisoners in a local maximum security prison had been beaten because a few had had the temerity to vote for opposition candidates. We agreed that this was a good reason to visit the prison. After lengthy processing and checking to ensure that we were not smuggling weapons, the warden, a colonel in this latest incarnation of the KGB, led us though a warren of iron gates to his office. The wooden panels shone with a recent coat of varnish, a rubber plant drooped in a dry pot, and a portrait of the country's national poet hung over the warden's desk. "This prison," the warden told us, "has 1,250 inmates, of whom 170 are incarcerated for life. Most will vote – but not the youngest."

"How young are the youngest?" I asked.

The answer was fourteen. In response to the next question, he admitted that they are not separated from adult convicts because there is "no space."

The prison was built in 1914 under the czars, and in the intervening years it had been run by some of the world's most barbarous police forces, including the Gestapo. Although it was meticulously clean, there was little sign that amenities had changed in ninety years. After making our way through a labyrinth of corridors and iron doors, we reached a narrow chamber where voting was taking place, and where we were joined by a general from the Ministry of the Interior, presumably alerted by the warden. A civilian polling officer assured us that "guided" voting was not taking place. The civilian suggested that we should take his views seriously, because he was a former inmate, incarcerated in this same prison for twenty years for a political crime. We left, subdued, and skeptical about the fairness of the process. But as we walked away, I thought that if nothing else, my colleague Zevile, with her striking figure, mink coat, and purple hair had for a short time brightened that grim and sunless place.

Holy Archimandrite of Pochaev.

Over six hundred party loyalists from the eastern region of Ukraine spread out through our province with instructions to boost the Yanukovych vote by fair means or foul. Two of them had tried to set fire to ballots in one polling station, an attempt that was thwarted only because their ignition system burned too slowly. Ternopil province was not a hotspot, but it had become a microcosm of the abuses contaminating the whole process. Manipulation on a colossal scale was taking place in the east.

Next day the government declared that Yanukovych had won. Simultaneously my organization and other observation missions reported massive fraud, calculating that roughly 1.3 million votes were added to the count between 8:00 P.M. and midnight. Most pundits and embassies in Kiev had expected that the election would be stolen. They also expected that a compliant population with no solid democratic tradition would allow the government to get away with it. That the government did not get away with it – then – constitutes the astonishing saga of the Orange Revolution, but that is another story, and a story with a sad ending and dim prospects, at least in the short term, for a brighter future.[1]

PALESTINE

Good Elections, Bad Judgments

In January 2006 I joined a one-flag (Canadian only) observer mission organized by the Canadian International Development Agency (CIDA) to monitor elections on the West Bank and Gaza.

At about six o'clock in the evening at the end of January, thirty-eight Canadians, all short-term observers for the Canadian Observer Mission to the Palestinian elections, arrived at Ben Gurion Airport in Tel Aviv. Earlier that day a suicide bomber blew himself up in the city, wounding ten people. However, the airport was calm, and with the help of an embassy official we scooted through Customs and Immigration and onto the bus that took us east into the hill country and to Ramallah, the Palestinian capital on the West Bank.

Our group gave meaning to the term "eclectic": we were a congenial collection of volunteers from all parts of the country, comprising lawyers, a family physician, an ex-colonel, a former helicopter pilot, professors, an artist, an automobile export entrepreneur, a former MP, an aircraft designer, graduate students, consultants, a fisheries commissioner, a professional election expert, CIDA officers, and diplomats, one active and two retired. There was a good gender mix and a range of ages from the late twenties to the mid-seventies. Almost everyone had either previous election experience or direct knowledge of the Middle East.

Briefings in Gatineau and at a Canadian Forces Base in Kingston included a simulated kidnapping. This was arranged to prepare us for the unexpected. A military briefer offered this cheerful epigram from Thomas Hardy on what an abducted person may expect: "More life may trickle out of a man through his thoughts than through a gaping wound." There were more briefings in Ramallah before we were deployed across the West Bank to Jericho, East Jerusalem, Hebron, Jenin, Bethlehem, and Nablus. Except for a few daytime excursions, Gaza had been scratched from our list as too volatile. Eleven persons had been killed there in the preceding few days. The Palestine veterans kept repeating that the situation is "complex," and advising us that if we think we are understanding it, we should dig deeper until we realize that we don't.

Bearing that injunction in mind, a few details may provide some context. Since the 1967 war, the Palestinian territories have been under Israeli occupation. In 1993, negotiations under the Oslo Accord gave Palestinians a limited degree of autonomy in the administration of the areas allocated to them. Since 2001, the beginning of the second Intifada, and up to the time of our visit, over 900 Israelis and over 3,500 Palestinians had been killed. In December 2005, a relatively quiet period, sixty had been killed in the West Bank. Over 150,000 Israelis had been established in fortified settlements in the West Bank, East Jerusalem, and Gaza, although those in Gaza were removed by Prime Minister Ariel Sharon in 2005. Secure road links to the settlements, a vast network of Israeli Defence Force checkpoints, and the new concrete wall offer enhanced security for the Israelis and suffocate the Palestinian economy. As a consequence of policies under the British mandate, Israeli investment in universities, and particularly the schools set up by the UN refugee organization (UNRWA), education levels in Palestine, including those for women, exceed those of most countries in the Middle East. But there are few outlets for the skills and training that these educational opportunities have provided. Unemployment is very high and likely to increase as a result of the standoff between Hamas objectives (including the extinction of Israel) and the reactions of Western donors, who were expected to pull back from many programs.

My destination was Nablus (Sychem in Biblical times), a city of grim, overcrowded refugee camps, a centre of tension and periodic violence. It is beautifully situated, with tall sand-coloured buildings ascending steep hills on either side. Most of the villages in Samaria, the ancient province of which Nablus is the centre, have been built on the crests of arid, stony hills. In many, the archeological remains reach back 3,000 years, but the ruins are neglected, rimmed with ramshackle cinder block houses, daubed with anti-Israel graffiti, and festooned with litter. And except for people like ourselves with special passes, the monuments are inaccessible. Palestine reeks with the stink of burning garbage. But not everything is bleak. Back in Nablus we passed a shop with a sign in English, "Arafat's Sweets." We stopped and had the finest baklava pastries I have eaten.

At a small resort on the Dead Sea, we bought ice cream from a young woman from the kibbutz nearby who had a pistol tucked into her waist. Because we wanted to say that we had done so, we plunged into the Dead Sea – and almost bounced. The water was incredibly buoyant, so much so that normal swimming strokes were impossible. Walking in the shallow water was slightly hazardous. People have been bathing at this place for thousands of years, but no one has cleared away the salt crystal-encrusted rocks on which we cut our feet. There was no sun and we emerged cold (it was January) and splattered with allegedly medicinal black mud.

Back in Nablus, the busy and deceptively normal street life was quickly shattered by the appearance of irregular militia groups. Twice in one day we encountered these men in dark clothes with no insignia, carrying an assortment of Kalashnikovs and shotguns. The atmosphere had been heated by a political murder near one of our polling stations the night before.

Given this, and the invariable irritations with checkpoints, the election itself was extraordinary. I have been to many elections in difficult settings and seldom have I observed one as professionally executed. In our polling stations there was a slight preponderance of female staff, and in some of them women were in charge, which was remarkably positive for an environment known for its Islamic militancy. Despite active campaigning outside the polling stations, there was unexpected civility within them, and in the usually chaotic press of voters immediately outside. In other words, the Palestinian Election Commission, supported by CIDA and by Canadian expertise, had reason to be proud of a first-class performance. Another consequence was that the Hamas victory was fair and square.

However, the concept of a Canada-only observer mission was not such a good idea. Stand-alone missions from whatever country, particularly when they are inextricably identified with the government of that country, are problem-prone. Election missions must have credibility built on a cumulative track record if they are to be convincing in their endorsement or repudiation of an electoral process. Making judgments and recommendations that will be considered seriously by the country in question and by the international community requires a level of credibility that is very difficult for a single-flag mission to achieve. The National Democratic Institute, the Carter Center, and the International Foundation for Electoral Systems (all of which I have worked with) are all US-based, but are never uniquely composed of US citizens or even a majority of US citizens. National missions are susceptible to possessing political baggage that can compromise their essential credibility. It is not difficult to imagine what would happen if the Canadian prime minister or his foreign minister were perceived to be obviously partial to Israeli or, for that matter, Palestinian policy. Multilateral missions like those from the EU, OAS, and OECS are largely insulated from this predicament. In this case CIDA and the Canadian government succumbed to the temptation to look upon Canadian observer missions such as this one, and the mission in Ukraine, as opportunities to burnish the Canadian image both at home (especially in politically congenial constituencies) and abroad. We go down this road at our peril.

An example of the counter-productive instructions that can arise in such circumstances was the prohibition on contact with Hamas imposed by our government. Any observer mission that goes into an election environment subject to the proviso that it can have no substantive contact with one of the two principal contestants cannot be expected to be taken seriously. In very difficult and contentious election situations it is often precisely the ability of election observers to talk to all sides that promotes problem-solving.

A further complication was that some of the arrangements on the ground for the Canadian Observer Mission were not prudent. The day before the election, our regional team, together with other observers, was taken to a briefing in an Israeli Defense Force compound outside Nablus. A convoy of vehicles, each plastered with its respective observer identity, drove into the compound, where we were given an almost totally useless briefing by an Israeli colonel who was an expert at non-answers. Not only did this waste an entire morning, but, more seriously, it sent the wrong signal about our neutrality to the Palestinian authorities, who were certainly aware of our destination. There was no balancing meeting with Palestinian officials. We embarked on election day with inadequate intelligence about what problems to expect, which party controlled the different sectors in the Nablus area, and where the "hot spots" might be located. In the event, this was not a problem as the election, with its unusually small number of incidents, was exemplary.

Getting to the polling stations was another matter. For some tangled reason relating to security, our drivers were from East Jerusalem, and had no familiarity with the Nablus area. In an environment where there are no detailed maps available, no street signs, and, apart from major highways, no directional information, this was a problem. Scouting the terrain prior to the election, we were perpetually getting lost. One afternoon we inadvertently drove into an Israeli settlement area. We turned around and were making our way back when we were overtaken and stopped by an armoured Israeli Humvee. In the end there was no problem (the car was papered with CIDA/Canada signs), but Ayat, our local interpreter, was terrified.

Ayat was a delightful young woman from Ramallah. When the need arose she was also enterprising. After one long day, much of it spent getting lost, we reached a remote village at the furthest end of our route. Public facilities are almost non-existent in rural Palestine, and our bladders were stretched. She got out of the car and knocked on the door of the most prosperous-looking house in the village. The woman of the house welcomed us into her home and to her bathroom. She introduced her family and served tea. On the following day, in a different village, an elderly woman invited us into her tiny confectionery for cookies and then into her more comfortable house. As we sipped her tea amid a jumble of small children, she told us with some pride that she had forty-four grandchildren. The Palestinians have few defenses, and a high birth rate is one of them – a tactic known elsewhere as *la revanche du berceau*.

Tragically, frustration takes other forms. Three brothers, all below the age of ten, were playing with a ball on a village street. Hanging from cords around their necks were miniature photographs of their "martyred" suicide bomber cousin. Conversation with the kids revealed that the pendants were being worn not just in sad remembrance, but with pride. To take the life of the innocent, including children, is horrifying and unconscionable, and to do so with pride, almost unimaginable. It was equally horrifying to get inside the minds of these boys. There was no longer any place within their conceptual framework for innocence. If you were an Israeli, you were the natural enemy and therefore a target. Whatever your age or occupation, you shared the guilt for what had become of Palestine. Nothing I experienced on the West Bank was more troubling than this.

These kids and their parents, and others like them, represent a significant, fanatical,

segment of the population. Yet, from admittedly brief observations, I had the impression that the majority of voters were not deliberately opting for terrorism, and that, like voters in this country, many were simply voting against a government and a system in which they had lost confidence. Dignity, identity, and the Hamas record of social service at the grass roots, as well as frustration with corruption and incompetence, were among the motivating factors.

Did they, in fact, elect a dark and implacable force that will lead the Palestinians and their neighbours into a deeper vortex of misery? Was penalizing the freshly elected consistent with our encouragement of a free election? Did the swift rejection of Hamas by Israel and Western donors undermine the pragmatists and reinforce the hard line within that movement? I don't know the answers to all or any of these questions. The Palestine veterans, who warned us we shouldn't expect to understand, need not have worried. The closer you look, the more distant your understanding becomes.[1]

NICARAGUA

The Jaguar Changes Some of Its Spots

Over the past decade I have travelled frequently to Central America on behalf of the Carter Center. The expeditions in this story were made following the completion of election work for Friends of the Inter-American Democratic Charter, a hemisphere-wide group created by former US President Jimmy Carter.

There was a young man from Nicaragua
Who smiled as he rode on a jaguar.
They returned from the ride
With the young man inside
And the smile on the face of the jaguar.

Anon[1]

Nicaragua is a bundle of grim, but sometimes entertaining, contradictions. The country is ruled by the former Sandinista commandante, Daniel Ortega, whose ambition is to become president for life, or at least for much longer than the constitution will currently allow. With a tropical mix of guile, good works and dirty tricks, he may achieve his goal. His latest venture is a project with a Hong Kong tycoon to drive a canal with twice the capacity of the nearby Panama Canal across his part of the isthmus.

Digging has begun, and if completed, the geopolitical consequences will be huge and the environmental consequences not yet predictable. Its opponents call it a '*monstruosidad*'. Others call it perplexing. Completion would almost certainly require at least tacit financial approval by China, yet the Nicaraguan government is one of only a handful on the planet that still recognizes Taiwan.

With few exceptions the governments that have marked Nicaragua's institutional character have been piratical. After Haiti it is the most impoverished country in the hemisphere. Rhetorically, it's well out on the left and continues to move away from democratic norms and the civil rights of its citizens. At the same time it is open to business, especially big business. The International Monetary Fund regards Nicaragua's macro-economic policies as reassuringly conservative. Central America, together with Mexico, is the heartland for narcotics-fuelled organized crime, with a staggering daily toll of violent death. Yet Nicaragua is less corrupt and gang-infested and much less violent than its neighbours. In large part this is because it has the best and least corrupt army and police force in Central America.

With the dust still thick in the air from the traumatic 2011 elections, I took two days to explore some obscure parts of the Pacific coast. Setting off with my taxi driver, the laconic and in this regard un-Nicaraguan Euclido, and his fifteen-year-old Corolla, our first destination was the Chocoyero–El Brujo Nature Reserve, a wildlife refuge. We drove for an hour and then turned off onto a road that would not normally be recommended for elderly Toyotas. We bumped along for about six kilometres until the road stopped in front of a plain wooden building with a courtyard where a birding class was in progress. For a small fee I hired Andres, a local guide. As we walked along the forest path, he explained that I had chosen the wrong time of day to see the birds. Dawn or late afternoon were better times, but, because there was cloud cover, we might be lucky. Andres directed my eyes to a motmot, whose long tail feathers culminated in tufts of blue, cuckoos, guans, and other birds almost invisible in the foliage. We briefly sighted the iridescent blue wings of a morpho butterfly. The path ended at a steep cliff face over which fell a thin stream of water. Swooping over the water was a flock of green parakeets. As we walked back to the car we heard the baritone ululations of a howler monkey. A labba or capybara,

a thirty-pound member of the rodent family, jogged across our path. No jaguars or quetzals, but this was a good start to the day.

"What's next?" asked the morose Euclido. Waving my hands and feeling like Balboa,[2] five hundred years before, I said, "Let's go to the Pacific." I was keen to have a swim, a body surf, and fresh fish for dinner. It wasn't far. In an hour and a half we arrived in the small fishing village of La Boquita with its long beach of dark volcanic sand. However, a thundering surf meant no swimming and certainly no body surfing. Instead I settled for an early supper with Euclido at one of the thatched, sand-floored restaurants. We had just sat down when the wash from a huge wave flooded the restaurant, soaking my shoes and pant cuffs. We shifted our table further inland, and eventually our ceviche, beer, and huge grilled snapper appeared. Euclido showed signs of mellowing.

After dinner I strolled along the beach. The roar of the surf had softened, and I watched a group of fishermen preparing to launch their boat. Using palm trunks as rollers and picking the exact moment between the waves, they pushed their open boat into the surf, jumped in, and cranked the outboard. Aboard were hundreds of lines with hooks, and buckets of bait. They would fish all night and truck their catch into Managua in the morning.

It was a seductive place, but the election was still buzzing in my head. Nicaragua was a pernicious model of abusing judicial, constitutional, and electoral processes and getting away with it.

The OAS was also taking a hit. On election morning, Dante Caputo,[3] head of the OAS observation mission, was distressed to learn that about one-fifth of his observers had been denied access to polling stations. As this was a blatant violation of the rules, Caputo convened a press conference to express his alarm about non-compliance by the electoral authorities. They eventually responded by opening all polling stations to OAS observation, but by then the news was out that this was a contaminated election. Ortega had won, but the exclusion of the observers for several hours, together with a host of other irregularities, including the exclusion of six thousand domestic observers, opened the question of whether he had really won a key two-thirds majority in the legislature.

That evening José Miquel Insulza, the OAS secretary general, spoke to Ortega by phone from Washington. The following morning, he issued a communiqué congratulating Nicaragua – saying that "democracy and peace took a step forward." We were astonished.[4] I spoke to Luis Yanes, the head of the EU delegation. He was equally astonished. Why would the secretary general basically accept the Sandinista version and undercut his mission on the ground?

Possibly because he was concerned that Ortega, who denigrates the OAS and frets about American influence, might seize the excuse of an unfavorable OAS report to withdraw his county from the organization – a precedent that might be followed by other countries on the radical left – most of whom claim to be more politically comfortable with CELAC – the new hemispheric organization that excludes both the US and Canada.

If there are lessons in this episode, one is that no international organization should undertake an electoral observation in a country to which in some important respect it is hostage. Another is that the hemispheric community should not have stood aside allowing the potentially infectious precedent of democratic backsliding to go unchallenged.

On the way back from La Boquita we were stopped at a police checkpoint. Euclido and I both grumbled. However, we were spared a lengthy delay after Euclido paid a small bribe. He explained that checkpoints were the principal means by which the rural police supplemented their miserable salaries.

The next day Euclido was unavailable and, in any event, I was looking for a more cheerful companion. I hailed a taxi on the main square. It was a Honda of about the same vintage as Euclid's. I asked the driver if he could take me to Poneloya, a small town about two and a half hours away on Nicaragua's Pacific coast.

"*Si, Señor*," the driver replied briskly, pleased at the prospect of a windfall long-distance fare.

"Do you know Poneloya?"

A pause, and "*Absolutamente.*"

We negotiated a fare and set off. I had chosen Poneloya for my last free day because it is almost unknown to international tourism, is within a few hours drive of Managua, and I had never been there. The previous day when I told my friend David that Poneloya was my choice, he told me I was crazy. "It's a crummy down-market place, and the toilets don't work." David had lived for fifteen years in Nicaragua. I rejected his advice to travel south to a trendy resort area, but my confidence had been shaken.

Ambrosio, the driver, and I headed north. Conversation was desultory – not a big improvement on Euclido. He talked about his family and was less interested than I was in the country's perplexing politics.

The first crisis of our expedition arose when Ambrosio got lost in Leon, a city on our route. Fortunately it is not a bad place to be lost in – sleepy, baked a smoky yellow by the sun, and, like most of Nicaragua, almost totally devoid of road signs. Leon is a university town, and although the periphery is frowzy, the centre, with churches and other buildings dating from the seventeenth century, is beautiful. After asking at least four people for directions, we eventually found the road to Poneloya.

When we arrived it became clear that David, unlike Ambrosio, had been there. Poneloya's main street, in fact virtually the only one, ran between decaying cement and cinder-block houses, some of which were beach hotels. My guidebook described several. One was the Hotel Lacayo, which featured "sagging beds, shared bath and a dilapidated balcony overlooking the ocean." The price was five dollars a night. The blurb added, "Don't mind

the bats – they eat the mosquitoes." For another thirty dollars you could be air-conditioned in Poneloya's most "romantic" and expensive hotel. As far as I could see, all the hotels were empty. Worse, the few restaurants were closed. It was midweek, and nothing much happened in Poneloya except on weekends and holidays. Discouraged, we motored on to the end of town, climbed a hill, and wound down the far side, where a line of very shaggy thatched bars and restaurants looked out over a river basin that opened onto the Pacific. Here at least there were a few cars and motorcycles.

We stopped at the Club Chechi, where there were customers and a woman leaning over a wood fire. I asked if she was still serving lunch.

Big smile. "Yes, indeed. What would you like?" She removed the lid from an ice box and showed us half a dozen fish that had been taken out of the water early that morning by the small boat moored at the foot of the restaurant. Ambrosio only wanted soup. I ordered a fish and shellfish soup for both of us and a medium-sized *pargo* (snapper) for myself.

We climbed a spindly staircase to our table, which stood on a balcony overlooking the river, and more distantly the ocean. The restaurant's ambience was artisanal grunge. There were no real windows and hence no glass. The floor was a charcoal-coloured clay composed of a sort of volcanic porridge and soot. The toilet arrangements were on the dark side of basic, but the view over the water, and most especially the food, more than compensated. The fish soup was one of the finest I have eaten, and the snapper, filleted and fried, was sublime. We drank the local beer.

The next part of my program was a swim in the ocean. We drove about a kilometre from Club Chechi and parked close to some fishermen who were repairing their nets. The beach was lovely, with deep beige sand, and a heavy scattering of shells above the tide line. Huge rollers crashed about a hundred yards off shore. There were no swimmers and no warning signs. I asked a young woman who was collecting shells if it was safe to swim. She raised her head, considered the question, said, "Yes and no," and returned to her shells. When I stepped into the water I could feel the current on my legs, so I stayed in the shallows. I walked to the point where the river opened to the ocean, from which I could see the tiny village of thatch and bamboo where we had lunched. It was huddled by a bend in the river and looked frozen in time.

Back at the car, the fishermen said that I could use water from their well to wash the sand from my feet. The well pump was operated by a bicycle wheel contraption. Ambrosio turned the wheel and the water gushed out. It was while washing my feet that I noticed that the cover that capped the fisherman's well was an old metal sign with the faded lettering still visible: "Danger. Strong Maritime Currents."

Except for the cell-phone calls from Ambrosio's wife and many relations, the return drive was lovely. To the east, looming above Lake Xolatlan, was the almost perfect cone of the Zero Negro volcano. Its flanks glowed pink in the late afternoon sun, and we were favoured with a plume of white smoke from one of its infrequent mini-eruptions. The sun set, and the western sky was so drenched in vivid apricot that it looked like a cheap postcard.

Still some distance from the capital, we stopped at a thatched roadside *quesillo* bar, dimly lit from within. Outside were scooters, bicycles, and a horse hitched to a cart with a broken wheel. Ambrosio explained, "Señor, the *quesillo* is one of Nicaragua's famous delicacies. You should try it." The Nicaraguan *quesillo* consists of mushy cheese mixed with sliced raw onion, rolled in a tortilla, and topped with thick fresh cream. Like fermented mare's milk in Kyrgyzstan, it is an acquired taste.

EL SALVADOR

Off the Beaten Track

The purpose of my visit to El Salvador in 2011 was to attend the Annual General Assembly of the Organization of American States on behalf of the Canadian Foundation for the Americas. Like the trips described in the two preceding chapters, the expedition described below was initiated after the meetings were over. This visit also kindled memories of earlier experiences of El Salvador, when the country was mired in civil war.

After Belize, El Salvador is the smallest country in Central America. Its only sea frontage is on the Pacific, running in a saw-tooth coastline from Nicaragua to Guatemala. At the conclusion of work in San Salvador, the capital, it was my plan to spend several days on this coast.

The portents, however, were not all good. Before leaving the capital I had to deal with the consequences of an "official" dinner I had attended the previous night. The pharmacist dispensed powerful substances guaranteed to set concrete in my internal regions, warning me against gin and almost everything else, with the exception of rice and grilled fish.

Pharmaceutically fortified, I set off for the coast with my newly acquired taxi driver. "Benedicto," I said, looking at the strange configuration in front of me, "what happened to the dashboard?"

"Ah, Señor, it is because this was originally a right-hand drive car."

It was a beautiful day and we made good time, but after covering the specified distance along the coast road, we could not find the hotel. It had been awarded three stars by *Frommer's Guide*, which said prophetically, "This is the place to stay if you want an adventurous vacation." Eventually a local resident told us that we had to look for a gate bearing the sign "*Propriedad Privado.*" Why, I wondered, would the entrance to a prominent hotel be so peculiarly discreet? The gate was opened by Fina, the cook. There were no other signs of life in this small hotel on a cliff top overlooking the Pacific. I was the only guest, Fina the only staff member. But that was OK. It was gorgeous.

I climbed down steep steps to the base of the cliff, where a natural basin had been extended and protected by a low wall. At high tide the rollers would crash against the wall, pitching huge curtains of spray over the pool and delivering a novel aquatic experience. Back at the top of the cliff, I settled into my hammock with a book and a rum and coconut water.

The problems began when I went into my room to shower before dinner. The power was off. This meant no light, no air conditioning, no water, and, I soon discovered, no dinner. Fina and I searched for candles and flashlights in the remains of twilight. No luck. Joaquin, the night watchman, arrived, but he had no flashlight. He pointed me in the direction of a nearby hotel where there might be a generator and supper. Alas, neither were available. However, someone offered me a lift in a truck to the nearest restaurant that had power. I clambered aboard and clung to the top of the cab while the truck lumbered up, down, and around the corrugations of the coast road. There were about eight of us in the back, mostly hotel staff. The man beside me said that there would be nothing open until we reached La Libertad, and something about the road being dangerous at night.

"Dangerous from the cars and trucks?" I asked.

"No," he said.

I thought about the book I had been reading on crime in El Salvador, where the homicide rate is the third highest on the globe, and my guide book, which described La Libertad as a town with "a reputation for high crime." It was probably not a good idea to let hunger trump common sense. Ahead of us were flashing lights and police. A large articulated truck had crashed, snapping off a hydro pole, causing the blackout.

There were lights in La Libertad, dimly illuminating an unlovely town. I was dropped off at a seafood restaurant built onto a pier, and arrangements were made for a ride back to my hotel. I ordered a grilled dorado. Service was slow, and by the time the meal arrived my driver was waiting. The fish was enormous, its head and tail overhanging the plate. I explained to the waiter that I would pay, but had to leave. He wrapped the fish in aluminum foil and gave me two candles. Back at the hotel, Joaquin enjoyed most of the fish while I skinny-dipped in the freshwater pool. With one candle, a crescent moon, and no other guests, this was not a problem. Apart from the crump of the surf against the cliff below, it was also incredibly peaceful.

The quiet and the conversation in the back of the truck set my mind back to 1983, when the country was less quiet. It had been my first visit to El Salvador, and my friend Chips Filleul, our ambassador,[1] had arranged for us to meet Thomas Pickering, the American ambassador, at his embassy. The war in El Salvador between the government, supported by the United States, and the Faribundo Marti revolutionaries (FMLN), supported by Cuba, Nicaragua, and by extension, the Soviet Union, was in full spate. Both sides were responsible for war crimes, but the atrocities on the left were no match for those on the right. The guerrillas lacked air power, with the result that they were unable to hold any town, mountainside, or other space permanently. But the peasantry and the urban poor were largely on their side, and this enabled the FMLN to move easily about the country. At the time of my visit, there were frequent attacks against army barracks and buildings in the capital, against the US embassy, and occasionally against the Hotel Presidente, where Chips and I were staying. The US embassy has now been replaced by an enormous walled monster on the edge of town, but at that time it was in the heart of the capital. It was the most visibly embattled embassy I have ever seen. The perimeter walls were pockmarked by rocket and mortar fire. When Chips and I arrived, it was protected by two companies of Salvadoran troops, while inside there must have been forty well-armed US marines. Although the circumstances were less dramatic, the scene reminded me of photographs of the siege of Western legations in Peking during the Boxer Rising of 1900.

We sat down with Pickering to hear a considerably more candid and even-handed socio-political analysis of the situation in El Salvador than the bald spin presented by the Reagan administration.[2] Discussion continued over lunch at the ambassador's residence, but the journey from the chancery to the residence was more memorable than the ensuing conversation. Chips travelled with Pickering and a bodyguard in the armoured limousine, while I was in the second of two armoured vans. The convoy travelled at speed, but respected traffic signals. When we stopped, the lead van swung diagonally in front of the ambassador's car, while mine braked on the opposite diagonal behind the limousine. I was in the back of the van with two bodyguards who were armed with submachine guns. The bulletproof windows had three ports through which the guns could be fired.

At Pickering's well-fortified residence we talked about the people who were attempting, at enormous risk, to find a few moderately sane individuals on both sides who were prepared to talk about ending the conflict. One of the most significant of the intermediaries was Father Ignacio Ellacuria. Born in Spain, he was a Jesuit philosopher, a Salvadoran citizen, and the rector of the Catholic University. More importantly, he knew many of the FMLN leaders and had earned their respect. He was instrumental in securing the release of the daughter of the president, who had been kidnapped by the FMLN.

On this occasion and on many subsequent visits to El Salvador over the next five years I made a point of calling on Father Ellacuria. More than anyone else, he helped me toward an understanding of this bloody conflict and its roots. By 1988, the time of my last visit to El Salvador, his name had advanced to a top spot on the army's enemies list – and we had become friends. In a conversation in the Carter Center in Atlanta almost thirty years later, a former guerilla commandate, Joaquin Villalobos, and I discovered that we had both enjoyed a friendship with Father Ellacuria over roughly the same timespan – in Villalobo's case the relationship was infinitely more meaningful. He had been the principal FMLN interlocutor with Father Ellacuria in peace negotiations with the Salvadoran government. A target of the Salvadoran army and the CIA, he always carried two pistols, one of them in his hat. Interviewed after the war, he remarked, "*No hay peor cosa que matarse por ideas.*" (There is nothing worse than to kill for ideas.)[3]

I was in Caracas when I learned of Father Ellacuria's assassination. On November 16, 1989, troops of the American-trained Atlacatl Battalion, a counter-insurgency unit, entered the university campus and executed

Ellacuria and five of his Jesuit colleagues. Two witnesses, the rector's housekeeper and her fifteen-year-old daughter, were also shot. Subsequent investigation by the Inter-American Commission on Human Rights disclosed that senior officers of the army had been implicated. Eventually two officers were jailed, but later released under an amnesty agreement.

If any good came from this crime, it was that international outrage, including widespread condemnation in the United States, accelerated the push toward peace negotiations. But "good" was a long time coming. Archbishop Oscar Romero, another outspoken advocate of human rights, had been murdered by an army death squad while conducting mass, nine blood-soaked years before the murder of Ellacuria and his companions. The United Nations-sponsored peace agreement was finally signed in February 1992. The war had come to an end. However, El Salvador soon descended into a different kind of mess. In the first decade of this century the blood spilled by violent crime and "drugs and thugs" gang wars exceeded the casualties of the civil war.

Enough gloomy reflections. The next night the hotel was air-conditioned, and the morning after, I ordered a car to take me to the airport. The car turned out to be a van with a handicap sticker. Once inside I realized that the sticker was not a precaution taken for potentially mobility-impaired passengers, but belonged to the driver, Miguel, a one-legged civil war survivor, who took me safely to the airport.

HAITI

Goudau-Goudau: Return to Haiti

My last visit to Haiti was in December 2010, a year after the earth-quake, and a week after a deeply flawed election had plunged the country into another major political crisis. The purpose of the visit was to learn what, if anything, the international community might do beyond what it was already doing to help prevent further unraveling of the country. The team represented Jimmy Carter's Friends of the Inter-American Democratic Charter, and was to have been led by Joe Clark. Unfortunately, civil disorders closed the airport, and Mr. Clark was unable to join us. Almost no story in Haiti follows a straight line. This one has a switchback course.

"Goudau-Goudau" is the onomatopoetic Creole word for the deep rumbling that signals the approach of an earthquake. Unsurprisingly, Haitians remain sensitive to that sound. In Port-au-Prince and in a wide arc surrounding the epicentre, there was still so much rubble and dislocation that you would think that our hemisphere's most devastating natural disaster occurred only weeks, not, in fact, over a year before our visit.

Our small team[1] was in Haiti for eight days, and we eventually did most of the things we were supposed to do, but this was not easy. The night of our arrival, rioting broke out in Port-au-Prince and around the country. Most of the demonstrators were protesting widespread fraud in the recent elections. A few took advantage of the general disorder to pursue personal vendettas and criminal opportunities. The result was that the capital and much of the country were paralyzed. Port-au-Prince must be the most easily barricaded city on earth. With few exceptions, the streets are narrow and strewn with rubble. Add a tire, light it, and, if it's handy, throw in the carcass of an old car, and presto! you have stopped all drivers save a few enterprising motorcyclists.

The team was marooned in the Hotel Karibe for several days. If you recall the casting and circumstances of the old Humphrey Bogart film *Key Largo*, you will understand the change in social chemistry that takes place in a hotel when none of the guests can leave: some become bitchier, some more nervous, and most, in our case, more convivial. We were a mixed bag: journalists, staff members from international organizations, a Dutch builder, a Haitian "rubble removal" entrepreneur, and several Spaniards who, we discovered, were part of the political organization largely responsible for paralyzing the city and for masterminding the political campaign of Martelly, the successful presidential candidate. The hotel did not run out of rum or food, although the latter was all beginning to taste the same after the second day.

Before long most of us were getting cabin fever. In our case, although the embassy kept telling us not to move, we headed out on our appointments as soon as our driver gave us a "more or less" all-clear. There were still problems and the occasional road blockade. I was told by a pair of foreign journalists that they had been able to navigate the barricades by showing press credentials. I instructed our driver to make two placards reading "*Presse Canadienne*" for the front and rear windows of our battered jeep. If asked by the demonstrators at a barricade "*Quelle Presse Canadienne?*" I would reply, "*Le Manor Park Chronicle*," the community paper I often write for. Unfortunately, I never had to give this explanation.

The rioting died down. It seemed that there were few tires left to burn. One interview that we missed was with a leader of the Vodou religion. We were anxious to learn more about Vodou's role as "escape," and the teaching of fatalism (another barrier to change), as well as to discover how influential *houngans* (priests) might facilitate reconciliation. However, we were able to resume most of our program, and were exposed to the bewildering pressures and contradictions involved in "helping" Haiti.

The United Nations, the donor nations and organizations, and Bill Clinton, who co-chairs the rehabilitation commission, were all regularly chastised for the country's painfully slow recovery and the fact that over 200,000 Haitians still lived in tent cities. Some senior officials admitted mistakes, but of course the reaction time of international bureaucracies is slow, and collisions among these organizations are common. The international community's relationship with the Haitian government and with Haitians generally was suffering from fatigue and frustration.

Scapegoating the internationals had been for many years a popular and perhaps inevitable Haitian pastime. This time it was different. An already fragile relationship was shattered by the revelation that post-earthquake Haiti had been infected with cholera by Nepalese troops working for the United Nations. Since the 2010 outbreak, approximately 6 percent of the population has been infected and thousands have died. A major indictment, and one of the worst the UN has had to bear in this century, but I believe that it is wrong to argue (as some do) that most of the blame for Haiti's appalling ongoing misery can be placed at the door of the international community. Few issues are debated with such lively and at times intolerant passion as who or what accounts for Haiti's chronic chaos and poverty. Writing in the June 6, 2013 *New York Review of Books*, the novelist Mischa Berlinski concludes, "If you believe, as I do, that the presence of vast numbers of culturally insensitive, publicity seeking, bumbling, profiteering foreigners prevents Haiti's descent into some greater disaster, then you will accept some of the corruption as a necessary price of doing business, of alleviating still greater suffering."

Too harsh? Probably. And he does no justice to a number of remarkable and dedicated people, some of whom, including a friend, were killed in the earthquake. But the point that the positive outweighs the negative is fair. The misery of millions would have been beyond imagining if the donor countries and donor organizations had not moved massively to provide disaster relief. Take one example. Tents, blankets, towels, medicines, and all the paraphernalia of emergency relief were shipped in. Tent cities to shelter over a million refugees sprouted like mushrooms in and around Port-au-Prince and other urban areas. Canvas towns need toilets: thousands of portable toilets were sent by USAID, Catholic Relief, and other organizations. However, these would have become instant bogs of human waste and lethal disease if they had not been cleared and cleaned according to a regular timetable – and not just for a month, but for the years it is taking to clear the rubble and build new homes. Haitians drove

the trucks and performed the mucky jobs, but had neither the funds nor the skills to install the infrastructure according to the standards required by basic hygiene.

Our conversations about what was wrong moved in many directions. The country was preparing for a second round of elections to determine the presidency. Exposure to democratic governance had been very uneven, and the setting for the second round was not promising. Pursuing interviews in the interior, we spoke to two powerful political chieftains, one living in a tent beside his partially collapsed mansion and the other in an intact and splendid villa. We learned afterwards that both men apparently ran drug trafficking operations. We learned that all major political parties are beholden, at least in part, to criminal organizations for resources and local intelligence. The finalists in the runoff for president were a university teacher (and grandmother), a political lightweight selected by the outgoing president and his party as someone unlikely to rock the president's boat with investigations, and a pop star celebrated in the past for dropping his pants and mooning his audiences. The pop star, Michel Martelly, won.

Another issue is the almost hopeless legal swamp of land tenure. The corruption of the Haitian legislature has meant that expropriation of land to create new towns is blocked. Poor families attempting to assert claims to small parcels of land stand little chance when judges are easily bought.

But here again, blame comes too easily, and Haitian shortcomings are only part of the answer. Another complication was the collapse of the government building in Port-au-Prince that held the few existing land records.

Of course, there are other very poor countries, and many of them are showing improvement. Why isn't this happening in Haiti? There is no consensus among scholars, but setting aside the role of natural disasters (divinely inspired, according to the evangelist Pat Robertson, to punish those whose ancestors made a pact with the devil), a malignant history has conspired against national progress. Few countries on earth can have had their independence so blighted at birth. Its population ravaged by war and disease, its plantations and wharfs destroyed, and its forests cut to build French warships. Haiti was forced by France to pay crippling reparations for 127 years. It also had the colossal misfortune to have the United States as a neighbour. The slave-owning United States could not abide the emergence of a liberated slave state off the Florida coast, and imposed a trade embargo. Ongoing racial antagonism maintained this policy for almost fifty years beyond the civil war. From having been the most prosperous territory in the entire hemisphere in the eighteenth century.

One of our conversations was with the correspondent for *Le Monde*, an astute, well-connected journalist who had been in and out of Haiti for thirty years. Asked if he could see any potentially good exits from the crisis, he replied crisply, "*Pas de sortie.*"

Moving through this strange, at times mystical and disfigured physical kaleidoscope was always an adventure. Because it was sufficiently remote from the capital to have a distinctive political dynamic, we set off for Les Cayes, a mid-sized town near the extremity of a long finger of land that stretches westward below Cuba's Oriente province. We were still in the outskirts of Port-au-Prince, in the wretched garbage-clogged suburb of Carrefour, when the driver's cell phone rang. The customs house and other buildings in Les Cayes were on fire, and there was a report that the local UN military detachment had been shot up. We switched destinations to Jacmel – along the same road initially, but closer and less troubled. Travelling south on this road we passed very close to the epicentre of the earthquake. The asphalt was split as though with a pie knife. Cyril, our driver, expertly navigated past the crevasses. When we came back in the dark, the same road was crowded with ancient, badly- or unlit trucks loaded with fruit or bags of charcoal, "*tap-taps,*" the gloriously hand-painted buses jammed with people, and the occasional bullock cart. Cyril drove like a maniac, but a skilled maniac with lightning reflexes.

Our last drive with Cyril was to the airport, where a car, as usual stuffed with passengers, shot out of a side road directly into our path. Cyril braked, twisted, and barely squeezed past the vehicle. He stopped long enough to shout at the driver, "You son of a misbegotten goat, if you had been killed, I would still have picked you up and beaten the **** out of you!" It sounded better in the original Creole.

ଊ ଊ ଊ

Lou Quinn: A Profile

In these travels I met a host of remarkable people, and it is, of course, getting to know the good, the bad, the mischievous, and the fascinating that is most rewarding. I have drawn outlines of many, but they are at best thumbnail sketches. Before drawing the volume to a close with a scattering of final observations, I offer a brief close-up of just one member of this cast, my friend Lou Quinn.

The day after Father Quinn died in a Florida hospital in 2007, the father superior of the Scarboro Missions, a former nun, a cousin, and I met with his cardiac surgeon. Long acquainted with Lou, his wonky heart, his Parkinson's, his discs, and his other afflictions, the distinguished surgeon grumbled that this had not been a "compliant" patient, and then repeated what he had said to his medical team: "This is probably as close as any of us will get to a Mother Teresa."

This view was widely shared in the Dominican Republic, whose people Father Quinn had served for more than half a century. President Fernandez decreed a day of national mourning, and all flags on government buildings across the country were lowered to half-mast. Along with several thousand grieving Dominicans, the president attended the funeral held in Father Quinn's parish, the mountain town of San Jose de Ocoa. So did the previous president, with whom Lou and his parishioners had enjoyed a more materially beneficial relationship. But the ex-president was not seated on the specially constructed VIP platform, as he was not on speaking terms with the incumbent.

In his eulogy, the diocesan bishop spoke of the many things that Lou had done and of the many things that he had unsuccessfully urged the government to do. One of these was the construction of a solid all-weather road running down the mountains and linking Ocoa to the country's east–west highway, for which Lou had long campaigned. Six days after the funeral, the tropical storm Noel devastated the Ocoa valley. The town and the surrounding villages were isolated when flood waters and mudslides sheered away large sections of the road, the need for whose reconstruction the government had ignored.

I met Lou in 1961, a few months before the assassination of the dictator, Generalissimo Trujillo. It was my job as vice-consul in the tiny Canadian embassy to offer some sort of protection to members of Canadian religious orders who were being harassed and threatened by the secret police. As explained in an early chapter on the Dominican Republic, there was nothing that I could really do except visit and show the flag. I am neither Catholic nor especially religious, but my meeting with Lou was the beginning of a forty-seven-year friendship. Helping to sustain the relationship was a thin stream of limericks and risqué humour.

Lou's mettle was tested almost immediately after his arrival in the Dominican Republic, ruled at the time by the megalomaniacal dictator, who decreed that it was all right to worship God as long as the "Benefactor" was at least equally venerated. This arrangement did not fit Quinn's temperament, and his *lèse majesté* was soon reported by the spies assigned to his church; hence my visit. He survived, but Father Arthur McKinnon, his equally outspoken friend and former assistant curate, did not. McKinnon was murdered in the tumultuous period that followed the dictator's assassination.

Educated in Toronto, Lou was ordained in 1952 as a priest of the Toronto-based Scarboro Foreign Mission Society, and left almost immediately for the Dominican Republic. Appointed to Ocoa, he found a widely scattered community comprised mostly of *campesinos* leading lives of harsh subsistence. Access to the market town was by a tangle of narrow mountain trails for horse and donkey. A first challenge was to build roads.

A gifted organizer and ingenious fundraiser, he cajoled money and equipment from the Dominican government, mining companies, charities, and international organizations, including CIDA. As a result of his work with the local development organization that had been founded by his predecessor, 600 kilometres of dirt roads were carved, 69 schools were built, wells were dug, clinics were set up, over 2,000 houses with cement floors and foundations were erected, millions of trees were planted, a small hydro dam was installed, hygienically designed latrines in pastel fibreglass were distributed, irrigation pipes were laid out, agricultural counsel was provided, and cottage industries for cigar boxes, furniture, and jewellery were established. Work on many of these projects continues to be joined each summer by hundreds of students and adults from the Toronto and Hamilton areas.

I saw more of Lou during my visits as non-resident ambassador to the Dominican Republic, and was occasionally able to inflate my leverage on his behalf. On two occasions I persuaded the naval high command in Ottawa to allow Canadian charitable organizations supporting both Lou and the Grey Sisters at the eastern end of the island to take advantage of the visits of Canadian warships to the Caribbean. An assortment of building materials, irrigation equipment, dental chairs, and an old ambulance were carried as deck cargo from Halifax to the Santo Domingo docks, where Lou's almost mystical authority spirited the supplies intact past some of the Caribbean's most notoriously corrupt customs officers. On both occasions Lou invited the ships' officers and men to Ocoa. Toiling in the sun on their free time, the sailors dug foundations, poured cement, and laid irrigation pipes. After work, Lou provided fried chicken and beer. A unilingual Spanish children's choir trained by him sang "O Canada" in English and in French to the astonished sailors.

Gradually the lives of thousands of people were profoundly transformed – and inevitably feathers were ruffled. Concern in high places that his priorities were misplaced led to an order for his removal from the parish. The conservative church hierarchy was troubled that too much time devoted to the quality of life of the people meant not enough time for their souls. However, the people's reaction surprised the cardinal and his associates. After massive demonstrations, the order was rescinded. Devout, but possessed of a mischievous sense of humour, Lou once complained to me over the telephone that what he had most in common with Pope John Paul was Parkinson's. In the end, his integrity and his extraordinary achievements won the hearts of nearly everyone. In 2006 he received a

Father Lou Quinn OC, courtesy of Scarboro Missions.

high decoration from the same Pope. A year before, the National Congress had formally declared him to be "Protector" of the Province of San Jose de Ocoa. Six months after his death the municipal department was renamed "Padre Louis Quinn."

Nicknamed "Guyacan," after the country's strongest hardwood, he was for many years as tough physically as he was in determination. It was often Lou who drove the bulldozer on the precipitous sections of mountain roads. Inspired by the teaching to love both neighbour and enemy, he struggled, often with difficulty, to follow that canon. A fearless advocate for his parishioners, he once challenged a burly policeman to an arm-wrestling competition. If Quinn won, the policeman would liberate an innocent teenager from the local jail, crowded with brutal villains. Quinn won.

Belligerent with rogues, blasphemous when thwarted, Quinn could charm the whiskers off a cat. An alumnus of St. Michael's Choir in Toronto, he sang with a mellow baritone, sometimes accompanying himself in his own compositions on the guitar.

Twenty years ago, I put it to Father Quinn that he might be a candidate for the Order of Canada.

"Why would I want that?" he growled.

"Because, you old rascal, it will help you raise money in Canada."

"Ah," said Quinn. He subsequently became a member of the order.

I don't recall what is etched on Lou's gravestone on the floor of his church, but it could not be much better than this passage from Beryl Markham's extraordinary memoir, *West with the Night*:

"If a man has any greatness in him, it comes to light, not in one flamboyant hour, but in the ledger of his daily work."[2]

AFTERWORD

"When my generation set out, the going was good."

—Evelyn Waugh

The stories, especially in Book I, the period when I was working for the Department of External Affairs, reflect a more challenging and entertaining career than I could ever have imagined when I joined. My experience was not unique. Colleagues have different but similarly varied tales to tell. One common thread is that they were good years. Although the reasons for job satisfaction vary widely, I believe that my generation was blessed with some shared features which are less visible and in some cases non-existent for our successors. We were no brighter – just more fortunate in our timing.

When I joined the foreign service in the late fifties I caught the tail end of the much ballyhooed Pearsonian golden age. Although not always golden, it was a good time to be in External Affairs. The good times dipped a few times, but they did not come to an end with Mr. Pearson's departure. A shortlist of the favourable conditions for the next forty or so years would include the view that the main lines of our foreign policy were mostly sound and that much of the time we felt pride in being part of a national enterprise that was doing positive things for the country and for the international community. More often than not we had exceptional – as well as eccentric – role models. With few exclusions, we respected the judgment and skill of our foreign ministers. We were told by esteemed foreigners that we had a first class foreign service.[1] Also, there was, more often than not, a reciprocity of confidence between ministers and professionals. This last was critically important because it spoke to a culture of foreign service in which senior professionals were participants in the consultative process with ministers.

The Harper government's calculated departure from what had been a largely shared, small 'l' liberal approach to the world surprised all of our friends and disappointed most of them. There can be no doubt that Canada's new vision has significantly eroded our leverage in the international community. But policies can be rectified. What is not so easily salvaged is the damage done to the culture of foreign service and, of course, more broadly and more seriously to the culture of public service.[2] When deputy ministers are dissuaded from asking awkward questions of ministers or from freely offering to spell out the plusses and minuses of new policy proposals, the 'don't rock the boat' and 'top down only' messages are not lost on the ambitious. Contamination seeps down the chain. The worst part of this corrosive dynamic is that after a number of years, it becomes 'the new normal'. With each passing year, fewer people in the business remember the former culture and its values. Declining numbers mourn their passing. Equally unfortunate would be the temptation for incoming governments, whatever their complexion, to find that loss of memory and the new 'no questions asked' compliance convenient. The ultimate loser, of course, is the country whose vital interests can no longer be pursued with unencumbered professionalism.

Now, lest I oversell the joys of my time in harness and assign full responsibility for the present darkness to the Harper government, I should acknowledge that an adversarial attitude toward the foreign service preceded the Harper government. Under Messrs. Chrétien and Martin it was often carping; under Mr. Harper it has been hostile. There were occasions under Mr. Mulroney and Mr. Trudeau when we invited censure. Vanity was occasionally a contributing factor, no doubt swollen by the fact that our names (as ambassadors and high commissioners) followed the unfortunate and antique prefix "Excellency". In Latin America, imagine the cumulative effect of *excelentissimo*.

It was never my intention in pulling these chapters together to write a book of advocacy. If there are lessons to be drawn, the plan was to have them emerge without fanfare from the narrative. For better or for worse, I have already broken that resolution. The gate being off its hinge, I will add one more observation to this polemic. In my experiences in the Dominican Republic, Cuba, Central America, the Balkans, Ukraine, and Central Asia, one disturbing and recurring memory stands out: the secret policeman as king – unfettered, above the law, unrestrained by objective and non-partisan oversight, redefining the meaning and value of liberty, and recalibrating the measures necessary for a 'secure' society. In Canada we are still at a healthy distance from being a society where laws are malleable, but there are signs that we are letting the guard down.

These signs bring to mind one of those many days in Bosnia when the instructions of the OSCE head office in Sarajevo appeared to be generating the exact opposite of the goals graven in the Dayton Peace Agreement. Brooding at my desk in Bihac I recalled what Pogo the possum had said from deep in the Okefenokee Swamp in similar circumstances. Pogo was the creation of Walt Kelly, the best cartoon satirist of the McCarthy era in the United States. In my fortnightly dispatch to head office I quoted Pogo: "We has met the enemy – and he is us." Once again, head office did not reply.

NOTES

DOMINICAN REPUBLIC

1 Fandino's is one version. Others claim that Trujillo was in the coffin at the church in San Cristobal.

2 The bizarre details of the final unravelling of the Trujillo dynasty are set out in the chapter 'A is for Aristide'.

3 Restored to the status of embassy from consulate general after the forced departure of the remaining members of the Trujillo family.

4 During the civil war in 1965, the offices on the second floor became the headquarters of Colonel Caamaño, head of the 'Constitutional' forces then fighting both a right wing coalition and President Johnson's Marines.

5 Clark Leith later became provost and vice president of the University of Western Ontario.

CUBA

1 Peter T. Haydon, *The 1962 Cuban Missile Crisis: Canadian Involvement Reconsidered* (Toronto: Canadian Institute of Strategic Studies, 1993), 130.

2 This paragraph also notes that "the Prime Minister informed the President that the Canadian Government would maintain its diplomatic representation in Cuba but would do nothing to indicate support or sympathy for the Castro regime," and concludes by citing the president's "warm appreciation for Canadian assistance" relating to "restrictions on Communist bloc air traffic to Cuba." RG 25 series, Cuba 1960-65, Department of External Affairs, Library and Archives Canada.

3 David Coleman, *The Fourteenth Day* (Norton, 2012). Coleman's title is intended to signal that White House tapes, previously unreleased, reveal that the crisis did not end after two weeks, as generally accepted, but continued for several months, as President Kennedy and his colleagues attempted to secure the removal of as much nuclear weaponry from Cuba as possible.

4 Ibid., 168.

5 Subsequently I learned that standard equipment for covert

activity such as this were tiny cameras disguised as watches and pens. There was also a miniature camera which could take a series of pre-programmed snaps with one hand from a moving vehicle. These were not offered.

6 Historians agree that there had been a mix of motives behind placing nuclear missiles in Cuba, some suggesting that the leverage gained by the presence of missiles in Cuba would have been a vital bargaining chip for Krushchev's overarching plan to push the allies out of Berlin, a gambit that would have involved deceiving Castro.

7 Consular Activities in Cuba were concerned with Canadians in legal or other distress.

8 The April Fool of 1964 was so successful that the tradition of attempting to bamboozle Gaby once a year continues to this day, often with the help of confederates, including Chuck Svoboda. The success rate is impressively high.

9 Maureen, the wife of a British colleague, actually produced a Soviet jeep containing puzzled Czech technicians who were compensated with food and drink.

10 The scavenger hunt preceded the final selection and the raising of the new flag on February 15, 1965.

11 At this point the ambassador was Leon Mayrand.

12 Michael Arkus "Swimming with Fidel: The Toils of an Accidental Journalist," CreateSpace Independent Publishing Platform, 2014, 222.

UNITED KINGDOM

1 These lamps were also used for many years by coal miners.

2 Winner of the Governor General's award in 1974 for *The Siren Years* (MacMillan), the most famous of his four diaries, which chronicles his life from 1937 to 1945, including the London Blitz, when he was a young officer at Canada House.

3 These treasures were the legacy of Peter Larkin, a tea tycoon, appointed by Mackenzie King as high commissioner in 1922. Larkin secured the old Union Club, which became Canada House, and his widow donated the exotic furnishings. In my subsequent incarnation at Canada House (1981–83) I fought to prevent this collection from being sold at auction.

4 Nancy Gelber, *Canada in London* (Canada House, 1983).

5 Despite several near-death experiences at the hands of cost cutters, sanity and Canada House have survived. While diplomacy has changed in several fundamental ways, making an impression on the host and the host's entrepreneurial and cultural elites has not. This beautifully-appointed room, the receptions and concerts in it, and the location, have made Canada House cost effective.

6   I was minister for cultural and public affairs. At that time the high commissioner and the deputy high commissioner had offices in MacDonald House in Grosvenor Square. From 1939 to 1942, this office in Canada House had been occupied by L.B. Pearson.

7   Most clubs are now open to women.

JAPAN

1   Until dismantled by the Harper government in 2012. At that time there was a cadre of over 7,000 scholars in 55 countries focused on one or more disciplines of Canadian Studies.

GUYANA

1   This Alberta-based company is the one that supplied the Christmas trees.

TRINIDAD AND TOBAGO

1   Cuthbert dances to calypso and jazz.

GRENADA

1   External Affairs telegram LCR 1944 of October 24, 1983. The Canadian government had previously delivered a message to the Junta appealing for the avoidance of violence (same telegram).

2   Canadian Embassy Havana telegram 2654, October 31, 1983. At the time of the invasion there were 743 Cuban construction workers and 43 regular soldiers (same telegram).

3   Also a boost for tourism as it would accommodate large commercial aircraft more readily than at Pearls.

4   Speech by Bishop on March 23, 1983, in which he also referred to the "warmongering Reagan."

5   In speaking to Ambassador Gotleib, Deputy Secretary of State Ken Dam asked that the Canadian government bear in mind "the enduring psychological effects of the Iran hostage situation and of the very present psychological effects of the attack on US Marines in Beirut." Washington telegram 2373, October 26, 1983.

6   The OECS formally sought US military assistance on October 22. A similar request was issued by Grenada Governor-General Sir Paul Scoon.

7   The admonition of Napoleon's foreign minister to a group of foreign service cadets at the Quai d'Orsay.

8   Our assumption was almost certainly linked to the fact that a few days before when both Trudeau and his deputy prime minister (also secretary of state for external affairs), Allan MacEachen, were out of the country, it was Pepin who was acting prime minister.

9   RG 25 volume, 12551 Situation Report, Library and Archives Canada, October 20, 1983. There were more Canadian tourists, but they were unregistered and hence not included in the count.

10   LCD telegram 8386 of October 25, 1983. This telegram was also used in the briefing given to US

Ambassador Robinson the same day by Minister Pepin.

11   The title of the foreign minister at this time was Secretary of State for External Affairs.

12   Soon after this experience a fully equipped Operations Centre was established in the Pearson Building.

13   At a meeting in the State Department on October 26, and in response to blunt concerns expressed by Canadian Ambassador Gotlieb, Deputy Secretary of State Ken Dam offered the less than reassuring message that "consultation with Canada had been considered. Military and operational considerations had to prevail in decision not to forewarn Canada, but there was recognition that Canada had very specific interests in that region." Washington telegram 2373 of October 26, 1983.

14   Ann Elizabeth Wilder, Grenada Revolution Online.

15   Library and Archives file RG 21-3 Grenada vol. 11.

16   Operation Urgent Fury, Ronald H. Cole, Joint History Office. Office of the Chairman of the Joint Chiefs of Staff, 1997.

17   Grenada sitrep #14, 1400 hours, October 26, 1983.

18   Ibid.

19   UN documents A/RES/38/7 Meeting 43, November 2, 1983

20   Ibid.

21   My bureau added the condition, accepted by the US side, that the

agenda would also encompass Central America.

22   I kept the T-shirts as souvenirs.

23   Associated Press, April 30, 1985.

24   Edward Seaga, prime minister of Jamaica, subsequently telephoned Pierre Trudeau to apologize. *Globe and Mail*, October 28, 1983. Seaga also indicated that a Caribbean prime minister had been charged with informing Trudeau in advance, but had failed to do so. Prime Minister Adams of Barbados also apologized to Trudeau.

25   See "The Funeral of the Honourable Forbes Burnham" chapter.

CENTRAL AMERICA AND COLOMBIA

1   Composed by Keith Bezanson and the author.

PANAMA

1   General Noriega is now serving his sentence in a Panamanian prison.

2   Meredith Daneman, *Margot Fonteyn: A Life* (Viking Press, 2003).

CENTRAL AMERICA

1   Twenty-five years later, promising change has been undone by narcotics, corruption, and gang wars. The incidence of violent death now exceeds that of the eighties in El Salvador, Honduras, and Guatemala. Of the four countries beset by conflict in the eighties, only Nicaragua enjoys relative peace.

2   Speech by the Rt. Hon. Joe Clark, September 26, 1986.

3   Rt. Hon. Joe Clark, Secretary of State for External Affairs press release, August 5, 1987.

4   The Contras, originally a small Nicaraguan guerilla force opposed to the Sandinistas, became a US proxy force, increasingly armed and financed by the United States and supported by mercenary troops.

5   The passions ignited in Canada by the Spanish civil war led to the formation of the Mackenzie-Papineau battalion, whose members fought against Generalissimo Franco and Spanish fascism. Similarly, hundreds of Canadians went to Nicaragua, but unlike in Spain, they were almost entirely non-combatant, contributing instead in a variety of supportive roles and earning the nickname 'sandalistas'.

6   On a visit to Managua, Nicaragua, in 2006, a former officer in the Sandinista Foreign Ministry told me how pleased she and many others had been with the balanced approach Canada had taken to the Central American crisis.

7   Including Colonel Donald Ethell, subsequently lieutenant governor of Alberta.

8   Excepting on Grenada as spelled out in that chapter.

9   There was a relatively free movement of ideas which percolated both down and up. My experience ten years before as director of the tiny Academic Relations division is illustrative. See the Japan chapter and footnote #24.

Consultative dialogue between ministers and senior public servants has been largely dropped from the public service culture. This retrograde development has been especially evident under the Harper government.

VENEZUELA, HAITI, AND THE DOMINICAN REPUBLIC

1   At the close of the posting President Perez bestowed upon me the "Orden del Libertador, Gran Cordon," a distinction I share with Fidel Castro and the late Muammar Gaddafi.

2   It was no longer an embassy, because the United States, like all other states in the OAS, had broken diplomatic relations when Trujillo attempted to assassinate President Betancourt of Venezuela.

3   Following bitter disagreement with the Catholic Church, Aristide resigned from the priesthood in 1994.

4   This anomaly was, I think, first discovered by Alexander von Humboldt.

5   Jose Toribio Medina's *Relacion del Nuevo Descubrimiento por muy Gran Venturas del Capitan Francisco de Orellana* (1855) reproduces an account of Francisco de Orellana's epic voyage of discovery from Peru to the mouth of the Amazon, written in 1542 by Friar Carvajal, a member of the expedition.

6   Twenty years later the greatly diminished Waimari-Atroari

were paid compensation and provided health facilities and teaching in their own language. Attempted genocide under the military dictatorship has only recently been under investigation by a commission appointed by President Dilma Rousseff. Tribal numbers are beginning to recover.

7   Highway BR-174 is now resurfaced and linked to a newly built road, Venezuela route 10, which connects Santa Elena de Uairen to Ciudad Bolivar.

8   979 metres, or 3,212 feet, on Auyantupui.

9   University Naval Training Divisions (UNTD).

DOMINICAN REPUBLIC

1   A full account of my experiences with this election and its aftermath was published in book form by Fundacion Cultural Dominicana in 2011. It is in Spanish, and carries the title *La Crisis Electoral de 1994: Alejandose del Precipio. Una Cronica del mediador de la OEA.*

2   Peña Gomez' presidency had been thwarted by Balaguer and ultimately by his recognition that the compromise was a better choice than civil conflict. In the election two years later, he won a majority but insufficient votes to prevent a second round. Balaguer, who had denied his victory in 1994 did so again by transferring his third place votes to the second place, and now victorious,

Leonel Fernandez. Peña Gomez died two years later.

BOSNIA

1   While the basic Muslim faith remained in Bosnia, in many areas traditional discipline had been diluted by generations of aggressive Yugoslav secularism. During the Bosnian war, moral and material support for the embattled Muslims came in part from the Middle East. In post-war Bosnia, support often took the form of zealous efforts to restore traditional discipline, but in 1996 there were few signs of the new proselytism in Cazin.

2   Most of the money came from remittances paid by relatives working in Western Europe, and some from widespread criminal activities.

PARAGUAY

1   IFIS: the Washington-based International Foundation for Election Systems.

GUATEMALA

1   Portillo was eventually extradited to the United States and sentenced to prison. Released in 2015, he returned to Guatemala.

2   United Nations Human Development Report for Guatemala 2003.

3   Term for a White ruling class in Central America.

4   Beckett and Pedley, RAND.

5   Recent evidence indicates that the income gulf in Latin America as a whole is slightly diminishing, but not in Guatemala where the

gap is widening. *Encyclopaedia Britannica*, 2015 Book of the Year.

6   Ronald Wright, *Time Among the Maya*, 1989.

7   FRG: Guatemalan Republican Front.

8   Since the Dominican Republic election crisis of 1994, the OAS has usually been forthright in their election assessments even when this has involved questioning a sitting government's claim of electoral victory. Judgment on the Nicaraguan election of 2011, which glossed over serious irregularities (not the overall results), was one exception.

9   An independent tabulation of the presidential vote.

10   Author in FOCAL paper, October 2003.

11   The most frightening of these was Cyril, chapter 'Goudau-Goudau: Return to Haiti'.

VENEZUELA

1   Already in trouble under Chavez, Venezuela is sinking under the dysfunctional management of his successor, Nicolas Maduro.

2   I was chair of FOCAL at this time.

3   Jimmy Carter presided at the Carter Center press conference and unfortunately overstated the fairness of the election as a whole by failing to note government abuses during the campaign. Subsequently he was accused by the *Wall Street Journal* of obfuscating the real result and colluding with Chavez. Appalled

by this calumny, I wrote to the *WSJ*, which published my letter explaining the absurdity of this accusation.

UKRAINE

1   One of the reasons the government's deception failed was the courageous audacity of the interpreter for the deaf on the national (government controlled) television network. Using hand signals, instead of translating exactly the government's concocted version of the election results, she expressed incredulity and conveyed to her audience that what she was hearing was false. The deaf across the country were able to communicate this unvarnished version to a wider Ukrainian audience.

PALESTINE

1   These points and others about contradictory policies were made more strongly and, of course, much more publicly by President Carter in his book *Palestine, Peace not Apartheid* published soon after these elections.

NICARAGUA

1   The limerick is quoted by Salman Rushdie in his book *The Jaguar Smile: A Nicaraguan Journey*, (Picador 1987) and has been adapted from the nineteenth-century limerick about a tiger in Niger by William Cosmo Monkhouse.

2   Vasco Nunez de Balboa was a Spanish explorer and the first European to see the Pacific Ocean from the New World.

3 Former Argentine foreign minister

4 The small Carter mission had not been invited to formally observe the election. We were 'informally' assessing.

EL SALVADOR

1 Chips was resident ambassador in San Jose, Costa Rica, and non-resident ambassador to Panama, Nicaragua, and El Salvador.

2 This posting was early in Pickering's career. A very impressive professional, he was to become the deputy secretary of state many years later.

3 For the past decade Villalobos has been a fellow of St. Antony's College, Oxford.

HAITI

1 Carlo Dade, then executive director of the Canadian Foundation for the Americas (FOCAL), Marcelo Varela, associate director for the Americas at the Carter Center, and myself as a member of the "Friends."

2 First published by North Point Press in 1942.

EPILOGUE

1 For example, Sir Humphrey Trevelyan, one of the UK's great diplomats, cited Canada's and Yugoslavia's foreign services as among the best in the world: *Diplomatic Channels*, MacMillan 1973.

2 As Professor Donald Savoie explains in comments on the Duffy case, this condition is seriously exacerbated by the power of the PMO, a situation that is "fraught with danger for democracy, for national unity and sound public policy...". *Globe and Mail*, August 14, 2015.

INDEX

Betancur, Belisario, 117
Bezanson, Keith, 118–19, 293n1
Bihac, Bosnia and Herzegovina
    Bangladeshis in, 186–87, 210–12
    beauty contest, 199–200
    Bosnian War, 184–86, 211–12
    Canadian military in, 210–12
    OSCE election monitoring, 184–87, 190,
        200–205
Bishkek, Kyrgyzstan, 221–22, 227–29, *229*
Bishop, Maurice, 100–102
Black Lamb, Grey Falcon (West), 183
Boa Vista, Brazil, 144, *148*
Boccachiampe, Elsa, 135
Bogota, Colombia, 117
Bosansko Grahovo, Bosnia and
        Herzegovina, 184
Bosnia and Herzegovina
    Bosnian War, 184–86, 196, 198, 201,
        211–13
    Canadian military in, 186, 189, 191–92,
        195, 203
    Catholic Church, 201–2, 213
    Dayton Agreement, 183, 185, 188, 193,
        205
    elections (1996), 183–93, 207
    elections (1997), 214–15
    elections (1998), 190, 207, 215
    Ice Cream Men, 200–201
    international police, 213–14
    JG's election work, 183–216, *190*
    lack of democratic tradition, 189
    Muslims, 184–85, 196, 200, 210–14,
        294n1
    secret police, 187, 287
    UN role in, 184–86, 202, 210–11
    US role in, 193
    war damage, 184–86, 196, 198, 201, 212
Bouterse, Desi, 91–92
Bratunac, Bosnia and Herzegovina, *192*,
        213–15
Brazil, travel from Brasilia to Caracas,
        144–50, 294n7

Broadbent, Ed, 105
The Broken Road (Leigh Fermor), 216
Brossa, Dr. Jordi, 168
Bruce, Gordon, 15
Burgess, Betty, 55
Burnham, Linden Forbes
    dictatorship, 64, 67–68, 75
    funeral, 82–84, 110
Bush, George H.W., 140–41
Bush Negroes, Suriname, 88–92

C
Caamaño, Francisco, 161–62, 289n4
Calle el Conde, Dominican Republic, *22*
Canada, international relations
    Canada-only election observations, 255,
        257–58
    Central America, case study, 125–30
    foreign service culture, 285–87, 293n9
    military in Bosnia, 186, 189, 191–92, 195,
        203, 206–7, 211–12
    Palestine, election observations, 255–60
    peace processes and, 129–30
    Ukraine, election observations, 258
    US relations generally, 127, 129–30
    See also Cuban missile crisis; Graham,
        John, diplomatic career
Canadian Foundation for the Americas, 269
Canadian Studies Abroad program, 59–62,
        291n1
Caputo, Dante, 264
Carabobo, Venezuela, 244–46
Caracas, Venezuela
    Brasilia to Caracas, travel, 144–50
    Miss Venezuela Contest, 150–54
Carnival, Trinidad and Tobago, 93–98, *95*
Carter, Jimmy
    Dominican Republic's elections, 158, 175
    exile of Cédras from Haiti, 142–43
    Friends of the Inter-American
        Democratic Charter, 181
    negotiations on Bosnia, 211

Suriname
    Bush Negroes, 88–92
    JG's posting, 85–92
    sovereignty celebration, 85–88
Svoboda, Chuck and Lisa, 46, 290n8
Swartz, Anna Maria, 8

T

Takutu River, 63–64, *73*
Talbot, Strobe, 167
Tegucigalpa, Honduras, 115–16
Tel Aviv, Israel, 255, *260*
Ternopil, Ukraine, 247–48, 250–53, *253*,
    295n1
Thatcher, Margaret, 106
Thomas, Christopher, 163, 168
Tian Shan mountains, 223, *229*
Time Among the Maya (Wright), 231, 233,
    241
Tirado, Jorge, 158
Tokyo, Japan, 59–62
Trevelyan, Sir Humphrey, 296n2
Trinidad and Tobago, 93–98, *95*, 102
Trudeau, Pierre
    Central American policy, 128
    foreign service culture, 286–87
    US invasion of Grenada, 102–10, 292n24
Trujillo, Rafael, *16*, *22*
    assassination, 15–18, 134, 164
    attempted coup, 133–34
    Balaguer and, 163, 172, 173, 175
    Betancourt incident, 294n2
    Catholic Church, 12–13, 15
    dictatorship, 3, 5, 7–10, 12–19, 218–19
    family, 5, 18–19
    funeral, 16–19, 289n1
    See also Dominican Republic
TSE (Supreme Electoral Tribunal),
    Guatemala, 236–38
Tudjman, Franjo, 206, 212
Tuzla, Bosnia and Herzegovina, 215
Tyup, Kyrgyzstan, 223, *229*

U

Ukraine
    JG's election work, 247–53, 295n1
    power of secret police, 287
United Kingdom
    JG's posting at, 53–57, *54*, *57*, 99, 290n3,
        291nn5–6
United Nations
    Bosnian war, 184–86, 202, 213
    Haiti earthquake recovery, 276–77
    Haiti sanctions, 142
    impact on OSCE, 213
    Rwanda genocide, 213
    US invasion of Grenada, 107
United States
    Canada/US relations in Caribbean, 108
    Canada/US relations in Central
        America, 125–30
    Dominican Republic's elections (1994),
        166–67
    Grenada invasion, 99–110
    role in Guatemala, 232
    role in Haiti, 139–40
    See also Cold War; Cuban missile crisis
UPD (Unit for Promotion of Democracy),
    234
Upper Canada College, Toronto, 11
Urosa Savino, Archbishop Jorge Liberato,
    245

V

Valencia, Venezuela, 244–46
Varela, Marcelo, 296n1
Velika Kladusa, Bosnia and Herzegovina,
    205, 206
Venezuela
    Betancourt assassination attempt, 17
    Chavez's recall election, 243–46
    JG's diplomatic work, 131–54, *149*, 157
    JG's election work, 243–46
    Maduro's government, 295n1
    Miss Venezuela Contest, 150–54